TUPAC
A THUG LIFE

CONTENTS

Foreword by Kris Ex   5

Part One – Panther Baby

Bury Me Like a 'G' by Kevin Powell   9
An Interview with Tupac's Mom by Davey D   17
The Music is the Message by Bronwyn Garrity   22
My Brother by Benjamin Meadows-Ingram   26
On the Line with . . . 2pac Shakur – The Lost Interview by Davey D   30
Asking for It by Michael Small   36

Part Two – Hit 'Em Up

Violence is Golden by Danzy Senza   41
Dreaming America by Daniel Smyth   47
Thug Life by June Joseph   49
Q&A with Tupac Shakur: 'I Am Not a Gangster' by Chuck Philips   55
Interview on The Westside Radioshow by Sway   58
Have Gun Will Travel by Ronin Ro   65

Part Three – A Black De Niro?

King of Stage by Joshua Rubin   71
Conversations with Tupac by Veronica Chambers   79
Juice review by Roger Ebert   83
Poetic Justice review by Roger Ebert   85
Above the Rim review by Chris Hicks   86
Got Your Back by Frank Alexander   87
Bullet review by Micah Robinson   92
Rebel for the Hell of It by Armond White   94
Gridlock'd review by Roger Ebert   97
Gang Related review by James Bernardinelli   99

Part Four – A Thug Death

The Living End by Frank Williams   103
All Eyes on Him by R. J. Smith   108
The Day After Tupac Shakur Died by Amy Linden   112
Easy Target: Why Tupac Should Be Heard Before He's Buried
   by Mikal Gilmore   113
Rap Wars: Did the Violence Claim Another Life? by Dana Kennedy   118

The New Tupac Fans by Ruby Bailey   121

Deadly Business by Dana Kennedy   123

The Tupac Shakur Murder Investigation: One Year Later Still No Arrests
    by Bryan Robinson   128

Dead Poets Society by Cathy Scott   131

Who Killed Tupac Shakur? by Chuck Philips   137

Who Killed Tupac Shakur?: Epilogue by Chuck Philips   148

Dead Men Tell No Tales: Of Revelation and Speculation in the Los
    Angeles Times *Biggie and Tupac Story* by J. H. 'Tommy' Tompkins and
    Johnny Ray Huston   149

Interview with Suge Knight by P. Frank Williams   151

Biggie & Tupac *(Remix): Nick Broomfield Imitates Life Imitating Art*
    by Ernest Hardy   156

Part Five – Tupac Resurrected

Jackin' Beats by Veronica Lodge   161

Who Stole Tupac's Soul? by Allison Samuels   167

A Rose by Any Other Name: The Rose that Grew from Concrete *Review*
    by Theresa Micalef   169

For Heaven's Sake by Soren Baker   171

Eternal Truths and Dead Pop Stars by Frank Ahrens   175

All Oddz on Me: Think You Know Who Killed Tupac? Wanna Bet?
    by Jordan Harper   178

Hood Scriptures by Kris Ex   180

Hip Hop Requiem: Mining Tupac Shakur's Legacy by Neil Strauss   184

Tupac Resurrection by Rita Michel   187

Tupac's Book Shelf by Mark Anthony Neal   189

The Tupac Uprising: Outlaws with a Cause by George Wehrfritz   192

*Symposium Analyzes, Celebrates 'Thug': Legendary Tupac Shakur Looked
    at as Cultural Artifact, Force* by Ken Gewertz   193

G.O.A.T. by Kris Ex   196

Tupac Shakur's Legacy by Lucy Morrison   198

Tupac's Continuing Career: A Matter of Grave Importance
    by John Jurgensen   204

Contributors   206

Acknowledgements   208

FOREWORD by Kris Ex

'Hip-hop ain't been the same since Tupac moved to Cuba on us.'
– Eminem, 'Fubba U Cubba Cubba' (2005)

When I first heard that Tupac Shakur had been shot (the first time, that is), I was busy doing something that is part of a whole other tale altogether. The important thing is that I received a page on my beeper. It was a friend's code, three times, with a '911' at the end. I ran to a payphone and called him.

'Yo, you hear what happened to your man?'
  'Who?'
  'Tupac . . . he got shot.'
  I thought it was some kind of joke, but my friend said, 'You ain't see the paper? It's on the front page of *The Post*.'
  'Get the fuck outta here . . . He alright?'
  'That nigga's crazy. He's stickin' his middle finger up at the camera as they put him into the ambulance. How you ain't see the paper?'
  (As I said, that's a whole other tale.)
  We laughed at 'Pac's madness for half a second, then I cut the convo short and made another call to a friend who I figured would have proximity to the situation: 'Niggas shot 'Pac?'
  'Yeah,' he said. 'Everything they saying in the news is true, but there's more to it than that. I'll tell you about it later. I'm still getting the story. It's crazy.'
  Later that night, and over the next few years, I would find out more details about what took place in New York City's Quad Studios on that November 30, 1994. Some of it would be through official accounts like the ones collected in this book, many of them would be through urban legends and street palaver, and a handful would be from players interwoven into his legacy through threads unseen by most and acknowledged by few. Much of it would be contradictory, with various sides claiming innocence while others accepted responsibility.

Such was the power of Tupac Amaru Shakur. His life and art, then and now, was able to transcend worlds and resonate and connect with political organizers, street thugs, certified gangsters, casual music listeners and die-hard hip-hop fans. He was a thug, a revolutionary, a brother, a leader, a hope that inspired and protected, even as we, the mere men and women who knew we were witnessing a *force majeure* in human form, felt an instinctive need to protect him, sometimes from himself.

When I first heard that Tupac Shakur had been shot (the second time, that is), I was hungover. My brother had come over and after admonishing me for being asleep at two in the afternoon, told me that 'Pac had been shot. My reaction was much like that of the Notorious B.I.G.'s:
  'Again?' I chuckled. My first thought was that he had been shot in the leg or some place free of vital organs. The idea of any true harm coming to 'Pac didn't exist in my world.
  'Nah, bruh,' my brother said. 'It looks bad. Shit is all on the news.'
  I looked at the television set, cold and at rest. I was scared to turn it on. It wasn't until my brother left that I would see the bullet-riddled BMW, realize that my pager had been going off all night, see that my answering machine was blinking with thirteen messages. Thirteen. It's an unlucky number for

5

some, but for me it's always been about the completion of a cycle and the start of a new one. I knew it was an omen. But unsure of what kind.

On September 13, 1996, I was on my way to a celebrity-studded concert starring D'Angelo, the man who was single-handedly bringing a style of music dubbed 'neo-soul' to the forefront of the American psyche. I was meeting a friend in Bed-Stuy, Brooklyn, and had to pass the childhood home of the Notorious B.I.G. on my way. When I emerged from the train station, there was quiet in the air, as if the ability to speak had been removed from the atmosphere, leaving only silence in its void. There was no grief, no emotion, just barren space where dice games, gossip, cat-calls and music once permeated the hood's consciousness. It was like watching a movie without a score – something was missing.

When I got to my friend's house, she opened the door: 'Did you hear?'

'Yeah,' I said. But I had never actually heard. And we never actually said it. We just smoked a few joints, circled the truth in tangents, and then drove to the concert without the radio on. It wouldn't be until we were on line for the performance that it would be said. A news crew, jockeying for reaction from the people, shoved into my face and asked, 'What do you think of Tupac Shakur?'

'I think he's dead,' I said. Then I walked away.

Almost a decade later, we're still trying to make sense of it. What you hold in your hands stands apart from the pantheon of books on the life of Tupac Amaru Shakur. This is a chronicle from many angles – from those of us who knew him, those of us who championed him, those of us who tried to figure him out, those of us who gave birth to him, and, blessingly, from those of us who actually were Tupac Shakur.

There's not much that I can say here that is not covered within these pages. This collection is culled from observations of the man as he lived and breathed, conversations with him as he spat fire and spoke truth to power with amazing clarity and befuddling badassness, there are words here wrought with the pain, confusion and shock which overtook us in the aftermath of his passing. There are shadows of his greatness at every turn. The only thing missing is the man himself, telling us that he is, indeed, alive and well. Because, while he continues to be a beacon for countless emcees and his life continues to inform black men as to how to feel about their communities, Tupac Shakur is dead. Even as he lives on, we know he is dead. We may wish to believe, in spite of the facts, that he is in Cuba, protecting Assata Shakur, even as she protects him, but he is not. He is dead. *Tupac: A Thug Life* celebrates his life and his passing. Join us as we offer tribute to a thug immortal.

kris ex
Brooklyn, New York, 2005

PART ONE

PANTHER BABY

BURY ME LIKE A 'G'

by Kevin Powell

At 4.03 p.m. on September 13, 1996, Tupac Amaru Shakur, rapper and actor, died at the University of Nevada Medical Center in the Wild West gambling town of Las Vegas, the result of gunshot wounds he had received six days earlier in a drive-by shooting near the glittery, hotel-studded strip. Shakur, a.k.a. 2Pac, was 25. The rapper is survived by his mother, Afeni Shakur, his father, Billy Garland, and a half sister, Sekyiwa.

The official cause of Shakur's death was respiratory failure and cardiopulmonary arrest, according to a medical-center spokesman. At press time, the police still had no suspects and no leads in the September 7 shooting and were having a difficult time getting witnesses to cooperate in the investigation. 'The only evidence we have is the number of rounds fired and the physical evidence,' said Sergeant Kevin Manning of the Las Vegas Metro Police Department's homicide unit, 'and we can't reveal that.'

Another officer, however, offered his own theory about the shooting. 'In my opinion, it was black-gang related and probably a Bloods-Crips thing,' says Sergeant Chuck Cassell of the department's gang unit. 'Look at [Shakur's] tattoos and album covers – that's not the Jackson Five . . . . It looks like a case of live by the sword, die by the sword.'

At the time of Shakur's death, his fourth album, *All Eyez on Me*, was Number 65 on the *Billboard* Top 200 chart and had sold nearly three million copies, according to the Recording Industry Association of America; his previous release, 1995's *Me Against the World*, sold two million copies. In addition to making music, Shakur was also an actor. He appeared in three movies: *Juice* (1992), *Poetic Justice* (1993) and *Above the Rim* (1994). When he died, he had recently completed two new films, *Gridlock'd* and one tentatively titled *Gang Related*, in which he

plays a detective.

Shakur, whose songs often detailed the misery, desperation and violence of ghetto life, grew up a troubled and sensitive child, living with his family in one inner-city community after another. Along with his million-selling albums and massive following, the rapper had often come under fire in his professional life for his offstage behavior. Since 1991, Shakur had been arrested eight times and served eight months in prison for a sexual-abuse conviction. He was the subject of two wrongful death lawsuits, one involving a six-year-old boy who was killed in Northern California after getting caught in gunfire between Shakur's entourage and a group of rivals.

Four days after Shakur's death, his father, Billy Garland, told *Rolling Stone* in an exclusive interview that he wanted people to focus on the rapper's accomplishments. 'My son is dead, and he don't deserve to be talked about like some common criminal,' he said. 'He wasn't perfect, but he did do some great things in a little bit of time.'

The events leading up to Shakur's shooting remain sketchy, but this much is known: On September 7, he attended the Mike Tyson/Bruce Seldon fight at the MGM Grand Hotel with 31-year-old Marion 'Suge' Knight, the CEO of Shakur's label, Death Row Records. At 8.39 p.m., less than two minutes after it had begun, the boxing match was over when Tyson knocked out Seldon. At about 8.45, according to the Las Vegas Metro Police, Shakur and other members of the Death Row entourage – which reportedly included several bodyguards – got into an argument with a young black man while leaving the event. The quarrel escalated into a fight in which either Shakur or members of the entourage knocked the young man to the floor and began kicking and punching him; the altercation was captured by an MGM Grand security camera. The hotel's security staff quickly rushed in and broke up the squabble, and the Death Row entourage left the building at about 8.55. Shakur and the entourage then stopped by the Luxor Hotel on the Las Vegas Strip for reasons the police have yet to determine. Shortly thereafter, they drove to Knight's home in southeast Las Vegas. While there, they changed clothes for a highly publicized anti-gang youth event put together by a Las Vegas Metro Police officer. The event was to be held at Knight's Club 662 (which spells out 'MOB,' reputedly for 'Members of Bloods,' on a telephone pad), located at 1700 E. Flamingo Road.

About two hours passed before Knight, driving his black, tinted-window BMW 750 sedan with Shakur in the passenger seat, was back in downtown Las Vegas, headed east on Flamingo Road near the intersection of Koval Lane. Directly behind them was a parade of about ten other vehicles that were part of Death Row's entourage. At about 11.15, according to the police and witnesses, a white, four-door, late-model Cadillac with four people inside pulled up beside the BMW, and a volley of about thirteen gunshots from a high-caliber handgun ripped into the BMW. Four bullets hit Shakur (who usually wore a bulletproof vest but did not have one on at the time of the shooting). Some reports suggest that the Death Row entourage returned fire. Immediately after the shooting, the Cadillac fled south on Koval. Knight, who had been grazed by bullets, made a U-turn from the eastbound left lane of Flamingo and headed west at a high speed toward Las Vegas Boulevard, away from the nearest hospital. Meanwhile, two patrol officers on an unrelated call at the nearby Maxim Hotel had heard the gunshots and called for backup. Two other officers followed Knight's BMW, which took a left turn on Las Vegas Boulevard South, and stopped the car, with two flat tires, at the intersection of Las Vegas Boulevard and Harmon Avenue. Upon discovering that Shakur and Knight needed medical assistance, the officers called an ambulance, which transported the two victims to the University of Nevada Medical Center.

At the hospital, Knight was treated for minor injuries to his head and released; Shakur, who had received two bullets to his chest, was admitted and listed in critical condition. During the following two days, the rapper underwent two operations, including one to remove his right lung and to stop internal bleeding. To take pressure off his badly damaged body, doctors placed Shakur in a medically induced coma and on a respirator. Shakur died on September 13; his family had his body cremated and held private services for the rapper in Las Vegas the following day.

In the six days following the incident, rumors flew about who was responsible for the shooting. Some observers within the music industry, who spoke only on the condition of anonymity, have suggested that the young man with whom Shakur and the Death Row entourage had scuffled at the MGM Grand shot Shakur and Knight. According to Sergeant Manning, the police 'determined that the individual in question could not have possibly followed Shakur because the man was being questioned by MGM security as the Death Row entourage was leaving the hotel.' The police never filed a written report on the scuffle, and the videotape, Manning said, is not considered evidence and will not be released to the media. 'We have no idea who he was,' Manning said. Asked if that was normal police procedure, Manning said it was 'not abnormal.'

A second theory put forth by people in the industry and on the streets in the days following the shooting is that Knight, who has been associated with the Los Angeles-based street gang the Bloods and who has a great fondness for the gang's color, red, had been the actual target of the shooting. That theory is unlikely, considering that all of the shots were aimed at the passenger seat of Knight's car. In the week following the shooting, a Los Angeles police officer reported that three members of the Crips, a rival gang of the Bloods, had been found dead in the Los Angeles suburb of Compton, Knight's home turf. Compton Police Department Captain Steven Roller, however, would not confirm the gang affiliation of the three dead men. 'That quote from the L.A. police is like a cop from Boston commenting on a homicide in New York,' he said. 'There is no correlation to the Tupac murder.'

According to the Las Vegas gang unit, several gangs, among them the Bloods and the Crips, have proliferated in the city during the last few years. The gang unit's Cassell credits this to a gang migration from California dating back to the early 1980s. The weekend of the Shakur incident, Cassell says, six other drive-by shootings occurred, four of which were connected to Hispanic gang activity; none has been linked to the Shakur murder. 'Gangs are a serious problem in Las Vegas,' says Cassell. 'We call it disorganized crime. Everything they do seems random, but they are very powerful and violent.'

A twist on the gang theory is that Shakur may have been killed as a warning to Knight. Often, according to sources, rival criminals will execute individuals who are valuable to their foes in retaliation for wrongdoings. Knight is indeed no stranger to crime. In 1992, he was put on probation in Los Angeles after he was convicted for assault with a deadly weapon; he had also received three years' probation in Nevada for transporting weapons across the state line. Last year, Knight was given a 30-day jail sentence for conspiracy to commit a drug-related offense. According to a September 25 *New York Post* report, the FBI is investigating Death Row Records for alleged organized-crime connections.

A third theory for the Shakur shooting, which doesn't seem to hold a lot of water, is that the rapper's death is somehow related to the simmering feud between East Coast and West Coast rap artists. For some time now, Death Row, which is based in Los Angeles, has been at odds with the East Coast-based Bad Boy Entertainment and one of its artists,

Biggie Smalls (a.k.a. the Notorious B.I.G.). When I interviewed Shakur after he was shot five times during a robbery in November 1994 (in which thieves made off with $40,000 of his jewelry), the rapper implied that he felt Smalls and Bad Boy's chief, Sean 'Puffy' Combs, who were in a recording studio in the building where Shakur was shot, knew who was responsible for the shooting. Combs and Smalls have denied any involvement in either Shakur shooting. More recently, Combs sent his 'deepest condolences' to the late rapper's friends and family.

To compound matters, Knight and other members of the Death Row entourage have been remarkably silent about the shooting, consistently telling the police that they didn't see any of Shakur's assailants, only the white Cadillac. Nor have any credible witnesses who were at the intersection of Flamingo and Koval at the time of the shooting come forward. Death Row publicist George Pryce would not comment on Shakur's murder, although one man at the label's offices did say, 'Tupac ain't got nothin' to do worth my bread and butter.'

As people flocked to Las Vegas in the days after Shakur's shooting, there were constant whispers that the rapper's condition was improving. Many of us who had followed Shakur over the years – the legion of fans, the pop culture pundits and the Tupac haters – believed he would bounce back, just as he had after he was shot in 1994. 'I'm still waiting for Tupac to call me; I never thought he was gonna die,' Keisha Morris, a former girlfriend of Shakur's, would later tell me. 'I thought he was going to walk out of the hospital just like he did before.'

Word of Shakur's death traveled quickly on September 13 – via cellular phone, fax, beeper and e-mail. By the time I got to the medical center, a throng of wellwishers-turned-mourners, mostly young and black, already stood inside and outside the trauma center where Shakur had been hospitalized. Some wept hysterically, some stared into space, and others sipped on bottled water or malt liquor. A few homeys spilled liquid on the ground in honor of Shakur. One young woman with thick braids and a flowered dress said, 'I hope you tell the truth about Tupac. He was a hero to me, and he kept it real for the hood.'

Jeeps and cars drove ominously through the intersection of Goldring Avenue and Rose Street, transforming the blocks surrounding the hospital into Las Vegas' version of Crenshaw Boulevard in Los Angeles on a Sunday night. Some of the vehicles blasted Shakur's music. Inside one black Hummer, four young men slouched in their seats and stared blankly in the direction of the hospital.

Even though it was September, the temperature soared above 100 degrees, and a thick, melancholic feeling hovered in the air. Reports that there had been retaliation for Shakur's death sifted through the crowd. Las Vegas Metro Police smothered the area as television crews, newspaper stringers, magazine reporters and freelance photographers all worked the outer edges of the crowd. Some onlookers flashed the familiar West Coast 'W' hand signal on behalf of Shakur. 'The boss man is dead,' said one teenage boy wearing an all-black outfit of a baseball cap, T-shirt and jeans.

When a black Lexus drove up to the entrance of the trauma center, the crowd stopped what it was doing to see who was inside. The six-foot-four-inch, 315-pound Suge Knight emerged from the passenger seat, smoking a cigar. As he walked slowly into the hospital with three other men, Knight's face was emotionless. Several young black men in the waiting room flocked to him, including Death Row's teenage singer Danny Boy, the only person in the contingent who cried openly. The crew hugged for a moment, then quickly pulled apart.

After Knight was told that Shakur's body had been removed from the hospital, the Death Row CEO and his boys made their way, very slowly, back to the Lexus. Knight didn't appear concerned with his own safety, in spite of rumors that he was the target

of whoever had shot Shakur. A collective sigh went up when Knight and his buddies drove off.

Like Kurt Cobain before him, Shakur had become a living symbol of his generation's angst and rage, and for that he is now looked upon as a martyr. But his fame and the controversy and misunderstanding that surrounded his life have also rendered Shakur – like Cobain, Marvin Gaye, James Dean, Jimi Hendrix, Jim Morrison and even Malcolm X – an enigma.

'Tupac had an anger; he had a temper just like all people do – but it certainly didn't drive his actions,' says Wendy Day of the Brooklyn-based Rap Coalition, an organization dedicated to creating an awareness of issues associated with hip hop culture. 'When the media portrays him as somebody who goes around beating up video directors and limo drivers, and shooting at cops, that's not the reality. I'm not saying he didn't do that, because it certainly was part of his personality. But I found him to be a warm, sensitive, caring, sharp businessman. Tupac had a wonderful point that he used to make: He would say, "Before I made a record, I never had a record," referring to crime.'

That much is true, but the last five years of Shakur's life were fraught with arrests and tragedy. Shakur's most notorious arrest came in 1993, when he was charged with raping a Brooklyn woman. He was ultimately convicted of one count of sexual abuse and served eight months of a four and a half year sentence. While in jail, Shakur married his girlfriend, Keisha Morris, but the marriage was annulled shortly after he signed with Death Row Records. Shakur was also arrested in 1993 on charges of shooting two off-duty police officers in Atlanta. Because of a lack of evidence, that case never made it to a grand jury. Witnesses had testified that Shakur and his entourage had shot in self-defence after the officers, wearing civilian clothes, fired at Shakur's car.

In addition to these and other arrests, Shakur was hit with a couple of civil suits. In

Top Doggz: Along with Dr. Dre, Snoop and Tupac spearheaded Death Row Records' rapid rise to the top of the rap industry.

1992, at a festival celebrating the 50th anniversary of Marin City, a Northern California ghetto enclave nicknamed the Jungle, a confrontation occurred between members of Shakur's entourage and another group of festival-goers. A gun was fired by someone in Shakur's crew and a six-year-old boy was shot and killed. No criminal charges were filed, although a civil lawsuit against Shakur and his then-label, Interscope Records, was settled out of court for a reported $300,000 to $500,000. That same year, lawyers defending a man accused of killing a Texas state trooper claimed that their client had been influenced by Shakur's first solo album, 1991's *2Pacalypse Now*, which contains references to violence against police officers. The trooper's widow filed a multimillion-dollar civil suit against Shakur, Interscope and its then-parent company, Time Warner.

Shakur began his musical career as a roadie and dancer with the Bay Area rap group Digital Underground. He had appeared on that group's 1990 collection, *This is an EP Release*, and the 1991 album

Sons of the P. That same year, Shakur released *2Pacalypse Now*, which includes the singles 'Brenda's Got a Baby' and 'Trapped.' In 1992, then-Vice President Dan Quayle targeted the album in his war against the breakdown of traditional values in the entertainment industry. Shakur's second album, *Strictly 4 My N.I.G.G.A.Z.*, came out in 1993, but it wasn't until two years later, with the release of *Me Against the World*, that the rapper became a multimillion-selling artist, partly because of his high-profile legal cases. This year's double album *All Eyez on Me* – Shakur's first for Death Row, which is distributed by Interscope – debuted at Number One on *Billboard*'s Top 200 chart.

Shakur's success mirrored that of two other Death Row artists, Dr. Dre and Snoop Doggy Dogg. The label was co-founded in 1992 by Dre, a former member of the original gangsta-rap group, NWA, and Suge Knight, an ex-University of Nevada football player. Knight has successfully created a myth around himself as an executive not unlike a Hollywood mob figure who has strong-armed his way into the entertainment industry. Many people inside the music business, afraid of his perceived power, were reluctant to speak on the record for this article. In 1991, Knight was sued by former NWA member Eazy-E, who died of AIDS in 1995. Eazy-E, who ran the rap label Ruthless Records, claimed that Knight had assaulted him with baseball bats and pipes, forcing Eazy-E to release Dre from his contract with Ruthless. The suit was dismissed.

Since its founding, Death Row, whose logo portrays a man strapped in an electric chair, has sold nearly eighteen million records and grossed more than $100 million on the strength of Dre's *The Chronic*, Snoop's *Doggystyle*, Tha Dogg Pound's *Dogg Food*, and two compilation albums. Despite its successes, however, Death Row has suffered major setbacks during the past year. In 1995, Time Warner, under fire from conservatives like William Bennett and anti-gangsta-rap activist C. DeLores Tucker, sold its 50 percent share of Death Row distributor Interscope Records back to the label's founders, Jimmy Iovine and Ted Fields, who then sold it to MCA Music Entertainment. (Neither Iovine nor Fields would comment on the Shakur murder or Interscope's recent business dealing.) Earlier this year, Dre split acrimoniously with Death Row, telling *The Hollywood Reporter* only days before Shakur's shooting, 'Gangsta rap is definitely a thing of the past. I've just moved on.'

Even before Shakur's death, sales figures showed that rap has suffered a slump since its 1991 peak, when rap accounted for ten percent of all records sold. Rap's market share dropped to 6.7 percent in 1995. Gangsta rap's place has been largely filled by the more melodic, pop-oriented sounds of rap artists such as the Fugees and the more street-oriented R&B of artists like R. Kelly. Even Death Row has now branched out into R&B.

It's an unseasonably chilly night in Jersey City, NJ, four days after Shakur's death, and the rapper's father, Billy Garland, is sitting in the modestly decorated apartment he shares with his wife. 'Me and Pac's life is so similar, you wouldn't believe it, bro,' says the tall, copper-colored 47-year-old man with thick eyebrows, deep dimples, a long nose and a hoop earring in his left ear. Garland looks hauntingly like Shakur – or, maybe I should say, Shakur looked like his father. The husky baritone voice is there, the lean body, the punctuating hand and facial gestures, the bright eyes and toothy smile.

As Shakur's song 'Dear Mama' fills the space in the apartment, I am astonished that this man is the father whom Shakur had told me several times before did not exist. 'A lot of times I feel responsible,' Garland says matter-of-factly, his eyes wet as he sits nervously on the edge of a dining-room chair. 'A lot of times I shed tears, 'cause a lot of shit he could have avoided. My son talked about father a lot. He didn't know I was alive when he made "Dear Mama."'

Nor did Tupac Shakur know the world that created him. Garland and Afeni Shakur, Tupac's mother, were both members of the Black Panther Party in 1970 when they met; Garland lived in Jersey City, Afeni in New York. 'Just like Tupac,' says Garland, 'I moved around a lot and never felt like I belonged to any community or family, until I joined the Panthers.' A year earlier, Afeni and twenty other New York Panthers – including her then husband, Lumumba Abdul Shakur – had been charged with multiple felonies, including conspiracy to bomb public areas in New York. While out on bail, Afeni dated Garland and a low-level gangster named Legs.

'When Afeni told me she was pregnant,' says Garland, 'I knew it was mine.'

Afeni Shakur's bail was revoked in early 1971, and she found herself in the Women's House of Detention in New York's Greenwich Village, pregnant with Tupac. In a previous interview, she told me, 'I never thought he'd make it here alive.' In May 1971, Afeni and her co-defendants were acquitted of all charges, and on June 16, 1971, her son was born. Afeni called him Tupac Amaru, for an Inca chief whose name means 'shining serpent'; Shakur is Arabic for 'thankful to God.'

By the time his son was born, Garland, who had two other children from previous relationships, was, as he puts it, 'doing [his] thing, and Afeni was doing hers.' The couple drifted apart, although Garland would see Tupac off and on until he was five years old. After that, Garland didn't have any contact with his son until 1992, when Garland saw Tupac in a poster for the film *Juice*.

In the intervening years, Tupac and his sister, Sekyiwa, lived with Afeni in the Bronx and Harlem, in New York, in homeless shelters and with relatives and friends. Tupac told me a few years ago that the political idealism of the Black Panther Party did not mesh with the harsh economic realities of his family's life. 'Here we was,' the rapper said, 'kickin' all this shit about the revolution – and we starvin'. That didn't make no sense to me.'

Afeni attempted to channel the creative energy of Tupac – who was often teased by family members and neighborhood boys for being 'pretty' – by enrolling him in a Harlem theater group when he was twelve. In his first performance, Tupac played Travis in *A Raisin in the Sun*. A ghetto child who never quite fit in, Shakur said it was on the theater stage that a new world unfolded for him. 'I remember thinking, "This is something that none of them kids can do,"' Shakur told me. 'I didn't like my life, but through acting, I could become somebody else.'

What seems to have affected Shakur even more than a disillusionment with who he was and where he lived was the absence of a father in his life. He had assumed that Legs, once connected to the legendary New York drug kingpin Nicky Barnes, was his real father, and Shakur admired him. 'That's where the thug in me came from,' he said.

Legs was the person who would introduce Afeni to crack, a drug she was haunted by for much of the Eighties. After Legs was sent to prison for credit-card fraud in the mid-Eighties, Afeni, tired of her struggles in New York, moved her family to Baltimore.

When she called to alert Legs of her whereabouts, Afeni learned he had died of a crack-induced heart attack. 'That fucked me up,' Tupac told me. 'I couldn't even cry, man. I felt I needed a daddy to show me the ropes, and I didn't have one.'

In 1986, Tupac Shakur was accepted into the prestigious Baltimore School for the Arts. A natural actor, he immersed himself in school productions and felt he had finally found his niche. 'That school was saving me, you know what I'm sayin'?' Shakur told me. 'I was writing poetry and shit, and I became known as MC New York because I was rapping, and then I was doing the acting thing. It was a whole other experience for me to be able to express myself – not just around black people but also around white people and other kinds of people. It was the freest I ever felt in my life.'

That period ended when Shakur was seventeen and his family moved to Marin City. There, his life would drastically change direction. For one, he wouldn't finish high school. He spent the next few years selling drugs, hustling on the streets, crashing in different people's homes and watching his relationship with his mother deteriorate completely. In 1989 things began to look up. Shakur met Shock-G, the leader of Digital Underground, and landed a job as a roadie and dancer. The group's hit song, 'Humpty Dance,' was just about to become the hip hop rage. After a tour and some recording with DU, Shakur embarked on his solo rap and acting careers.

Garland re-established his relationship with Shakur two years later, in November 1994, just after the rapper had been shot in New York. 'I had to be there,' Garland says softly. 'He's my son. I've never asked him for anything – not money or nothing. I just wanted to let him know that I cared.'

Garland says Afeni OK'd the visit, and Tupac, though a bit groggy, was surprised and happy to meet him. 'He thought I was dead or that I didn't want to see him,' Garland says with a tinge of anger. 'How

15

could I feel like that? He's my flesh and my blood. Look at me. He looks just like me. People who I had never seen before immediately knew I was his father.'

Garland's voice trails off. '[Tupac] was a genius, and he was only 25,' Garland says. 'I just hope all of them kids who sent all these letters learn something from Tupac's life. And I hope the people who murdered my son pay.'

During the past three years, I talked with Tupac Shakur on numerous occasions – at his home in Atlanta, inside a New York jail, at a barbecue joint in South Central Los Angeles – and had gotten to know him rather well. He was a complex human being both brilliant and foolish; very funny and deadly serious; friendly and eager to please, but also bad-tempered and prone to violence; a lover of his people and of women but also a race divider and a convicted sex offender; generous to a fault but also a dangerous gambler when it came to his personal and professional life; incredibly talented but at times frivolously shortsighted. To me, Shakur was the most important solo artist in the history of rap, not because he was the most talented (he wasn't), but because he, more than any other rapper, personified and articulated what it was to be a young black man in America.

But the demons of Shakur's childhood – the poverty, the sense of displacement, the inconsistent relationship with his mother, the absence of a regular father figure – haunted the rapper all his life. In his song 'Dear Mama' from *Me Against the World* he sings, 'When I was young, me and my mama had beefs / Seventeen years old, kicked out on the streets.'

Shakur's lyrics were all over the map. Sometimes you didn't know if he loved black people or if he absolutely despised them. When you juxtapose the deeply uplifting 'Keep Ya Head Up' with the venomous 'Hit 'Em Up' – on which he refers to the rapper Biggie Smalls and his wife, R&B singer Faith, in the line, 'You claim to be a player, but I fucked your wife' – you get a clear picture of Shakur's schizophrenic nature regarding issues of race and gender. What made him special, however, was that he wasn't afraid to put himself out there, conflicts and all, for public support or ridicule.

Shakur's music is part Public Enemy and part NWA, and his rapping is part preacher and part street hustler. The sound has a chaotic urgency, reflecting Shakur's East Coast roots, but it isn't as sophisticated as the cut-and-paste artistry of PE's *Bomb Squad*. The beats are very spare, the loops and samples are straightforward. Yet his most popular hits – like the recent 'How Do U Want It?' – are more melodic than most New York-based hip hop, more along the lines of West Coast artists like Warren G or Dr. Dre.

By 1995, Shakur seemed tired of the hip hop game. 'I don't even got the thrill to rap no more,' he told me. According to his long-time friend Karen Lee, ''Pac always carried the weight of a lot of people on his shoulders. All he ever wanted was to hear himself on the radio and to see himself on the movie screen.' Given Shakur's iconic status, it's no wonder that some people have already begun to speculate that the rapper is still alive, that he faked his death. Shakur has become a symbol, an anti-hero.

Now that Tupac Shakur is gone, some will charge that it was the music that killed him or that he had it coming because of the choices he made in his life. To me, those are cop-out, knee-jerk responses. Shakur, in spite of his bad-boy persona, was a product of a post-civil rights, post-Black Panther, post-Ronald Reagan American environment. We may never find out who killed Tupac Shakur, or why he did the things he did and said what he said. All we have left are his music, his films and his interviews. Shakur lived fast and hard, and he has died fast and hard. And in his own way, he kept it real for a lot of folks who didn't believe that anyone like him (or like themselves) could do anything with his life.

AN INTERVIEW WITH TUPAC'S MOM

by Davey D

This interview took place one week before the one-year anniversary of Tupac's untimely death. His mother, Afeni Shakur, who has been the subject of so much of Tupac's work, talked very passionately about her son. During the interview his godfather, Geronimo Pratt, rolled through, and his sister Set also stopped through . . . .

Davey D: *The first thing I want to do is thank you for granting us this interview. We're up on the anniversary of your son's untimely death. There are so many of us that are still in the shock, so many of us who can't believe it and so many of us within the Hip Hop Generation that are trying to heal from this. And one way we can bring about this healing is to continue to study and learn about Tupac. I guess the best way to really do that is by talking to you, his mom, Afeni Shakur. You're the person who can provide us with that bridge of information. After all, you're the woman who raised him, you're the person who helped shape him, and helped make him into the person whom we've come to admire. I guess the first thing I would like you to do is let our listeners know who Afeni Shakur was. You were a member of the Black Panther Party, you were pregnant with Tupac while in jail, as one of the infamous New York 21. Who is Afeni Shakur?*

Afeni Shakur: Basically, first let me just say peace and respect to all of the listeners, and all of the people who care about my son, who care about his work and who care about his music. And the first thing I would like to do is give encouragement to brothers and sisters who are artists or trying to be artists. From the bottom of my heart, I encourage them to work on their art and to not allow anyone or anything to keep their artist spirit down. And that to me is really important.

And then having said that, let me say that I was a member of the Black Panther Party. I joined in 1968. When I joined, I wasn't a student. I did not come off the college campuses like a lot of known Panthers did. I came from the streets of the South Bronx. I had been a member of the Disciple Debs, which would have been the women Disciples in the Bronx. What the Panther Party did for me, I used to always say it gave me home training. The Party taught me things that were principles to living, and those principles are the principles I think most Panthers have tried to pass on to their children and to anybody else that would listen to them. You know that one of those principles was like, don't steal a penny, needle or a simple piece of thread from the people. It's just general basic things about how we as individuals treat a race of people, and how we treat each other as a people! And those are the things I think the people recognize in Tupac . . . .

We discovered, within the BPP, that you try and live by these principles and you have attached to those principles a willingness and a desire to protect and defend your family and your people. Also, if you have a large mouth and you're willing to speak openly about those things, that you are going to be the victim of all kinds of attacks. That's basically what has happened to all of us. Tupac was and remains in my mind a child of the BPP. I think that I always felt that even though this society had destroyed the work of the BPP. I always felt that Tupac was living witness to who we are and who we were. I think that his life spoke to every part of our development and the development of the Party, and the development in this country that I don't think will die.

Davey D: *One of the perspectives that people have put forth about Tupac was that he*

Afeni Shakur confers with fellow Black Panthers Elbert Howard and Ray Massi Hewitt at a 1970 press conference.

was a gangster, and that he was somebody who invited trouble. How do you address that? How should we, especially those of us within the Hip Hop Generation, perceive Tupac?

Afeni Shakur: First of all, the difference in people's temperament and my temperament, our temperament is such that it's just like you were asking me about a song, 'Wade in the Water, God Gonna Trouble the Waters.' We want the waters troubled. We are trouble makers, it's what we are here for. We don't make apologies for it. Why would we? We are revolutionaries, the children of revolutionaries . . . I believe that this is true, basically of young people in any generation. And that's just true naturally. For us, we're trouble makers, because why wouldn't we be trouble makers in a society that has no respect for us? The fact is that it is a miracle

that we sit here. I don't think that we are supposed to be anything but trouble makers. Tupac used to comment on people who criticized him for cursing, as a matter of fact he said this just about verbatim, 'As I walked into this hall, I passed a young child who was hungry. There is not a bigger curse than a young child hungry. If we are not concerned about the incest, the rape, about our children dying at the rate that they are dying, I cannot imagine why we would be making all this noise about a word, any word.'

Davey D: *Do you think his music influenced people to move in a direction of violence? That was one thing, I remember the police in Houston wanted to sue him and say that he caused an officer to be shot . . . .*

Afeni Shakur: They did sue him in Houston and, as a matter of fact, that campaign was

18

started by C. Delores Tucker who has now sued Tupac's estate, namely Tupac's music. Has sued him for interfering with her and her husband's sexual life. Now, don't you think that's preposterous? Of course it is. And I think it's okay for us to say that it is, and it's just as preposterous to think that music could influence you to do anything else. If that were possible, will someone please make a song that will influence us to not kill each other. Please, I beg any person to do that. That should be simple under that mentality. But obviously, that's an irrational concept, and that's what I mean about us thinking. Don't allow people to think for you. Let's use ration. It's okay for us to do it. I'll tell you something else, for people who feel so bad about Tupac's leaving this planet, we should remember that each of us come here with a beginning date and an ending date. Tupac's beginning was June 16, 1971 and his end was September 13, 1996. In the 25 years that God gave him on this earth, he shone like a star, and he did all that he was supposed to do, he said all that he needed to say. You need not weep for Tupac, but weep for yourself, because we are left here with these contradictions that we still must face.

Davey D: *The whole rivalry between Tupac and Biggie and to see both of them at the height of their careers, as far as a lot of people are concerned, gone . . . . Have you ever talked to Biggie's mom? You know you guys are looked at in a way where it's like, well, wow if we can't get next to them, we have to get next to their mothers. What words do you pass on about that? And what are your thoughts on that?*

Afeni Shakur: Let me say that my son was

killed on September 13th 1996, and on November 10, Yafeu Fula, one of the Outlawz and a member of my son's group and a member of our family, was murdered . . . and on January 12 a daughter of another member of the BPP was murdered in her bed with her baby playing in her bed while the killer, her husband, watched all day long. What I have known from the beginning is that I am not alone. And that I am not alone does not mean that the only two people that got killed were Biggie and Tupac. I am so sorry, but every child's death is painful. To me, it's painful because it's this process that we have to stop. We are right back to the same thing which is about ration and reason . . . and about winning. And as I said, Tupac had 25 years and he did 25 years worth of wonderful work. What the next person needs to know in whatever years they are allotted to them, is what have they done? And I'm sure that Biggie's mother must feel the same about her son. It's no use in people trying to swage their own guilt for their own deficiency by debating or spending that much time on Tupac and Biggie.

Davey D: *What do you mean by swage?*

Afeni Shakur: I mean that we all have to speak about our own issues. When we talk about rivalries, with East/West Coast, I don't have any idea what that is. But let me say this, my son was shot on two separate occasions; the first was five times, twice in the head, and at that time we thought he could have died. So a year later he was shot again and he did die, but there wasn't a rivalry. My son was injured by gunshots and my son reacted through his music to what had happened to him and, as I say, Tupac spoke elo-

> ## 'Growing up, I could cook, clean, and sew, but I just didn't feel hard.' — *Tupac*

quently about how he felt about all of that East/West Coast stuff. I would not try and change one period of a sentence that Tupac spoke about that, because Tupac was an honorable young man. He did not lie and whatever Tupac said happened, happened in that way. And I think that people have to deal with their responsibilities for whatever they have done or not done. That's a part of life also. Tupac dealt with his responsibilities, I think other people have to do the same.

Davey D: *You talk about Tupac being honorable and speaking truth. How did you feel when he said things about you in records?*

Afeni Shakur: He told the truth. I live with truth. I have no secrets. Neither did Tupac, neither does my daughter. We don't live behind secrets, we don't live lies, we are who we are, and we are pretty happy to be who we are. We are proud of who we are and we stand tall and defend who we are.

Davey D: *Was it painful to hear him talk about you having a drug addiction? Was it something that you had to discuss or did you know that he would put some things that happened in his life in music for the public to look at and hear and formulate their own opinion?*

Afeni Shakur: Let me first say that any of those songs that Tupac wrote was primarily the way he felt about something. You have a right to express your feelings. I do not have to agree with them. I needed him to say how he felt, specifically about the pain that I had caused him. That's how we heal, and so you know for me it was Tupac explaining something that happened to his family, his reaction to it and his feelings about it. I think they were honest and I respect him for that. Absolutely and completely.

Davey D: *Tupac has done a lot of things in his career. What do you think he should*

have done differently in terms of the decisions he made? What sort of path do you think he should have continued on? Do you think he deviated, or went down the wrong corner in any of the things that he did?

Afeni Shakur: I think that Tupac made perfect decisions for himself. I would like to encourage young people to make decisions for themselves. You make decisions that you stand by and you take responsibility for them. Really, this is life, you try to make a difference in people's lives, because you stand firm for something. So really, for me, Tupac was perfection.

Davey D: *What do you think are the misperceptions that you as his mom would like to clear up about him?*

Afeni Shakur: The misconceptions are that Tupac was a rapper, that Tupac wasn't political and that Tupac was a gangster. But primarily I really think that time will take care of that. I have faith in Tupac's legend. I really believe in the divinity of legends. I believe that God chose Tupac and I believe that no human being can destroy his image, his legend, his life, his music or his work. So in reality I don't care what people say, because I truly believe that God sent him here. He sent him with a mission. He fulfilled his mission and he went back where he came from.

Davey D: *What is it about Tupac that so many people admired, and still admire about him?*

Afeni Shakur: His truth in the face of anything. And I think that you know that's why people don't want to believe that he is dead. Because they believe that Tupac could face anything, and come out on the other side. Let me say, so can you.

Davey D: *It's been a year and there's been a lot of controversy surrounding his death in terms of who owns the estate, recording* *rights and situations involving the record company Death Row. What is happening with that? Can you give us an understanding on where things stand and where you hope to have things going?*

Afeni Shakur: As it relates to Death Row, we have reached an agreement, a settlement of some sort and I'm sure that's probably resolved.

Davey D: *There has been an iron hand placed upon people who might have had affiliations with Tupac in terms of them releasing his earlier music. I guess that's good, because they have always had to come through and somehow deal with you one way or the other before materials are released. Where does that stand now? Will we start to hear some of his earlier recordings? Some of the things he left with Death Row, will they start to come out or are there other plans for releases of his music materials, movies, etc?*

Afeni Shakur: Well, some of Tupac's extended and biological family have started Amaru Records, which is a record company that Tupac would have started had he still been here. We are going to first release his earlier material so that people have a more comprehensive understanding of what his journey was. We have the end of his journey, it would probably be okay to have the beginning also, so that's what we are attempting to do with his first release. And after that, we would like to do a tribute album and an audio book of his poetry. We also are committed, within the next two or three years to developing and releasing up to eight new artists. So prayfully we will be able to do what we want to do in our business in a principled and ethical manner. Outside of that, we are trying to negotiate a documentary about Tupac's life. Possibly and probably a feature film with HBO with a producer by the name of Marvin Worth . . . what we wanted is for people not to steal Tupac's material.

It had really less to do with control than it had to do with stealing. And the problem I have with stuff is that, I always say if Tupac were here would you do it? And to answer the question, you wouldn't do it if he were here. First of all I have no respect for you because you are a coward. And I know if Tupac was here he would call you one of those names that he knew oh so well. And that's pretty much the way I feel about the *Vibe* pictorial book. I found out about it when it was reviewed in *Essence* magazine. I had been speaking to Quincy Jones all year and he never mentioned it. I have no respect for that kind of behavior. People can buy what they want, but just don't expect me to say it's cool . . . and further more I ain't mad at nobody . . . .

Davey D: *What individuals do you see today that embody the revolutionary spirit that has often been associated with Tupac? Who has that mindset?*

Afeni Shakur: Well, I really think Sista Souljah has that type of spirit. I think Geronimo Pratt also has it ⋅ . . . and so does Mumia Adul Jamal . . . . The fact is . . . that I'm not wailing off the names of young brothers and sisters a mile a minute . . . it's not like Tupac was the most excellent person . . . I just ask for people to be honorable, honest, and honest to themselves about themselves and to be courageous about truth. When I can see more of that, I'll just feel a little better, but whether I do or don't I'm not mad at nobody . . . .

Davey D: *Is this a lost generation? Are we a lost generation?*

Afeni Shakur: Absolutely not! Thank you Treach for your song. Thank you Scarface for your song. Thanks for the respect Bones Thugs N Harmony. Thanks for the respect and at least musically understanding what my son was about and saying. They've done that. I thank them from the bottom of my heart . . . .

THE MUSIC IS THE MESSAGE

by Bronwyn Garrity

At Crenshaw High School, the students boo before Leila Steinberg gets a chance to greet them. When she goes downtown to a group home for troubled teens, they kick aside their chairs and yell, in not so many words, that they aren't up for any empty talk. At Beverly Hills High, they just yawn.

Steinberg, 40, is used to ruthless adolescent judgment – she faces it weekly as the founder of Assemblies in Motion, a nonprofit organization of hip hop artists who perform at socially minded assemblies for high schools, detention centers and foster homes. Steinberg confesses that being a white Jewish mother can undermine her image as a force in rap. But she also points out that her fair complexion and last name made helping launch the careers of early hip hop stars, including Mac Mall and the late Tupac Shakur, possible. 'Doors were opened to me [in the record industry] that were still closed to them because they were black.' The kids in the audience sit up a little straighter.

Steinberg grew up in Watts and is herself an artist who once performed with world music greats O. J. Ekemode and the Nigerian Allstars. She ultimately decided to focus not on performing, but on raising art out of the inner cities and, then, taking it back in – as education. 'We have really failed children in the school system [by undervaluing the arts],' she says, preferring to emulate a time in human history when art was used to educate, to connect, to reform, to vent and to document. 'One artist can have more impact on an entire school system than all the academic classes put together, but there are no educators for artists and artists don't understand that they're educators.' She believes it is high time to call on today's performers to be teachers, voices and tools of social change.

To this end, Steinberg, who relocated her family and work to Los Angeles from the Bay Area less than a year ago, runs an ecosystem of projects, including Moses Soul (a record label and film production company), the Microphone Sessions (a raucous Monday night performance workshop) and Assemblies in Motion (the education-oriented top of Steinberg's food chain).

Benefiting from any cash flowing out of Moses Soul, Assemblies in Motion also pulls the best talent from the open-to-the-public Microphone Sessions, held at legendary Studio 56 in Hollywood, where Elvis Presley, Billie Holiday, Charlie Parker, Ella Fitzgerald and John Coltrane all recorded soundtracks.

As it happens, the current members of Assemblies in Motion – or AIM, as it is most often called – still attend the workshops, perfecting new pieces in front of the mostly black inner-city adults who are themselves present to work on their own poetry and music. This week, Steinberg, in collaboration with Quincy Jones and his son, Quincy D. Jones III, will see the DVD release of *Thug Angel: The Life of an Outlaw*, a documentary about Shakur, with whom Steinberg worked in the Bay Area's Microphone Sessions and AIM projects of the Eighties. Steinberg also was executive producer with Tracy Robinson and Jones III on the film's soundtrack, to be released in May.

It was as one of the only white kids in Seventies Watts that Steinberg recalls discerning her privilege. 'I always understood that I could very easily get away with anything; the other kids asked me to do things for them, to get people's attention because they couldn't.' In the early Eighties, she and her then-husband Bruce Crawford, a prominent black DJ from Los Angeles, moved to Sonoma, where she found work as the artistic director of the Petaluma Cultural Center. On the side, Steinberg organised her husband's musical events and concerts.

With her love of world music and his of rap, the duo became well-known in the Bay Area for hosting some of the most rousing concerts of the time, with thousands of revelers trudging in from all over to check out the unusual combination of African, reggae, rap, rock and world music. 'We had thousands of kids at the events, so I knew what I could do in terms of bridging cultures and communities and aligning artists.' Pretty soon, she also had the biggest names in hip hop headlining, including New Kids on the Block, Tone Loc, Digital Underground and Egyptian Lover. But Steinberg always made room on the stage for talented unknowns.

In producing the shows, Steinberg saw the tremendous power and political potential of rap. She set out to create a multicultural performance company that would combine poetry, rap, hip hop and dance that were also relevant social statements, 'so that people would walk away transformed,' she says.

Whether it was her agenda or their own, artists turned out by the hundreds to her weekly tryouts. Word on the street at the time was that if you wanted a record deal, you had to meet this 'white girl of hip hop.' Not only did she produce huge events with big stars, she was rumored to know everyone in the industry, and to be able to get in the doors of record companies. The influx of people desiring a chance on the tryout stage never ebbed, however, and Steinberg realized that it was in itself a movement. Thus began the Microphone Sessions.

Somewhere in the same city, a young artist named Tupac Shakur heard the rumors about Steinberg and set out to find her. But, the afternoon in 1986 that he met her, he was not thinking about music. She was a white woman sitting on the grass outside Bayside Elementary School in Marin County, quietly reading a book about Winnie Mandela, and, Shakur, on a school-time ramble about town, stopped in his tracks to scold her.

'Give me a break,' he said. 'What do you know about Winnie Mandela?' Steinberg, who taught an art class at Bayside, said she would be able to tell him something, but not until she'd finished the book. But Shakur, who was a prolific reader, proceeded to grill her – until he was impressed enough by her grasp of black culture to ask for her name. When he learned it, he laughed at destiny. He'd found his mentor.

So, it turns out, had Steinberg. At only sixteen, Shakur was already celebrated on the street for his explosive and articulate talent. Friends who had seen him perform reported that the boy's gift for writing and captivating audiences was just what her group needed. Indeed, the evening of their first meeting, Shakur accompanied Steinberg to the Microphone Sessions. Soon after, the two launched AIM, performing at one crammed Bay Area high school assembly after another. As their work with high school audiences progressed, Steinberg distanced herself more and more from the concerts on which she'd worked so hard. Her priority now was AIM – and helping Shakur find his place in the world.

'What made Tupac special was the fact that he put his soul on the record. There are very few artists who give it up like that anymore,' says Jones III. 'I think [Steinberg] taught him how to do that, how to not be afraid to say who he was.'

Steinberg's role in the young artist's life was pivotal, says Shakur's mother: 'We are all indebted to Leila, Tupac's first manager and adult friend, for her integrity in looking after the safety of [his] work,' says Afeni Shakur.

When Steinberg recounts the story of how she and Tupac Shakur met, her teen audience at an AIM assembly at Beverly High settle, finally, into their seats. Steinberg laughs, knowing that while the ice is breaking, the kids still aren't convinced that she can entertain them. 'But once I bring my artists out, every one of these kids transforms,' she says. 'Whether they're white, black, in jail or in Malibu, young people respond to music.'

Out slides Kumasi, the handsome black

schoolteacher and Islamic fundamentalist who raps in a smooth voice about life in the streets. 'I'm a soldier,' he intones, 'in the war of life . . . . Where are the captains? We're losing men . . . .'

Then, Java, an actor in the recent film *Baby Boy* and the one expected to make it big for his brilliant writing and acting talents. There's Hope, whose voice stirs goose bumps, and Fatso, who wrote a song about his mother's crack addiction and his life without a role model. When the kids see Mo, they giggle and point – he plays a character on the television show *Boston Public*. GaKnew, for whom the kids stand up and cheer, closes with a story about forgiving white people for the historical treatment of blacks, and about being an American.

Steinberg was right: The audience is rapt.

At Beverly, students rush the stage to slap hands, hug and get autographs.

At Crenshaw, hecklers are moved to tears.

At a group home for troubled teens, boys stay an extra two hours to talk politics and social issues.

But Steinberg's theme of music and transformation has been important for the young artists as well as for the teen spectators. As AIM members, GaKnew and the others were culled from the large, regular crowd that attends the Microphone Sessions.

The Microphone Sessions, as the classes became known in the Bay Area because of Steinberg's mandate to 'get up to the stage' and perform, are composed mostly of young African Americans from the inner city. While many are now successful actors, producers and publicists, many more have histories as drug addicts and dealers, gang members and felons. Many tell stories about addicted mothers. Steinberg, who has been a foster parent – officially or informally – to more than fifteen kids in the last ten years, has heard it all, and encourages her artists to write about those experiences. There is no censorship in her sessions, and no rules except honesty.

On a Monday night at the Microphone Sessions, Steinberg perches on a large speaker near the stage inside Studio 56. She opens the evening with a discussion about current events, and then asks for volunteers to perform. No one moves.

'What's up, Fatso?' Steinberg calls out. 'Come up here, please.'

The young man, who is confident on stage at AIM assemblies, seems suddenly self-conscious. 'I don't got anything tonight, Leila.' He waits with his head down.

'Yes, you do. You're up. Get up there.' Steinberg points to the stage. The class, reclining in chairs and couches scattered about the room, watches intently.

'Send it!' cries a woman moving into his abandoned hiding place. There is laughter at the familiar blessing.

'I'm Fatso. Fatso Fasano,' he declares, all coolness now. 'This is to you, little brother,' he says, nodding to a sixteen-year-old near Steinberg. The boy has just told the class he's going to be the father of twins.

Fatso explains that he wrote the song for his friend Hope to sing, but she's not here tonight. Fatso goes for it himself, but Steinberg stops him and sends another artist, Molly, to the stage. Although she has never seen the lyrics, she leans in, her voice wavering at first and then rising, booming out into the room.

Fatso and other AIM members often attend both the Microphone Sessions and once-or twice-weekly assemblies, work Steinberg considers crucial to the artists' – and society's – growth.

'They want to be stars, of course,' she says of her artists. They know she can help them with record deals when the time comes, but her plan is to make sure they are giving back to the community before then.

Fatso, a former hustler, says that 'working with Leila inspired me to make a difference and help change the world, to be a part of the solution instead of the problem.'

Being socially responsible isn't always financially easy. It costs money to put on AIM assemblies, even though the artists perform

'Pac talked a lot about death in his songs . . . A lot of people believed that he was foreseeing his death rather than creating it.' – Leila Steinberg

free. To keep AIM going, Steinberg pours money earned from Moses Soul into her workshops and the early careers of her artists. Additionally, Paul Schwartz donates the use of Studio 56 because, he says, he believes in the art that springs from the sessions.

At the end of her high school assemblies, Steinberg usually opens a forum for free discussion – about race, political issues and society. For a person to be truly powerful, she says, as an artist or otherwise, she must be articulate, well-read and understand the strength and meaning of what she is saying. 'The more you look at [history] through the music of the times, the more you under-stand what was going on. Textbooks tell us what the government thought. Music tells us about the people.'

Steinberg talks of a final and important lesson – ironically, one Shakur never learned before his death in Las Vegas in 1996: the need for artists to believe in the power of their words.

''Pac talked a lot about death in his songs,' she recalls. 'A lot of people believed that he was foreseeing his death rather than creating it.' His words had power that he didn't respect, she says. ''Pac wrote himself out of his script. He didn't understand the real power of what he was saying.'

MY BROTHER
by Benjamin Meadows-Ingram

As the mastermind behind the influential Oakland collective Digital Underground, Shock-G (born Gregory Jacobs in New York in 1963) provided a P-Funked-out, party-time alternative for a hip hop era otherwise defined by the political angst of Public Enemy, KRS-One and NWA. But, as Shock is the first to admit, DU's larger legacy stems just as much from introducing the world to Tupac Shakur.

Referred by DU's manager Atron Gregory, an eighteen-year-old Tupac dropped by Oakland's Starlight Studios for an impromptu audition in 1989. Impressed, Shock offered 'Pac a job the following year when the group went out as part of Public Enemy's *Fear of a Black Planet* tour. Officially hired as a roadie and dancer, 'Pac earned a chance to freestyle during each night's set, and made his first recorded appearance on DU's playful 1991 hit, 'Same Song.' Shock would go on to produce three tracks ('Rebel of the Underground,' 'Solja's Story' and 'Tha Lunatic') on 'Pac's solo debut *2Pacalypse Now* (1992), as well as his breakout single 'I Get Around' in 1993, and 'So Many Tears' in 1995.

Although they grew apart over the years, the foundation of their personal and professional relationship stayed strong. At the time of 'Pac's death in 1996, Shock was working as his musical director, constructing a show for his upcoming tour. Says Shock: 'Way beyond Digital Underground, 'Pac would always shout us out in interviews and give us props on his albums. Even though his thing was bigger than what we were doing, he never forgot and he never dissed.'

Benjamin Meadows-Ingram: *What was 2Pac like when you first met him?*

Shock-G: I was in the studio, mixing down *Sex Packets*. He came in real businesslike, like, 'Yo, are you Shock-G? Wassup. I'm Tupac. You want me to spit right now?' And I could just feel 'Pac's energy, feel him wanting to do this. Some people come in and they're a little nervous, they wanna hang out first, but 'Pac wanted to get right to it. So I took him to the piano room and he did one looking at me fierce, eye to eye. 'You wanna hear another?' . . . He didn't have that '2Pac' style yet, though. He was a Chuck D-head. The first rhyme he spit was MC-ish, but it was a pro-black political rap, educational and full of struggle. Most of his first demo was Public Enemy-ish, X-Clan-ish. I really thought he was hot, because at the time I was living in Oakland, and I couldn't understand most of the local cats. Most of them rhymed country and slow and that wasn't hot yet. 'Pac rhymed articulate. He didn't sound square, but he sounded clear.

Diction was different then. All the cats that were considered hot – KRS-One, Rakim, Craig G spoke good, articulate English. But he always sounded how you're supposed to sound that year, so when the West and South hit hip hop, and it started to sound like NWA, Cube and Scarface, he sounded like them niggas.

It was still political, but in a different way. Like, 'Fuck speaking the Queen's English.' That was part of the pro-African American, pro-poor, pro-have nothing thing. 'Pac was always a thug. He just didn't think to put it in his music yet. Nobody did, 'cause NWA hadn't happened yet. He'd put positive shit in his songs, and then be a nigga in the streets. But once he saw that being a nigga in the recording booth worked as well, he incorporated that into his style.

Benjamin Meadows-Ingram: *What was he like on tour?*

Shock-G: He knew that was the opportuni-

26

ty for him, and every chance he got to rhyme, he rhymed. When it was his turn to rhyme on stage, instead of rhyming to the audience, he'd be rhyming to the backstage, making sure Ice Cube and Chuck D heard him. 'Pac's flow was average, but his lyrics were incredible, and he didn't waste words. You could feel he really meant what he said.

One time 'Pac came busting into our dressing room, like, 'Yo, guess what! Chuck D just told me I got flows, Chuck D! Whoooo!!' Then he'd run out the room and tell the next person.

Benjamin Meadows-Ingram: *What was 'Pac like around women?*

Shock-G: I knew he was a star, 'cause even when he was the unknown new guy, he would bury as many chicks or more than me and Money-B – and we were video stars. When the girls came to the room, they sweated 'Pac, just because of his demeanor, and the way he was walking and talking. Sometimes he'd unzip in the dressing room and hit a bitch before we even got to the hotel. But he was tactless. A lot of us would shake girls after we had sex with them, but his tact was bad. On the surface he'd be mean like, 'Yo, why is this bitch still here?' But deep down he was scared, like he didn't know what to do with the chick. Looking back, it's clear that he was worried that she might find something in him that she wouldn't like.

Benjamin Meadows-Ingram: *What was 'Pac's creative process like in the studio?*

Shock-G: He showed up late and left early. I'd spend eight hours on his song, and he'd be there for 40 minutes. He'd get pissed if you asked him to do [his vocals] again.

That's the way it was, 'You straight? If you need me, holla.' Then he'd go buy some weed, meet this chick, whatever he had to do . . . . He was always high. I never really saw him sober, 'cause if he was sober he wasn't happy. And he was just always thinking and writing. He'd be on the toilet shitting, and if the phone rings, he'd go to the other room to get the phone . . . and you come in. 'Yo let me use the bathroom,' and there's piss and shit all over the toilet. He just didn't have time for it. He felt like Martin Luther King or Malcolm X or something – he knew it could come and he had to get shit done before it came.

'All I ever wanted to do was make a record and make a movie.' – Tupac

Benjamin Meadows-Ingram: *What about when he wasn't working?*

Shock-G: Outside of his poetry book and his music, 'Pac was a weirdo. He was the worst basketball player. His shots would miss the whole backboard. But he would throw a fit, like, 'Yo, how come I can't play?' He wrecked every car he owned in the first week or two he had it. As far as we were concerned, he couldn't handle police well, 'cause he was always the one getting us arrested. His house was a mess. And all he ate was barbeque wings. I knew 'Pac wasn't planning on living long, 'cause I never once saw him eat a vegetable. He might eat a French fry, never saw him drink water. I never saw him drink nothing but beer and Hennessy. Beer, Hennessy, hot wings, Newports and weed – that was that nigga's diet.

And we all knew 'Pac had a boil-over point. His eyes would water up easy whenever he got mad, frustrated or sad, and you couldn't challenge him without it being a scene.

As big of a celebrity as 'Pac was, deep

'Don't fuck with the Underground' – Tupac backstage at a DU concert in 1990.

down he had that same gap foster kids have. That whole shit from relative to relative. Never feeling loved, like he didn't fit in, didn't have a foundation. He didn't feel like anybody loved him unless he was 2Pac the character. Tupac the thug was a celebrity, but Tupac Shakur, just the man, the boy at one point, felt like nobody loved him. So when we'd step to him like, 'Pac, you need to calm down, these muthafuckas out here are trying to kill you, he'd just look at you with this confused look, like, 'What the fuck do you mean? I had nothing. Now have everything.' And it's from being this wild person.

Benjamin Meadows-Ingram: *How much did you see him after he left DU? When you did see him, how had he changed?*

Shock-G: After he came to my wedding reception in 1994, I only saw 'Pac four or five times, and you could tell he was different. His jewelry was sparkling a little more, he had more tats, and he wasn't a skinny nigga anymore. The stress in his eyes was more grown, and his eyes were redder. The bags

of weed were bigger and there was Hennessy in the studio now. He's important and there's important muthafuckas standing around. Sometimes you see 'Pac, and he's with an entourage of cats, there's press all around, and he's moving. You just go up there to put something in his hand and say wassup, and he just gives you that look like, I can't stop right now, it's bigger than me.

Benjamin Meadows-Ingram: *How did you feel about Suge? How did 'Pac change with Death Row?*

Shock-G: I thought it was a good thing. When I used to look at the cover of *Vibe* with 'Pac, Snoop, Ore and Suge, I was proud of that nigga. I was like, Goddamn, look at that muthafucka. He was just fooling around with us and these little labels. Now look at him. As for Suge's intentions, I can't speak on shit that I don't know. But I do know that Suge was the only one that could hold that nigga down the way he wanted to be held down.

Benjamin Meadows-Ingram: *What about*

in the studio in those later years?

Shock-G: In the studio, we were working. We talked about music, and he was so excited to play you his new shit, I'd try to tell him what I liked about *All Eyez on Me* and he's like, 'Yeah, yeah, I did that for Suge. Listen to this . . .' and he put *Makaveli* on. There was too much bad shit going on to be hashing that shit. You could see it in his eyes, he didn't want to talk about it no more, and you didn't even wanna bring it up.

Benjamin Meadows-Ingram: *What was it like hanging out with 'Pac?*

Shock-G: 'Pac would do stupid shit, but you never did not invite that nigga. If 'Pac was there, I felt better, safer in some ways. I knew some stupid shit could go down, but when you rolled out with 'Pac, you knew you were rolling at maximum output. We gonna look good, roll big, floss, pull the bitches. Like, I'm about to have a great night. And only 'Pac could lead it. But there was no quiet time for 'Pac. I'd be going to bed and he'd be off to the craziest session on the craziest side of town. The shit he was getting into, I didn't have the energy for that shit. He had to be where the action was. He had to learn it, see it, tell it. And it got to the point where being around 'Pac was usually stressful.

Benjamin Meadows-Ingram: *What was your personal relationship with 'Pac like?*

Shock-G: Tupac was like a relative to me. When he called me to the studio, I was there. When I needed him, he was there. One time when I wasn't seeing him that much, a lot of people were asking me to talk to him. Even his mom, like, 'He'll listen to you, Shock.' But I felt like he wouldn't listen to me either. I was like, 'Yo, 'Pac, I'm on tour, here's a key to my condo. It's quiet, nobody will know that you're there. When you feel this is too much, here's a spot you can go, hide out, watch *The Jeffersons* and just chill.

He's like, 'But I gotta go to Europe tomorrow.' I'm like, 'Man, there's two or three new hits out on you, and we're all worried about you, bro.' He said, 'All I've ever wanted to do was to make a record and make a movie and I've done that, and now I can't stop.' I was like, blah, blah, blah . . . 'But, Shock, you don't understand. I don't give a fuck.' And he rushed back to the party or the video or whatever. When a cat you're trying to help looks you in the eye and says, 'You don't understand, I don't give a fuck,' that's that. You're still worried about him, but you're done.

Benjamin Meadows-Ingram: *What were your feelings when he died?*

Shock-G: Anybody who knew 'Pac and won't admit this is lying: When they pronounced 'Pac dead, first it was emotional, but the next day it was like, peace . . . . This nigga survived police shootings, beat so many charges, walked on this, walked on that. It was almost like anytime the phone rang and it was news about 'Pac, it was like, 'Oh really, 'Pac's OK? OK.' And when you hung up the phone you went back to what you were doing, like, that's just 'Pac. You knew he was searching for something he couldn't find, and he found it in death. When he was alive, he wasn't happy. A black man, he grew up without a father, raised in the hood, left out of the whole social system, got fronted on by police who have the right to kill us without reason. 'Pac didn't like that shit to the point where he couldn't sleep at night, and he hurt so much when he was alive that it hurt you to know him.

I grew up hearing about Huey Newton and Malcolm X, Kennedy, Gandhi, Jesus, Bob Marley and all those cats, but I had nothing to do with it. I feel blessed and fortunate to be connected to his career in any way. 'Cause 'Pac would have happened no matter who he came through. It was just luck that he came through Digital.

ON THE LINE WITH... 2PAC SHAKUR
The Lost Interview
by Davey D

One of the most interesting, and intense, interviews I've ever conducted was with Tupac Shakur. He had just filmed the movie *Juice* and had everyone wondering was he just acting or putting forth his real life persona in the movie? Although I had known him for a couple of years it was hard for me to tell, 'cause he had a loaded gun on him as we spoke . . . . If I recall it was a 38 . . . . 'Pac explains in this interview his then recent encounter with the Oakland Police Department which resulted in him getting beat.

I had run excerpts from this interview in a newsletter I used to publish back in the early Nineties. I had completely forgotten about this interview and had misplaced the tape. A couple of months ago, while working on liner notes for Digital Underground's *Greatest Hits* which recently came out on Rhino records, I came across a tape that had an old interview I did with Shock G. I flipped to the b-side and, to my surprise, I discovered the missing Tupac interview from 1991.

So today, in celebration of his birthday, we are sending off the transcript of the entire interview. We are also going to be playing the entire interview on our *Hard Knock* radio show. If you happen to be located in the San Francisco Bay Area or anywhere throughout Northern and Central California tune into KPFA 94.1 FM. If you happen to be listening to us up in Seattle where we are also heard tune into Radio X. We will be airing this interview at 4pm Cali time. Everyone else peep us out on line at KPFA.org or radio-x.org. We will be putting excerpts of the interview up on the site tomorrow. Enjoy the interview.

Tupac Shakur considers himself the 'Rebel of the Underground' [Digital Underground] and for good reason. He stirs things up and does the unexpected. Such a person is bound to generate excitement because they have impact on both the people and situations around them. Tupac in 1992 promises to have a major impact in the world of hip hop. He's kicking things off with a sensational acting debut in the movie Juice, *where he stars as the character Roland Bishop. His debut LP,* 2Pacalypse Now, *is beginning to cause a bit of a stir on retail shelves around the country. And if that's not enough, Tupac is branching out and signing new acts to his production company, including his older brother Moecedes, who raps in the Toni Tony Toné song 'Feels Good.' I recently had the pleasure of interviewing this outspoken and very animated individual at his apartment, where he told his tale.*

Davey D: *Give a little bit of background on yourself. What got you into hip hop?*

Tupac: I'm from the Bronx, NY. I moved to Baltimore where I spent some high school years and then I came to Oaktown. As for hip hop . . . all my travels through these cities seemed to be the common denominator.

Davey D: *Tupac . . . Is that your given name or is that your rap name?*

Tupac: That's my birth name and my rap name.

Davey D: *You lived in Marin City for a little while. How was your connection with hip hop able to be maintained while living there? Was there a thriving hip hop scene in Marin City?*

Tupac: Not really. You were just given truth to the music. Being in Marin City was like a small town so it taught me to be more straightforward with my style. Instead of being so metaphorical with the rhyme where I might say something like . . . I'm the hysterical, lyrical miracle, I'm the hypothetical, incredible . . . I was encouraged to go straight at it and hit it dead on and not waste time trying to cover things . . . .

Davey D: *Why was that?*

Tupac: In Marin City it seemed like things were real country. Everything was straightforward. Poverty was straightforward. There was no way to say I'm poor, but to say, 'I'm po' . . . we had no money and that's what influenced my style.

Davey D: *How did you hook up with Digital Underground?*

Tupac: I caught the 'D-Flow Shuttle' while I was in Marin City. It was the way out of here. Shock G was the conductor.

Davey D: *What's the D-Flow Shuttle?*

Tupac: The D-Flow Shuttle is from the album *Sons of the P*. It was the way to escape out of the ghetto. It was the way to success. I haven't gotten off since . . . .

Davey D: *Now let's put all that in laymen's terms* . . . .

Tupac: Basically I bumped into this kid named Greg Jacobs, a.k.a. Shock G, and he hooked me up with Digital Underground and from there I hooked up with Money B . . . and from there Money B hooked me up with his stepmomma . . . and from there me and his stepmomma started making beats . . . [laughter]

Me and his stepmomma got a little thing jumping off. We had a cool sound, but Shock asked me if I wanted a group. I said, 'Yeah but I don't wanna group with Money B's stepmomma 'cause she's gonna try and take all the profits . . . She wants to go out there

and be like the group Hoes with Attitude,' but I was like, 'Naw, I wanna be more serious and represent the young black male.'

So Shock says we gotta get rid of Money B's stepmomma. So we went to San Quentin [prison] and ditched her in the Scared Straight program . . . [laughter] After that Shock put me in the studio and it was on . . . This is a true story so don't say anything. It's a true story. And to Mon's stepmomma I just wanna say, 'I'm sorry, but a man's gotta do what a man's gotta do. I'm sorry but it was Shock's idea, Bertha.' But don't worry, she can get her half of the profits from the first cut after she finishes doing her jail time. [laughter]

Davey D: *What's the concept behind your album* 2Pacalypse Now?

Tupac: The concept is the young black male. Everybody's been talkin' about it but now it's not important. It's like we just skipped over it. It's no longer a fad to be down for the young black male. Everybody wants to go past. Like the gangster stuff, it just got exploited. This was just like back in the days with the movies. Everybody did their little gunshots and their hand grenades and blew up stuff and moved on. Now everybody's doing rap songs with the singing in it. I'm still down for the young black male. I'm gonna stay until things get better. So it's all about addressing the problems that we face in everyday society.

Davey D: *What are those problems?*

Tupac: Police brutality, poverty, unemployment, insufficient education, disunity and violence, black on black crime, teenage pregnancy, crack addiction. Do you want me to go on?

Davey D: *How do you address these problems? Are you pointing them out or are you offering solutions?*

Tupac: I do both. In some situations I show us having the power and in some situations I show how it's more apt to happen with the police or power structure having the ultimate power. I show both ways. I show how it really happens and I show how I wish it would happen.

Davey D: *You refer to yourself as the 'Rebel of the Underground.' Why so?*

Tupac: 'Cause, as if Digital Underground wasn't diverse enough with enough crazy things in it, I'm even that crazier. I'm the rebel totally going against the grain . . . I'm the lunatic that everyone refers to. I always want to do the extreme. I want to get as many people looking as possible. For example, I would've never done the song 'Kiss U Back' that way. I would've never done a song like that – that's why I'm the rebel.

Davey D: *Can you talk about your recent encounter with police brutality at the hands of the Oakland PD?*

Tupac: We're letting the law do its job. It's making its way through the court system. We filed a claim . . . .

Davey D: *Recount the incident for those who don't know . . . . Where is all this now?*

Tupac: We're in the midst of having a ten million dollar lawsuit against the Oakland Police Department. If I win and get the money, then the Oakland Police Department is going to buy a boys' home, me a house, my family a house and a 'Stop Police Brutality Center,' and other little odd things like that.

Davey D: *In the video for the song 'Trapped,' do you think that would've had the police want to treat you aggressively? After all, the video is very telling, especially in the unedited version where you have a cop get shot . . . .*

Tupac: Well, the ironic thing is the cops I came across in that incident didn't know about that video. The second thing is that everything I said in that video happened to me. The video happened before the incident. In the video, I show how the cops sweat me and ask for my ID and how I can't go anywhere.

Davey D: *Let's talk about the movie* Juice. *How did you get involved? Where's it at and what's it about?*

Tupac: Mmm, what led me? Well, we have the Freaky Deaky Money B and Sleuth [road manager for Digital Underground]. Money B had an audition for the movie. Sleuth suggested I also come along, so I went. Money B read the script and said to me, 'This sounds like you – a rebel.' He was talking about this character named Bishop. I went in cold turkey, read, God was with me . . . .

Davey D: *Have you ever had acting experience before?*

Tupac: Actually I went to the School of Performing Arts in Baltimore, and that's where I got my acting skills.

Davey D: *OK, so you weren't a novice when you went up there . . . . So what's the movie about?*

Tupac: The movie is about four kids and their coming of age.

Davey D: *Is it a hip hop movie?*

Tupac: No, it's not a hip hop movie. It's a real good movie that happens to have hip hop in it. If it was made in the Sixties it would've depicted whatever was down in the Sixties . . . . My character is Roland Bishop, a psychotic, insecure, very violent, very short-tempered individual.

Davey D: *What's the message you hope is*

gotten out of the movie?

Tupac: You never know what's going on in somebody's mind. There are a lot of things that add up. There's a lot of pressure on someone growing up. You have to watch it if it goes unchecked. This movie was an example of what can happen . . . .

Davey D: *Can you explain what you mean by this?*

Tupac: In the movie my character's father was a prison whore, and that was something that drove him through the whole movie . . . .

Davey D: *This was something that wasn't shown in the movie?*

Tupac: Yes, they deleted this from the film. Anyway, this just wrecked his [Bishop's] mind. You can see through everybody else's personality, Bishop just wanted to get respect. He wanted the respect that his father didn't get. Everything he did, he did just to get a rep. So from those problems never being dealt with led to him ending four people's lives.

Davey D: *Do you intend on continuing making movies?*

Tupac: It depends on whether or not there are any good parts. I want to challenge myself.

Davey D: *What is your philosophy on hip hop? I've heard you say you don't like to see it diluted?*

Tupac: Well when I said that, it made me think. It brought me to myself. Now I have a different philosophy. Hip hop when it started, it was supposed to be this new thing that had no boundaries and was so different to everyday music. Now it seems like I was starting to get caught up in the mode of what made hip

hop come about. I would walk around and hear something and start saying, 'That's not hip hop.' If someone started singing, I would walk around and say, 'That's not hip hop.' Well, now I've changed my mind. That could be hip hop. As long as the music has the true to the heart and soul it can be hip hop. As long it has soul to it, hip hop can live on.

Davey D: *I guess my question would be, how do you determine what's soul and what isn't?*

Tupac: Well you can tell. The difference between a hit like 'Make You Dance' [C&C Music Factory] and 'My Mind is Playing Tricks on Me' [Geto Boys]. You have to ask yourself, which song moves you?

Davey D: *Well actually both. Both songs move me.*

Tupac: Really? Well . . . . OK, there you go.

Davey D: *So they both would be hip hop, right?*

Tupac: I guess so, at least in your opinion. The 'Make You Dance' song didn't move me. But the Geto Boys song did move me

Davey D: *Well for the record, Bambaataa says both of them are hip hop. I asked him what he thought about groups like C&C Music Factory. He said they were part of the hip hop family . . . . But that's his philosophy on things. So what's your plans for the next year or so?*

Tupac: To strengthen the Underground Railroad. I have a crew called the Underground Railroad and a program called the Underground Railroad . . . I wanna build all this up, so that by next year you will know the name Underground Railroad.

Davey D: *So what's the concept behind the Underground Railroad?*

Tupac: The concept behind this is the same concept behind Harriet Tubman, to get my brothers who might be into drug dealing or whatever it is that's illegal, or who are disenfranchised by today's society – I want to get them back into [it] by turning them onto music. It could be R&B, hip hop or pop, as long as I can get them involved. While I'm doing that, I'm teaching them to find a love for themselves so they can love others and do the same thing we did for them to others.

Davey D: *How many people in the Underground Railroad? Is it a group that intends to keep constantly evolving? Also, where are the people who are a part of Underground Railroad coming from?*

Tupac: Right now we're twenty strong. The group is going to be one that constantly evolves. The people that are in the UR are coming from all over, Baltimore, Marin City, Oakland, New York, Richmond – all over.

Davey D: *What do you think of the Bay Area rap scene compared to other parts of the country?*

Tupac: Right now the Bay Area is how the Bronx was in 1981. Everybody is hot. They caught the bug. Everybody is trying to be creative and make their own claim. New York just got to a point where you could no longer outdo the next guy. So now you have this place where there isn't that many people to outdo. Here you can do something and if it's good enough people will remember you. So that's what's happening. Here in the Bay Area, it's like a renaissance.

Davey D: *In New York the renaissance era got stopped for a number of reasons in my opinion. What do you think will prevent that from happening in the Bay Area?*

Tupac: Well at the risk of sounding biased, I say Digital Underground. They are unlike any other group. I'll give that to Shock G. He

made it so that everything Digital Underground does it helps the Bay Area music scene. It grows and goes to New York and hits people from all over the country. That helps the Bay Area. Our scene is starting to rub off on people. We want everyone to know about Oakland. When other groups come down, like Organized Konfusion or Live Squad and they kick it with Digital Underground, they get to see another side of the Bay Area music scene. It's a different side than if they kicked it with that guy . . . I don't wanna say his name, but you know who he is, he dropped the 'MC' from his name.

Davey D: *So you think Digital Underground will be more strength to the Bay Area rap scene because they help bring national attention. What do you think other groups will have to do?*

Tupac: What we have to do is not concentrate so much on one group. We have to focus more on the area. It's not about just building up Too Short, Digital Underground and Tony Toni Toné and say, 'That's it. They're the only groups that can come from the Bay Area.' We have to let the new groups come out. Nobody wants to give the new acts a chance. Everybody wants to only talk about Too Short and Digital Underground . . . . We have to start talking about these other groups that are trying to come in that are coming up from the bottom.

Davey D: *When you say 'come up,' what do you mean by that?*

Tupac: It's like this. Instead of letting them do interviews where nobody ever reads them, let a good newspaper interview them. Instead of putting them on the radio when nobody is ever going to hear them or where nobody is going to hear them, have them where people can hear them and get at them where they had a better chance, just like if they were Mariah Carey.

Davey D: *Do you find the Bay Area sound is being respected? Do you find that people are starting to accept it around the country?*

Tupac: I feel that the Bay Area sound hasn't even finished coming out. It's starting to get respected more and more everyday.

Davey D: *Your brother Moecedes is a rapper for the group Tony Toni Toné. What's the story with him? Are you guys gonna team up?*

Tupac: He's in the Underground Railroad. He's also about to come out with another guy named Dana.

Davey D: *Who produced your album and are you into producing?*

Tupac: I co-produced it with the members of the Underground Railroad, which is Shock G, Money B, Raw Fusion, Pee Wee, Jay-Z from Richmond, Stretch from the Live Squad. It's really like a life thing – this Underground Railroad. It affects everything we do.

Davey D: *Is there anything else we should know about Tupac?*

Tupac: Yeah, the group Nothing Gold is coming. My kids are coming out with a serious message . . . NG is a group coming out that I produce. All the stuff I say in my rhymes I say because of how I grew up. So to handle that, instead of going to a psychiatrist, I got a kids' group that deals with the problems a younger generation is going through. They put them into rhymes so it's like a psychology session set to music. It'll make you come to grips with what you actually do.

Davey D: *What do you mean by that? Are they preaching?*

Tupac: No, they're just telling you straight up like Ice Cube or Scarface. They're being blunt and it comes out of a kid's mouth. If you're a black man, you're going to really trip out 'cause they really call you out and have you deal with them . . . NG will make us have responsibility again. Kids are telling you to have responsibility . . . .

Davey D: *What do you think of the current trends in hip hop like the gangsta rap, Afrocentric rap, raggamuffin and the fusion of the singing and rap? Some people call it 'pop rap.'*

Tupac: I think all the real shit is gonna stay. It's gonna go through some changes. It's going through a metamorphosis so it will blow up sometimes and get real nasty and gritty, then the leeches will fall off and hip hop will be fit and healthy. Hip hop has to go through all of that, but no one can make judgements until it's over.

Davey D: *What do you think the biggest enemies to hip hop are right now?*

Tupac: Egotistical rappers. They don't wanna open up their brain. It's foul when people are walking around saying things like, 'Oakland is the only place where the real rappers come out. New York is the only place where the real rappers come out. They booty out there or they booty over there . . .' All of that just needs to die or hip hop is gonna have problems. It's gonna be so immature. That's just conflict in words. We can't be immature, we gotta grow.

Davey D: *Cool. I think we got enough out of you, Tupac.*

Tupac: Yes I think you got enough.

ASKING FOR IT

by Michael Small

'It's sad, there ain't no hope for the youth / And the truth is there ain't no hope for the future / And then they wonder why we're crazy . . . . We ain't meant to survive.'

'Keep Ya Head Up.' Tupac, 1993

After Tupac Shakur's death, my friends who knew that I had interviewed him started calling me with questions. Did I know the inside details? Who killed him? Was it gang-related? Was he really a bad guy? Did he deserve it?

In a way, those questions make me angry – partly because I had such a tough time getting anyone to listen to me talk about Tupac five years ago. At that time, rap was being blamed for creating all the violence in human history, and I was trying to counteract the hype by pitching an article about Tupac's positive qualities. Not only had he written a sympathetic rap about unmarried mothers ['Brenda's Got a Baby'], but he was starting a mentor program to help poor kids in his Oakland neighborhood. 'We read together, and write rhymes,' he told me. 'They're learning how to express themselves, and they're all doing better in school. I call this my Underground Railroad. Just like Harriet Tubman from South to North, I want to take them from illegitimate to legitimate.'

I had a strong positive angle about a gangsta rapper. Not one publication was interested.

As other rappers have learned – to their financial gain and often to their personal harm – violence is the best way for them to get attention. Tupac proved this more than once. Back in 1992, when Dan Quayle blamed a Tupac song for inspiring a murderer to kill a Houston policeman, this made headlines. Later, it was discovered that the murderer didn't even own Tupac's tape. This did not make headlines.

Now that he's dead, conservatives will probably try to link Tupac's violent lyrics to his violent death, and this also makes me angry. Tupac was living amid crime and violence long before he started writing raps. By his own account, his father was a 'gangsta' who 'died of a heart attack from freebase;' he and his mother, Afeni Shakur, a founder of the Black Panthers, were homeless for part of his childhood; and he grew up around drug dealers and policemen who vented their own frustrations – sometimes brutally – on the people in his neighborhood.

'I want people to know,' Tupac told me, 'that I'm not just out there holding my dick, cursing. I'm not just saying, "Kill, kill, kill." I'm talking about true-to-life incidents. It makes you a violent person. It makes you a caged animal. And that's how we act. And that's how my lyrics are. It's a state of emergency.'

Though I didn't see Tupac's home, I visited enough gangsta rappers on their own turf to know that guns and violence are not just a fantasy. As Compton rapper/producer DJ Quik was driving me down Crenshaw in South Central LA, he told me that we were passing the spot where strangers recently shot at him from another car. When I asked him why he didn't find a safer place to live, he told me that he couldn't imagine a place on earth where he wouldn't need a gun to protect himself. Then he showed me the automatic pistol hidden under his dashboard.

During the year that I spent writing about rappers and their music, I made many attempts to find out if someone – a government official, a philanthropist, a vastly profiting record company executive – was doing

Tupac backstage with Spice at the KMEL Summer Jam 1992.

anything to provide an alternative to the violence. I ended up feeling the same anger and cynicism that Tupac expressed to me: 'Nobody gives a fuck about some juvenile delinquent from the ghetto.'

While Quayle was grandstanding about violent lyrics, I saw crumbling, overcrowded schools that made me understand what incredible luxury I had enjoyed at my own entirely white suburban high school. I also heard from rappers that the budget cuts of the Reagan/Bush era had dismantled every positive activity for city kids in order to decrease taxes for middle-class parents. When Queen Latifah was growing up in East Orange, New Jersey, she played basketball at a local boy's club. Now, it's closed.

Oddly enough, the only people who seemed to make any serious attempt to help the community were a few rappers with awful reputations: Tupac, Eazy-E, Parrish of EPMD. 'I don't have to be calling every newspaper and say, "Guess what I'm doing,"'

Tupac told me about his mentor program. Basically, he was too smart to waste his time: He knew that no one would write about a rapper's benign side. I can't help but think the program ultimately fizzled out because no one offered him support.

Like other rappers, Tupac indicated that his violent lyrics had an underlying social cause: It was his duty to write about the violence in his world so people around the world would know about it, and perhaps do something about it. But, as the years passed, he and other gangsta rappers seemed to get more cynical about their mission. Too Short, another rapper who used to be based in Oakland, told me that he began by writing positive raps and no one would listen; as soon as he put sex and violence into the lyrics, he was a star. Tupac, it seems to me, eventually picked up that same attitude. His positive, uplifting raps (and he wrote several of them – more than any other gangsta rapper) didn't make him a millionaire, but going to jail – even if he regreted it – made his album sales soar.

When I spoke to Tupac, he seemed to have two different people inside of him. At one moment, he was completely likeable, intelligent, and more articulate than other rappers who have greater rhyming skills. He was also idealistic. He told me that he believed rap could erase racism among the members of the younger generation who would then grow up and pass this onto their children. 'The sneaky shit,' he said, 'is that nobody knows that rap is educating a whole race of people. Now the white kids are coming up listening to the black experience. And when they get jobs, they're gonna be in a position to hire, and when I walk in there they're going to remember this young black kid. Not the black kid that they got on TV. The real black kid. The one that watched your ass. The one that talked with you. The one you had a lot in common with. And he'll give me a job because we'll be understanding each other.'

A moment later, Tupac would become someone else: the ultimate angry young man, a hothead lashing out at some general injustice. Just a few minutes after telling me about his mentor program, he told me about beating a kid who stole something from his trailer on the set of the movie *Juice*. 'I was like, "OK, I'll take justice into my own hands." And I got some of my niggas, and we went and found the little n-i-g-g-e-r who stole from me and beat his ass. Because I'm a true nigga. Not a fake film nigga. And you cannot rob from me. You can see I'm fiery. But that's just how I am.'

Ultimately, the hothead personality brought Tupac more attention and more rewards as it crowded out his other side. 'Tupac's not a bad individual,' the East Coast rapper Tragedy told me a few years ago. 'The problem is that he's trying to be real in a fake world. It's eating him up inside. He's struggling with himself, and he's putting himself in some fucked-up situations because of it. You're gonna have bad elements around you, especially when you're young and making money. I do feel he should lose some of the crowd he's around.'

But Tupac didn't lose that crowd. In 1992, he was at a Bay Area arts festival with a gang of cronies, one of whom fired a gun in a scuffle and accidentally killed a young boy. The gun was traced back to Tupac, though he was never found guilty of firing it. After that, he was arrested six times and served time for various charges, including assault, battery, weapons violations, and sexual abuse of a fan. Even on his final night, Tupac was driving with Suge Knight, the owner of Tupac's label, Death Row Records. The late rapper Eazy-E, whom I liked and trusted, warned me to steer clear of Knight – the only such warning I received during a year of interviewing rappers. Knight reportedly has boasted that he has ties to the Bloods gang and that there's a contract out on his life. In light of Tupac's previous troubles, I wonder why he still chose to ally himself with people like Knight.

For me, the saddest thing about Tupac's death is that it shows just how little hope he had for the future. He had wealth and plenty of talent, but he didn't see where he could go in this world without the gangsta persona. Like DJ Quik, he couldn't picture himself in a safe place. He couldn't imagine a world where he could find peace by taming his temper and creating his Underground Railroad. Tupac was a good actor, and in the end, he did a much too realistic job of acting out the gangsta role that his audience – both black and white – asked him to play. Because of that, he died, and now everyone's asking about him.

HIT 'EM UP

PART TWO

VIOLENCE IS GOLDEN

by Danzy Senza

It's a lazy afternoon, and Bishop is just kickin' it in a friend's living room, watching television and mulling lunch. The 1949 James Cagney gangster classic *White Heat* flickers on the television screen, as Bishop looks on. Cagney, a tough guy who loves his mom, climbs atop an oil tank, and, in a burst of defiance and nihilism, sets himself ablaze rather than give himself up to the police. Cagney's infamous farewell – 'Made it, Ma, top of the world' – is spoken simultaneously by a mesmerized Bishop. As Cagney burns, Bishop launches into a passionate diatribe about courage and risks, yelling at his baffled friends, 'That motherfucker took his destiny in his own hands. You've got to be ready to stand up and die for shit if you want some juice!' Bishop, until now, has cowered in the face of local gangsta bullies, passively accepting the poverty of his family and neighborhood. No longer. From this moment on, Bishop is transformed into a trigger-happy madman who 'don't give a fuck' about his friends, his freedom, or his life.

Tupac Amaru Shakur played Bishop in the 1992 film *Juice* with a chilling intensity that stunned critics and audiences alike. But now, those same fans of Shakur are wondering if what they witnessed onscreen was art imitating life, or a startling blend of the two. Like Bishop, Shakur seems to have turned some irrevocable corner, consumed with rage and destined for self-destruction.

Late '93 was a rough time for rap music. Rapper Snoop Doggy Dogg, riding high on the hype of his *Doggy Style* debut, was arrested on charges of murder. Only days later, Flavor Flav of Public Enemy was brought in on charges of shooting his neighbor. And then came Shakur. The enigmatic rapper, actor, and sex symbol lit up the nation's nightly newscasts with an alleged spree of criminal activity. 1993 had been a good year for him. He had starred in the John Singleton film *Poetic Justice* and released a multi-plat-

inum second album, *Strictly 4 My N.I.G.G.A.Z.* He had even been nominated for an NAACP Image Award. But last fall his life took an ugly turn when he was arrested twice in a three-week span. First, on Halloween night in Atlanta, he was charged with shooting two off-duty police officers. Then, on location in New York to film his latest movie, *Above the Rim*, Shakur was accused of forcibly sodomizing a young female fan in Suite 3809 of the midtown Parker Meridien Hotel.

'You wanna sweat me / Never get me / To be silent / I'm giving them a reason / To claim that I'm violent,' Shakur intones on *2Pacalypse Now*'s 'Violent.' 'Thug Life,' brazenly tattooed across his stomach like a banner, is Shakur's street manifesto, an expression of the rage of young black men in America – rage against the system that denies them and fears them. 'I'm a product of this society,' he once said in an interview. 'You know, I'm a revolutionary. I'm straight thuggin' out here. Thuggin' against society. Thuggin' against the system that made me.'

At the center of all this fury is an individual who was nearly born in prison, and who to this day doesn't know who his biological father is. An individual whose politically active mom suffered through a debilitating addiction to crack, and whose two father figures whilst he was growing up are both presently behind bars. And now, an individual who faces a long haul in jail if convicted of either violent offense.

'Fuck no! He didn't rape nobody,' Afeni Shakur says, over the phone from her home in Georgia, in defense of her son. 'Nothing in his life speaks to the kind of things that he's being accused of. He's a financially independent black man trying to take care of his mama and his sister. I'm very proud of him for who he is.'

Tupac's 47-year-old mother was one of the star defendants in the 1971 trial of thirteen Black Panthers, accused of conspiracy to bomb a public spot. *The New York Post* wrote of Afeni in March of that year:

'In some respects the most exotic of the thirteen defendants, with her Afro and relentless Panther rhetoric. The 23-year-old firebrand is now being viewed from several different perspectives . . . . The prosecution has complained at a bail hearing that Mrs. Shakur was discovered singing in court. "Singing!" the prosecutor exclaimed. The prosecutor also depicted her as a homeless fly-by-night . . . bouncing from place to place while free on bail . . .'

Upon acquittal on the conspiracy charges, she continued 'bouncing from place to place' with her son, living in Harlem, Baltimore, and Marin, California. Afeni says she tried to get him into acting as a way of keeping him on the right track, channeling the anger that she knew would grow. At the Baltimore School for the Arts, Shakur had his first experience as a 'flyboy in the butter-milk,' surounded by middle-class white kids.

In a rap scene where your geographical roots often define your identity, your crew, your style, Shakur never had a 'hood. Poverty was the constant in his life, Shakur's root-lessness emblematic of the post-civil rights generation, into a world of dispersed, not quite integrated mutinies, a world of slain heroes and jailed parents.

To the black folks who live there, it's called 'the Jungle,' though Marin City looks more like a desert – a wide, dusty field spotted with yellow grass and anonymous public housing. Known to outsiders as the 'the gilded ghet-to,' couched between the cafe-lined towns of Mill Valley and Sausalito, it's the only poor black neighborhood in Marin, California's richest county. In Sausalito, a blonde woman on her mountain bike gives me directions to Marin City, remarking, 'I didn't even knew it existed until recently, when I saw a bunch of kids getting off a bus by the side of the road.'

In the dusty parking lot outside Hayden's Market – the only store in town –

the older folks play dominoes and barbecue a side of ribs. On the other end lot, men relax against cars, showing off their stereos and sipping forties. Around the bend, at the basketball courts, bare-chested teenagers run some ball, girls sit at the picnic tables and watch the court.

Arriving with his mother in 1988, Shakur's two years in Marin City were painful and formative. It was there that Afeni got hooked on crack. Their small apartment was bare of furniture and Shakur bounced between neighbors' homes, low on cash and hungry for a way out.

Shakur escaped from Marin City in 1990 after a successful dance audition for Digital Underground. In the three years that have passed since he fled the ghetto, the town's feelings toward this local hero have gone from pride to hatred – many refer to him as 'Tu-faced.'

Much of the town's resentment can be traced to a tragic occurrence at the annual Marin City Festival. For fifteen years the festival had been trouble-free until the warm summer evening last August Shakur and his entourage showed up. Soon after his arrival, a fight broke out, gunshots were fired and a six-year-old boy named Qa'id Walker-Teal killed by a bullet wound to his head. Late evening, Shakur was chased out of town by an angry mob who pelted the windows of his Jeep with rocks and bottles. Charges were filed against his half brother, Maurice Harding, but later dropped. The killer was never brought to justice.

'Me, I'm with the Jungle,' says 'S.S.,' a former running mate of Shakur's. 'I'm proud to be with the Jungle, but Tupac got no respect for it. All I know is when the fes-tival came to town, he wouldn't get onstage and perform. It was like he didn't even like the town.'

A short, light-brown-skinned fellow with braids in his hair a la Snoop, who calls himself Klark Gable, ambles over. Even on this warm afternoon, Gable wears a plaid flannel shirt and baggy jeans. He's soft-spoken but friendly, and we stand together watching the game in the fading afternoon sunlight, reminiscing about the days when he and Shakur were tight. 'Then he met up with those brothers from Oakland,' Gable says, 'started carrying a 9mm, and you couldn't tell him nuthin'. Back when he had nowhere to sleep, people here put him up, clothed him. We showed him a lot of love. There's no reason for him to be actin' this way. We didn't have any beef.

'When he was here, he was very political, very wise and intelligent. He used to say that when he got enough status, he was going to help black people. But he went downhill. He wanted to live the gangsta life,' Gable reflects, sad and bewildered. 'He wasn't brought up like that. He knew the ghetto life, not no thug life.'

Even before the Atlanta shoot-out, Halloween hadn't been much of a holiday for Shakur. He had given an uninspired performance at a late night Clark-Atlanta University homecoming celebration and was exhausted. Sometime after 2:00 A.M., Shakur and his entourage left the campus. At the intersection of Peachtree Street and Fourteenth Street, a well-lit midtown shopping area, they got in a beef with two white men, whom they would later discover were off-duty police. By the end of the encounter, Scott Whitwell had been struck by a bullet in the derriere and his brother Mark in the abdomen.*

The Whitwell brothers initially characterized the encounter as a drive-by shooting. Out on the town with Mark's wife to celebrate her passing the Georgia bar exam, they claim to have been nearly run over by a black BMW and a grey Mercedes while crossing the street. Whitwell told the Atlanta police that they began to argue with the men in the cars, and were then fired upon.

But as the initial media deluge subsides, and more evidence is presented, Shakur's guilt in the Atlanta case seems less certain. A witness to the shooting, 26-year-old Edward Fields, says he saw one of the off-duty police officers draw his .9mm Glock first, yell, 'Get down! Get down!,' and fire a shot at the

Mercedes. It was only then, says Fields, that a man he recognized as Tupac Shakur got out of the car, leaned over the roof, and returned three shots at the two white men. An Atlanta officer has testified that the Whitwells, in a police report taken that evening, labelled Shakur's entourage 'a bunch of niggers.' Shakur's legal representatives plan to bring forward a white couple who were present at the scene of the shooting. 'They thought it was a white gang attacking black people,' says Chokwe Lumumba, one of Shakur's lawyers in this case.

Meanwhile, Scott Whitwell, who was found to be drunk the night of the shooting, has since been suspended from duty for two weeks for stealing a gun seized in an arrest. In a separate matter, his brother Mark faces charges of aggravated assault, reckless conduct, and falsifying information. The conduct of the Whitwells, both prior to and during the Shakur incident, casts some doubt on their version of the incident. What's irrefutable is that once again, trouble had found Shakur, and it didn't have far to look.

'Tupac acts on his emotions. He does what he feels and he's hyper,' says Digital Underground's Money B, an old playmate of Shakur's from his Oakland days. 'But with the hotel thing, everyone knows Tupac ain't gotta rape nobody. Just knowin' how that goes, it sounds kind of suspicious.'

Shakur is accused, along with two other men, of forcibly sodomizing a young woman on the night of November 18. Shakur, who has admitted to having sex with the woman prior to that night, claims that he invited her back to his hotel room after she left several sexually explicit phone messages on his hotel answering machine. Then, he says, the woman gave him a back massage while 'talking dirty' to one of his friends. Shakur proceeded to leave the room, presumably so his friend and the young woman could get busy. 45 minutes later, his friend woke him up and told him the woman had burst into hysterics after giving one of the men a blowjob.

'She cried and said to me, "Why did you

let them do this to me?"' Shakur told the *Daily News* shortly after his arrest. 'Then she said: "You think you got a problem now? You haven't heard the last of me."'

Michael Warren, one of the attorneys representing Shakur in this case, charges that she gave consent. Witnesses say they saw her get down on her knees and give Shakur a blowjob on the crowded dance floor of Nell's, a trendy nightclub in the West Village, only four days before the hotel incident.

'You've got to ask the necessary question, "Who is this woman?"' says Warren. 'You don't know her personally, very few of us do. But we do know that in the midst of maybe 100 people, in the middle of a crowded club, she pulls Tupac out to the dance floor, begins to massage him, and thereafter zips down his pants and performs oral sex for approximately five to ten minutes. It raises issues of consent and credibility.'

The prosecution dismisses the importance of the alleged incident at Nell's. Attorney Michael Kapien says, 'Anything that happened or did not happen at the discotheque that night is totally irrelevant to the complaint made and the charges she's brought. Michael Warren's statements are demeaning to all women. They imply that a person doesn't have the right to say no when they're sexually assaulted by several people. No means no.'

Meanwhile, Shakur's lawyer Michael Warren believes the police have been tampering with the evidence – such as the sexually explicit answering machine recordings that Shakur claims the young woman left him before the alleged incident, but which he now says the police erased during their search of the hotel suite.

Shakur is not exactly known as a friend of the police. He is still facing in civil court a multimillion-dollar product liability suit from the widow of a slain policeman in Texas who claims Shakur's music incited a young black man to kill her husband (the criminal case was dismissed). The same case led to Vice President Dan Quayle's infamous defamation

of Shakur's 1991 album, *2Pacalypse Now*.

And the major media have depicted Shakur as a sociopath. Outlets from *Newsweek* to *MTV News* saw his arrest as another example of how gangsta rappers conflate art and life. *Newsweek*'s cover asked 'When is Rap 2 Violent?' over a picture of a snarling Snoop Doggy Dogg.

Shakur's mother likens all this to 'the McCarthy era, where a whole lot of faceless people waged a campaign that began with fear. Everything was fine when he was doin' the Humpty Dance,' says Afeni, 'but now that he's singin' about "Keep Ya Head Up," he's a threat.'

America, with its 'lift yourself up by your boot-straps' myths, has often romanticized poverty, conferring 'authenticity' on the experiences of the poor and dispossessed. The Beats of the 1950s found their 'ultimate hipster' in 'the Negro.' Now, for the moment at least, mainstream American youth are mesmerized by the image of the authentic urban homeboy.

'Rap is of great importance to the suburban kids because they have no culture,' says poet and scholar Ishmael Reed. 'Whites paid a terrible price when they abandoned their native traditions. So now white people are looking for an authentic culture in black people.'

And Shakur, to the American imagination, seems the authentic black everyman, a composite of clichés of black manhood that have graced the screen and page since the turn of the century. He's a gun-toting revolutionary, a sexual dynamo, a loose cannon with a 400-year-old chip on his shoulder. Rap music, as largely bought by both blacks and whites, favors ultraviolent simplified depictions of urban life rather than multidimensional portraits. There are exceptions; a song off of De La Soul's recent album rejected the current mindset – 'Gangsta shit is outdated / Posdnuos is complicated' – but this album has stalled on its way up the charts.

Bill Stephney, vice president/general manager at label Def Jam, says the pressure

A youthful 'Pac hangs with his homies, New York 1989.

for black youths to act out the violence of the music has gotten worse as rap has moved into the suburbs. 'Back in the day, all rap was considered hard-core and underground. Now anybody who doesn't think about dusting off the police or carrying a .9mm is seen as a sell-out, as crossover. That's a hard image to live up to.'

Shakur's thug persona has certainly aided his record sales. And while the charges brought against him probably won't hurt his standing in the rap community or his box-office appeal, they've served as a reminder to Hollywood that the gangsta images they profit from can come with a price tag. Columbia Pictures recently dropped Shakur from a role in John Singleton's upcoming film, *Higher Learning*. A source close to the film explains simply, 'We would really like to work with him, but we can't do it if he's in jail.'

But rumors still fly that Columbia sacked him because of his volatile reputation. One woman who worked as a production assistant on the set of *Juice* says that although she didn't see him do anything violent, 'He used to run off the set at odd moments, for no apparent reason. It's like there's something chemically unbalanced about him.'

A leading rap executive was less polite: 'To be perfectly honest, Tupac's a full-fledged, mother-fuckin' nut.'

Nobody wanted to speak badly of Shakur on the record, and it's no surprise. Only last year, Shakur attacked director Allen Hughes with a lead pipe after hearing that one of his songs was being dropped from the *Menace II Society* soundtrack. He has admitted to the fight, but said it was fair since it was two against one. The case is still unsettled, and the Hughes brothers won't comment on the incident. Shakur is also alleged to have beaten up a limousine driver outside the set of the Fox network comedy *In Living Color* when the older black man wouldn't let him smoke weed in the back of the limo.

But others have only good things to say about their experiences with Shakur. Jeff Pollack is the director and writer of *Above the Rim*, Shakur's most recent film in which he plays a drug dealer named Birdie, trying to steer a promising high school basketball player in the wrong direction. Pollack had heard the negative rap on Shakur and was prepared for the worst. 'I've had none of the problems that people have complained about,' says Pollack. 'He always came to the set prepared. He has all the expected natural talent, but he also has the craft of acting that goes behind it. Tupac is irreplaceable. There isn't anyone who can do what he does. He's

'Bullet to 'da head' – Tupac with his bodyguard Frank Alexander (right) at Club USA, March 1994.

riveting. He's the guy you love to watch.'

Like De La Soul's Posdnuos, Shakur is also 'complicated,' and there's little doubt that his timing complicates matters further: Being charged in two serious crimes just as the nation has suddenly galvanized itself around the issue of violence in America makes him especially vulnerable to attacks, even by black organizations.

In Washington, D.C., the National Political Congress of Black Women has waged a full-fledged campaign against gangsta rap, and Tupac is a prime target. National Chair C. Delores Tucker, says, 'We've found negative gangster rap, misogyny, and a promotion of violence in Tupac's lyrics. It's nothing more than pornographic smut.'

Ishmael Reed, who believes rap music 'has injected new life into American poetry,' says that the middle-class blacks who are trying to censor the likes of Snoop Doggy Dogg and Shakur are simply 'embarrassed in front of whites. The black bourgeoisie has always tried to repress art. They think this is perpetuating stereotypes. But in reality, they don't respect art. They're Philistines.'

America, as writer Jake Lamar remarked, likes its black men 'badass and on CD format.' Whether Shakur is guilty of all he stands accused, or he is being targeted because he is a young black man in America, the fact remains that he and other gangsta rappers are not so different from the culture that claims to be offended by them. As cultural critic bell hooks puts it: 'At no point do people interrogate why huge audiences, particularly young white male consumers, are so turned on by this music. Gangsta rap is not at the margins of what this nation is about, but at the center. People unwittingly assume that black males are writing their lyrics off in the jungle, far away from the impact of mainstream values and desires.' From the metaviolence of such critically acclaimed white filmmakers as Quentin Tarantino and Abel Ferrara, to Kurt Cobain's recent admission of gun possession, to the Spur Posse's cocksure sexploits, violence and misogyny are not and have never been the exclusive domain of black manhood. 'The Jungle' lies closer to white America than it would like to believe.

* In July 1998, a default judgement against the estate of Tupac Shakur for $210,000 was awarded to Georgia state deputy sheriff Scott Whitwell. This judgement related to the alleged shooting by the rapper in 1993. Shakur had filed a $2-million counter suit claiming that Scott Whitwell had made false accusations and the shooting was justified. But a judge subsequently issued the default judgment against Shakur's estate and in favor of Whitwell after the rapper's lawyers failed to make court-required disclosures.

DREAMING AMERICA

by Daniel Smyth

As I remember, it was Tupac Shakur's eighteenth birthday. Shock G of Digital Underground rented a stretch limousine for the celebration. There were eight or nine of us.

(Tupac Shakur is 22 now. *Juice* and *Poetic Justice* behind him. *Strictly 4 My N.I.G.G.A.Z.* and *2Pacalypse Now*, both complex and underrated. His forthcoming *Thug Life* will surely be listened to more closely. By the time he turned eighteen, I'd known Tupac for about eighteen months. He has been pleading insanity from then till now. He feels his mania is what we all have and deny, that insanity is a rational adjustment to an insane world.)

Tupac met a white girl. Maybe her name was Jennifer. She and her friend were with us as we walked back to the car from a club. Jennifer wasn't quite sure she wanted to come along and neither was her friend. Tupac coaxed and Jennifer got in, but her friend was adamant about not, as she said, 'getting in a car with a bunch of strangers.' Then Jennifer's friend decided to come along. She sat on the floor and crossed her arms, angry. We were the picture of revelry and Jennifer's friend was stiff and stared straight ahead.

(Tupac is the quintessential wronged black man-urban youth-crazy motherfucker. You wish he would articulate his complaints more diplomatically, without firearms. You purchase those complaints though, and enjoy them – within the confines of a song or film. You quake when his hatred manifests itself in assault or gunfire or verbal pummeling. And you are weak if you desert him, if you don't respond to the call of his profane soliloquies. Because you are not driven as crazy by U.S. cultural norms, because you grit your teeth and swallow 'the way things are' with more of the highly regarded 'restraint,' you are a punk ass nigga. Brothers like Tupac remind us that all ain't fresh up in Bel Air. Brothers like him are the sirens.)

Tupac got mad and, as I remember it, said something to the effect of 'You think you're too good to be in here with a car fulla niggas? Fucking whore. You think just because the hair on your pussy is ugly-ass blonde, every motherfucker in the world wants to get with you? I'll put your ass out right here on this motherfucking bridge. I'll put your ass out in the middle of West Oakland.' Jennifer's friend cried, while Jennifer pleaded with Tupac.

(The cool night was a tiny precursor to the Reginald Denny incident and case: excuse or encourage or join the black man who is institutionally wronged, or help the individual white – in this case – women who bear, this rare time – the key phrase, remember, is black-on-black crime – his wrath? What is the black owed? For what can he or she be excused? *Save the whites . . . join Tupac . . . watch . . . avert eyes . . . be morally superior . . . revel in vindictiveness.* Options with historical and sociological significance. I stared out the window and hoped the situation would play itself out without violence.)

The names got more filthy, the words – *should have left your ass up there, fuck both y'all, fuck these stupid white bitches man* – loud and bitterly enunciated. Add some bass and it could have been a song. Jennifer and her friend were on their own. The driver kept looking back to check on them and us. He kept on driving, hugging the freeway and the low hills that lead to Shock G's place.

(Tupac is a daredevil, a time bomb. Held for questioning in the shooting of a six-year-old black boy in Marin County; called out by the former Vice President for promoting black man-on-police violence; sued for assault in one state; filed suit alleging police brutality in another. Tupac's guns are the mirror. The straight-up muthafuckin' bullseye. Instead of dodging, he takes the offense

Tupac arrives at a launch party for the thriller Red Rock Rest, *April 1994*

and lives dangerously, crazily. And so regardless of the recent sexual assault charge – sexual dominance is the spine of the manhood that Tupac and the rest of the world fetishizes – but we'll probably never know if he 'held the girl down' or not – he'll be a hero, perhaps go to prison a hero. And if he dies while he's still young, bleeding on the sidewalk, Tupac Shakur will be posthumously knighted, a champion, his funeral packed with devastated homies, all feeling verified, Pac's death proof of their truth. They are already living and dying through Shakur in the streets. And in Bel Air, but quietly.)

We passed through the security check-point at the sprawling complex that would burn to the ground a year later during the Oakland firestorm. And amid the landscaped greenery, right above the turquoise swimming pool, we left the long black car quickly, like there had been a stink there. From a window in the apartment, I saw Tupac tongue-kissing Jennifer or her friend. The girl's arms were relaxed and hung loosely crossed at the back of his neck. Another guy was also kissing Jennifer or her friend. And Sleuth, Digital's road manager, who had spent and would spend more time being Tupac's sometime friend and sometime keeper, said, 'You wonder why these niggas is crazy.'

THUG LIFE

by June Joseph

'A thug is an underdog, 1000 against one and still fighting. We have nothing. To make something out of nothing is what America's about. This all started with me being mad and now there's two groups doing the real music I love and on my own label (Outt Da Gutta), and here I am, a high school drop-out. I'm proud of that achievement. That's what Thug Life is all about. If we're not thugs, we don't survive . . . .'

Tupac Shakur, August 1994

It's all about survival. No one really addressed the problems in the African-American ghettoes nationwide . . . except hip hop – the genre Chuck D dubbed 'the black CNN.' Politicians paid lip-service when it mattered – at election time – and then conveniently forgot their campaign promises to pay attention to the ever-expanding ghettoes. The nation, and the world, sat up in April 1992, when South Central burned to the ground. Over two years later, talk to anyone still living in the poverty stricken district, they'll tell you there's no significant change . . . . blacks are still second-class citizens. There's hardly any new business in the neighborhoods, because entrepreneurs fear they'll lose heavily on their investment. One thing is constant, the 'gangstas' are still vying for supremacy. Killing each other with alarming regularity. What was it MC Ren said? 'Same ole shit!' . . . and then some.

Against this bleak backdrop come Thug Life, five young black men who've lived hard and grown up fast. They're thugs, but not in the literal sense – they fight to make good, to feed their children, make a bit of cash and maybe one day escape all the shit. More importantly, they fight to stay alive . . .

It's a surprisingly warm Thursday in autumn-kissed New York City. And there's an excited buzz – Thug Life are in town from Los Angeles and rumor has it that part-time frontman Tupac may show up at one of the interview sessions. If he does, journalists have been pre-warned not to mention his recent bout with the American judiciary sys-

tem. The elusive Tupac is currently in New York for a week shooting final scenes for his upcoming movie *Bullet*, a low budget shoot-'em-up, alongside pugnacious actor Mickey Rourke, so there's a good chance he might materialize.

As it happens, the rumors turn out to be unfounded. Tupac *doesn't* put in a much-anticipated appearance, but that doesn't mean the quartet gathered in a hotel room, 51 floors above Manhattan, aren't any less interesting without their famous founder.

After again being reminded not to mention Tupac's well documented brush with the law, even though some charges have actually been dropped against him, the interview begins . . . well, almost. The four bundle out of the hotel room for a little light refreshment and return fifteen minutes later with the sweet smell of Hennessy Brandy on their breath.

After literally waiting in the wings for two years, while Tupac allowed them to perfect their emceeing skills and established himself as one of hip hop's more prominent figures, Thug Life are finally a force to be reckoned with. Anyone who's familiar with Tupac's recent spate of videos from his platinum-selling *Strictly 4 My N.I.G.G.A.Z.* album, or who's been fortunate to see him perform live, will be familiar with the words tattooed in four-inch Gothic-style letters right across his stomach. Of the phrase Tupac has said, 'Crowds were screaming Thug Life and I realized I started something. When I saw more and more people like me,

'And the best thing about it is he's just like us . . . . A regular person' – Tupac hooks up with Thug Life, 1992.

it made me want to organize those thugs. We got power in numbers. If it's me and a million more, you'd have to think about messing with us . . . . '

Ask Rated R, Macadoshis, Mopreme and Syke what Thug Life means to them and they'll give you a collective smile, a look of relief and pride.

'I know a lot of teachers and people thought a lot of us [blacks] wouldn't make it to any of the positions that we're in right now,' begins Syke, fixing his wrap-around sun-glasses on his face. 'Because anything can go from here, the world could be ours. We're just showing the li'l youngsters in the ghetto and the people that you can make it, because there's older people that have nothing too. Because I always thought that I couldn't do nothing really. I didn't know what I wanted to do. I finally found something that I love doing. And I can get paid for writing my life on paper.

'When I was a young guy, who didn't

know where I was going . . . did things . . . I did a lot of bad things. I always said I wanted to be a trash man, because I know they got paid and nobody wanted to do that! I was that type of kid in the class. Now I'm a rapper, but yeah, I did a lot of bad things . . . . '

Macadoshis was given an incentive to stay in school. Sports. But even he had to run the gauntlet of petty gangstas and hoods lurching in corners near his home. Fortunately, while he says he was 'affiliated with gang-bangers' and taking part in the odd scrap, that's as far as it went. He says he had an enduring role model, who had a profound influence on his life. It was American football player Howard Studdard, who played for University of South Carolina, then professionally for the San Diego Chargers and the Seattle Seahawks.

'I idolized my uncle, he played professional football and I always wanted to play ball. He was one of my idols, so I had someone to look up to. A lot of these kids don't .

. . That's why they're turning to banging and shit, they don't have no father figure . . . but there aren't no father figures no more for the kids.

'That's the main thing that kept me in school – females and football. You had to keep a C-average just to play on the team. So that kept me in school a lot. I just used to go to school, come home, and I felt good about that. But on my way home from school, getting off the bus, I had to pass all those niggas hanging out on the corner doing nothing, banging and shit. They all knew me. I had scraps with the same niggas on the corner . . . I was more or less trying to make something about myself. At the time it wasn't about rap, it was about sports . . . . '

Third member, The Rated R, isn't talking much about his formative years, except to say he too is from South Central. He also says that life was difficult. The fourth member of the group, Mopreme, is Tupac's older brother by four years. Though the two are close now, they never spent much of a childhood together. When Tupac talks of a chequered childhood with his Black Panther mother, Mopreme lived apart from him, moving from state to state. Tupac says he's grateful having his brother with him, though he admits they haven't had a 'family moment' yet. Mopreme himself is evasive when asked to be specific about their blood relationship. He refuses to say whether they're step, half or full brothers.

'We just brothers, that's all. I've been down from day one doing my own thing, struggling solo. I was moving around so much, I never got to stay in one place and create a clique. I was just a nomad, staying true to the art. I grew up in Queens, New York, and spent a lot of my time there, but I moved all over though. I lived down south – [Washington] DC, Virginia. Then I lived in the West Coast.'

The two were reunited just four years ago.

All the members of Thug Life pursued music in some form. While their peers chased felonious routes, each group member aspired to make some good of their lives. Tupac was part of the West Coast's rap funksters Digital Underground. Mopreme had a taste of fame with Tony, Toni, Toné on their 'Feels Good' single. Sykes was producing 'street tapes' with a friend Johnny J for a group he helped form called Evil Mind Gangstas. Of the five, only Rated R and Macadoshis were friends. Moving amongst the influential rappers and deejays in L.A.'s burgeoning hip hop culture garnered them a chance meeting with Tupac, through their friend Coolio and his deejay Wino.

'Me and Macadoshis was close friends with them,' Rated R recalls in his distinctive, sometimes hard to understand drawl. 'When Coolio's solo deal was going through with Tommy Boy, we were all kicking it over at Coolio's house. Treach was going to be out there at a radio station out in L.A. called 92.3 The Beat one day and Coolio asked if we wanted to go. We went and met Tupac and Naughty By Nature.

'After that we all went to roll up at a room in Hollywood and kicked it for like about six hours straight, and everybody respecting each other's flow and was just loving our (rap) styles. We got a different style, so they were just loving the shit at that time. We were just trying to get us a deal at that time. And Pac slid us his number and said, "Hook up with us." So next day me and Mac got with him, since then it's been on. That was two years ago.'

Mopreme's career has seemingly stagnated compared to the success of his younger sibling. Tupac's pursuit of a solo career proved fruitful. His debut long player, *2Pacalypse Now*, garnered him praise from the rap media and legions of fans. Mopreme says there was no bad feeling towards Tupac. No rumbling of envy, just a need to be there for his brother. He believed that if he sacrificed his career, Tupac would return the favor.

'We are our own individual people, but we still love each other. Actually I was making records before him. I actually did some things with Tony, Toni, Toné in 1991, but then 'Pac came out and got a better opportunity, a better chance and more love. It would be selfish to hold myself back and not help. His career was large, so I just stopped and held myself back to help him and what he was doing. I'm always going to be a part of it. It always takes one to propel you, a catalyst. The thing that brought all of us together was 'Pac. He blew up and he needed us and we needed him.'

The project took two years to come to fruition. In the meantime friends and acquaintances pursuing rap careers were having major success. The list reads like a roll-call of West Coast hip hop – Snoop Doggy Dogg, Coolio, Warren G, even Y?N-Vee. And still, Tupac's band of men waited.

'We did a Thug Life tour about a year or so ago, 1992-93. A year went by. We were waiting for a long time, getting real impatient,' Sykes explains. 'We've seen a lot of groups blow up before us.'

'We weren't too hard about seeing everybody come up,' Macadoshios interjects. 'Even though, basically, we were waiting for our time to come up. We knew when we came out it was going to be the right time and it would definitely do good. We were impatient, definitely, but we weren't sour about people coming out before us. We weren't knocking nobody.'

Autumn/Winter 1994 and Thug Life can finally enjoy the fruits of their labor with their impressive debut album, *Volume 1*. Not only does Tupac prove his creativity is no fluke, but his cohorts are also allowed to shine with their lyrical flow and musical knowledge. Beat-wise the album sways between jeep-beat funk and soothing, soulful melodies.

'We had good thoughts about the album all the way through doing it,' drawls Rated. 'As for me I felt it was going to do good regardless. There's negative publicity about the album, so what? There's always someone that'll say it's good.'

'If the beat is funky, that's all we care

about,' says Syke, the burliest member of the group. 'It doesn't matter what it is, we'll rap on a funk track, we'll rap on a jazz track, we'll rap on a R&B track. It don't matter what it is, we'll make the track and the track makes us . . . We're just no gimmicks.'

The West Coast-based group aren't worried about all the attention their famous and conspicuously absent fifth member garners. They're also not worried if people view them as Tupac's band or credit their success as a whole to the former DU rapper.

'Can I answer that?' Macadoshis chuckles. 'We're not worried about playing in the back. In actuality, it's helping every member of the group because we all plan to do solo projects and stuff like that. Basically we're enjoying exposure. It's not like we're playing second string. It's a privilege working with him . . . we're all a unit.'

'And the best thing about it is he's just like us . . . a regular person,' Syke interrupts with a voice that resonates throughout the room. 'So we ain't trippin' over that. He showed us so much love. We played so many places with him that I would never have seen in my life . . . . '

'We're getting our start. We're going to be there too,' Rated adds his two cents.

And if people insist you're nothing without him?

'That's when your solo project comes out, you have to show the people you can do it on your own,' Syke grins. 'Right, like the saying goes, we can show you better than we can tell you,' Rated continues. 'I can talk all day long, but you ain't seen shit I did. But when you see it for yourself then you know . . . . '

With tracks like the ritualistic 'Pour Out a Little Liquor' – a hip-hip practise where homeboys pour a mouthful's worth of liquor on the ground in respect to their deceased friends – 'Cradle to the Grave' and 'Bury Me a G,' there's a morbid death theme running through the album. While records such as 'Gangsta Lean,' a trite tribute to dead gangstas that might drive you to use your AK, Thug Life's on-wax treatment of death is both harrowing in its matter-of-factness and at the same time poignant.

'That's why we're smoking marijuana and drinking Hennessy every day. It's right there in our faces. It's so scary and it's so real. I mean death is so scary. Everybody is scared about death. It's so real and it's happening around us every day, every week and we don't know how to react to it,' says Rated R. 'That's all we can write about. We try and stay calm off of it. One minute we're here, next minute we gone. It's real . . . . Some people are in the tragic accident [seeing a friend or relative die] when it happens and they've got to bounce back.'

During the making of their first album, Thug Life lost two close friends in gun-related incidents. One was shot while waiting for friends in his car, while Rated R was unfortunate to witness the death of one of his close friends. He is bemused at the pathetic way people treat life. Though he hears of killings from around the neighborhood, he's still not desensitized to it and the way the killings go on perpetually.

'I had a friend. I was standing outside with him and people rolled by and he got shot. I just stayed there with him, but he died right there . . . . So I'm supposed to go back to the house and just accept it, act like nothing happened. Can't no one help me with my problem. My friend just died. That's something tragic. Eventually you got to just move on. It's nothing nice. Nobody likes death. That's why the world's so crazy now, because of death. Everyone can't accept their loved one being dead, so they want revenge . . . . '

'That's why we writing about it now,' says Macadoshis. 'I got two kids – two sons. One's six and one's four. I want a daughter, but I don't want to bring another child into this world because I don't think it's going to last that much longer. That's why I think I write about death so much and sad things . . . . '

'It's a reality,' adds Rated R bluntly.

'We can move out of the ghetto, but it don't matter,' the talkative Syke continues. 'If you leave the ghetto, when you come back you're still involved in the stuff that's going on there. If you come back, you'll still get shot, if you still chill with the homeboys acting like you're not Mr. Big, you're going to get shot just like anybody else hanging on the corner.'

With their album, Thug Life want success badly. They say with success they can help themselves and their family and friends attain the things they've aspired to for so long. But they promise not to forget where they come from and to support those that supported them. There'll be others who are envious, but Thug Life vow to give something back to their ravaged community.

'Some homeboys think once you start rapping, you're weak now, you're not doing the things you used to. You got more to lose now. If the homies are talking madness to you, you don't want to scrap as quick as you used to scrap before,' Sykes explains. Mo agrees. 'Yeah, you might have a photo shoot the next day . . . . That's what rappers got to deal with.'

Rated R explains why it's important that rappers give something back to the very communities that supported them. 'Some people that have fame are real, like you hear about Luke from Florida. You hear about how he give it back. He's got much love for giving back. Ice-T, he give it back. Ice Cube! There's rappers that give it back to the community.

'Basically that's how I came up. I was influenced by the street and I was always influenced by the hip hop and dancing and pop-locking and locking. But I was just influenced by the streets, because there was nothing else for me to do as far as go to a summer camp or be on a basketball team, nothing like that, so I hung out with the same everyday homies and dealt with the next man. Back then we thought it was cool. But as I got older, I realized this wasn't the thing to do . . . . If you're smart, you realize that only the strong survive and the weak die. That's the

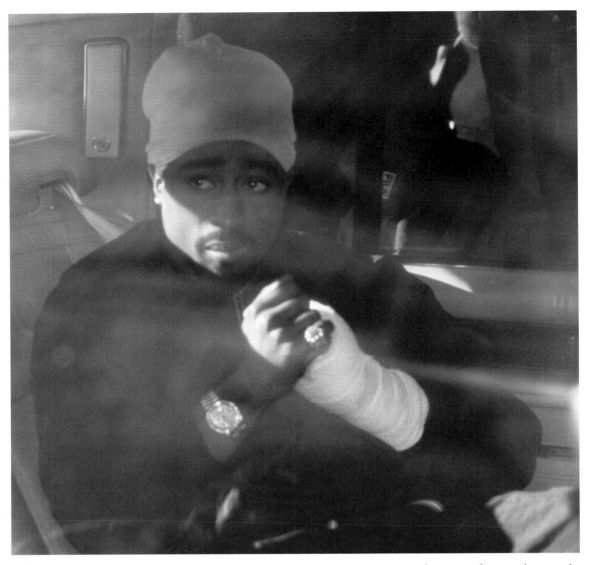

Tupac leaves court following his initial appearance to answer charges of sexual assault, December 1994.

way it is in the 'hood, everybody's so weak they don't even have any faith in themselves, they're just out there doing their same old thing . . . .

'Whites are doing it, Japanese are doing it. They hustling, getting their people on. They weighing the books, that's the way they do it. Learn everything they can, then they go get the biggest jobs, making Sony Walkmans and videos. They go back to the people – their family, the people they grew up with and put them down, then they go do the same and their whole race just got it under control. Same thing with the Mexicans. They doing their illegal business on the West Coast, but they got their Mexicans. They just want to work with Mexicans, because they all on each other's level. That's what the blacks just need to do.'

Thug Life are, at least for now, genuine in their convictions. Devoted and true to the game. Whether they will stand by their philosophies with the onslaught of success, only time will tell. But if there's any group more deserving of success, it ain't Snoop and it ain't Dre, it's these guys. Props.

Q & A WITH TUPAC SHAKUR

by Chuck Philips 'I Am Not a Gangster'

Six days after his release from a New York prison, Tupac Shakur is holed up in the control booth of a dimly lit Tarzana recording studio.

Bobbing his head and grinning, the 24-year-old rapper turns up the volume on a funky duet called '2 of America's Most Wanted,' which he just finished with label mate Snoop Doggy Dogg [a.k.a. Calvin Broadus, whose murder trial is set to begin Monday in Los Angeles Superior Court].

It's the fourteenth song Shakur has recorded since emerging from behind bars. Death Row Records, which recently signed a contract with Shakur, posted $1.4 million on October 12 to spring the rapper from Riker's Island maximum-security penitentiary, where he was serving up to four-and-a-half years for two counts of sexual abuse. The charges stemmed from a 1993 incident at a Manhattan hotel in which Shakur and an associate were accused of holding a female fan down while a third man sexually assaulted her.

Shakur denies the allegations but was advised by his attorneys not to discuss the case during his first interview since his release. It was the biggest in a series of confrontations involving the rapper, who was shot five times last December by a robber in New York. He has also faced criminal charges on four other occasions since March, 1993, including a weapons violation in Los Angeles, where a trial is set for November 16.

Shakur comes across as a man of many contradictions – someone who has the words thug life tattooed across his stomach but complains about being misrepresented by the media as a gangsta rapper.

His best-selling music, which covers topics ranging from police shootings to teen-age pregnancy, polarizes listeners. It has been both widely acclaimed by numerous critics and frequently attacked by parent groups and politicians. While Shakur was in jail, his last album, *Me Against the World*, entered the national pop charts at Number One and held that position for a month. It has sold nearly two million copies, fueled by the poignant Top Ten single 'Dear Mama' – an ode to the struggle of single mothers. Some of his more violent songs have been accused in a pending Texas civil suit of influencing a teen-age car thief to kill a state trooper.

Dressed in a baggy sweat suit and bandanna, Shakur – who hopes to have a new album out by Christmas, just days before arguments begin on his appeal – spoke about prison, the media and his music.

Chuck Philips: *How does it feel to be free again?*

Tupac: I'm so glad to be out. It was tough sitting in jail listening to Jay Leno and Rush Limbaugh and everybody making jokes about me getting shot. And watching the media report all kinds of lies about me, like that I got raped in jail. That never happened. But at least while I was locked down, all the inmates gave me props, and so did lots of mothers and kids, who wrote me letters of support.

One of the best letters I got came from [actor] Tony Danza. I've never even met the guy, but he wrote me to say he liked my album and to keep my head up and to just come out stronger. I can't tell you how great that made me feel.

Chuck Philips: *How do you look back on the last couple of turbulent years?*

Tupac: It's been stress and drama for a long time now, man. So much has happened. I got shot five times by some dudes who were trying to rub me out. But God is great. He

'Pac gets to grips with actor Stephen Baldwin at a 1996 AIDS fundraiser.

let me come back. But, when I look at the last few years, it's not like everybody just did me wrong. I made some mistakes. But I'm ready to move on.

Chuck Philips: *Did you write this new album in jail?*

Tupac: No. I only wrote one song there. But I've been in the studio every waking hour since I got out. Me and my producer Johnnie 'J' keep coming up with new songs 'til people start passing out. Then we come back early in the morning and start over. You're going to feel the entire eleven months of what I went through on this album. I'm venting my anger.

Chuck Philips: *A number of your songs*

deal with – and some people say glorify – drug dealing and gang violence. What do you say to people who say you are a bad social influence?

Tupac: Let me say for the record, I am not a gangster and never have been. I'm not the thief who grabs your purse. I'm not the guy who jacks your car. I'm not down with people who steal and hurt others. I'm just a brother who fights back. I'm not some violent closet psycho. I've got a job. I'm an artist.

Chuck Philips: *So why is gangbanging and violence so often the focus of your music?*

Tupac: Everything in life is not all beautiful,

not all fun. There is lots of killing and drugs. To me, a perfect album talks about the hard stuff and the fun and caring stuff. What I want to know, though, is why all of a sudden is everybody acting like gangs are some new phenomenon in this country? Almost everyone in America is affiliated with some kind of gang. We got the FBI, the ATF, the police departments, the religious groups, the Democrats and the Republicans. Everybody's got their own little clique and they're all out there gangbanging in their own little way.

The thing that bothers me is that it seems like all the sensitive stuff I write just goes unnoticed . . . the media doesn't get who I am at all. Or maybe they just can't accept it. It doesn't fit into those negative stories they like to write. I'm the kind of guy who is moved by a song like Don McLean's 'Vincent,' that one about Van Gogh. The lyric on that song is so touching. That's how I want to make my songs feel. Take 'Dear Mama' – I aimed that one straight for my homies' heartstrings.

Chuck Philips: *You studied at the Baltimore School of Performing Arts. Does your theater background influence your songwriting?*

Tupac: It influences all my work. I really like stuff like *Les Miserables* and *Gospel at Colonus*. And I love Shakespeare. He wrote some of the rawest stories, man. I mean look at *Romeo and Juliet*. That's some serious ghetto shit. You got this guy Romeo from the Bloods who falls for Juliet, a female from the Crips, and everybody in both gangs are against them. So they have to sneak out and they end up dead for nothing. Real tragic stuff.

And look how Shakespeare busts it up with *Macbeth*. He creates a tale about this king's wife who convinces a happy man to chase after her and kill her husband so he can take over the country. After he commits the murder, the dude starts having delusions just like in a Scarface song. I mean the king's wife just screws this guy's whole life up for nothing. Now that's what I call a bitch.

Chuck Philips: *Why do you use such derogatory terms to describe women? Doesn't that play into the hands of critics who say rappers are misogynists?*

Tupac: If the shoe fits wear it, that's what I say. What if all the guys started complaining when women call them dogs? In real life, just like in *Macbeth*, all women are not just pure and true. Just because I write some songs about bad women, though, that doesn't mean I hate women. I've written songs that show great love and respect for women too. Songs that talk about strong, upstanding women and their pain.

Look around you in this studio right now. I have women working on my music. They understand where I'm coming from. So does my mama. I always play my music for her before it comes out. Why do you think I wrote 'Dear Mama'? I wrote it for my mama because I love her and I felt I owed her something deep.

INTERVIEW ON THE WESTSIDE RADIO SHOW

by Sway

(transcribed by Davey D)

On Friday April 19 1996, Tupac Shakur graced the airwaves of KMEL Radio's Westside Radio program in San Francisco. Here, in an historic interview, he let the entire Bay Area know exactly what he was feeling and thinking at that point in time.

For those who weren't up on the backdrop at the time that interview aired, Tupac had not spoken to anyone extensively since joining Death Row. His album, *All Eyez on Me*, was the album of choice for more than a few headz, especially here in the Bay Area. The Bad Boy/Death Row conflict was at an all time high . . . . No one from the Death Row camp had spoken on co-founder Dr. Dre's departure. More importantly, Tupac had not been through the Bay in what seemed like years . . . . My boy Sway of *The Wake Up Show* was the person asking the questions.

Sway: *First of all Tupac, congratulations on your success . . . . Most people from the Bay Area couldn't be there by your side, but we felt like with every episode you went through we were there, we saw you through the media and we were right there. Brothers got a lotta love for you here in the Bay Area and we wanna know when you're planning on coming back?*

Tupac: I'm comin' back for sure, and I love the Bay. Everywhere I go, and every episode I've been through, I always felt like I was sharing it, both the good times and the bad times, with the Bay Area. I felt like, whatever I am, the Bay Area had something to do with making me. So if I'm bad they had something to do with making me and if I'm good they had something to do with making me. Between the East Coast, the Bay Area and L.A. and Baltimore, those places made me . . . I owe them everything. It's not like I just got love

for one block. I got love for those communities, I got love for those areas because everything about those areas made me who I am . . . . From the crackheads to biggest ballers to the teachers to the principals in schools to the police that pulled me by the arm to the mammas on the block. To everybody who helped raise me and I appreciate it . . . . With all my fans I got a family again. When I started rappin' I was talkin' about broken homes and now everybody is alright again just because of my fans being behind me, they made it more then just an artist thing, instead it was like them saying, 'Hey, that's our homeboy and we support him. I appreciate that . . . I went to jail and they made me number one. I appreciate them stickin' up for me when everyone was kickin' me when I was down . . . . That's love and I'll never trade that, so for the Bay and Philly and all those areas and all those ghettos and towns, I love y'all, don't let this East Coast/West Coast thing get to you . . . I love you with all my heart with everything. I do this for y'all . . . .

Sway: *It seems like every time you come up something happens to bring you back down. When you're caught up like that, what is it that goes through your mind when you got millions of fans wondering about you?*

Tupac: It hurts me in one way because they be lookin' at me saying, 'Damn, you got everything, why are you doing this?' In my heart I'll be saying, 'Damn, you know I don't wanna go to jail, I'm trying to live.' On the other hand, I can't really take it personal because I'm a reflection of the community . . . . All young black males are going through that. It's happening with a lot of young black females also, young white males . . . . A lot of minorities are going through that where they try to come up and get pulled back five steps . . . . To me it's not personal because they're all going through it. The only thing that makes it different and original with me is that people get to watch it from beginning to end like it's a soap opera. You get to watch mine and with everyone else they get to hide and go to their homes and get over it. With me, you see me dealing with my greatest pains. You see me get over things . . . .

Sway: *What went through your head when you got shot in New York and that whole complication?*

Tupac: I can't front. It slowed me down. What went through my mind was like, 'Damn, I'm shot.' I used to believe I could never be touched. So now I'm more careful. Some people may say I'm disrespectful, but I'm more cautious because I have been shot. I know what that feels like. I'm not trying to be in that predicament. I know we all have choices to make and my choices have already been made even if I wanna change it. What I learned in jail is that I can't change. I can't live a different lifestyle, this is it. This is the life that they gave and this is the life that I made. You know how they say, 'You made your bed, now lay in it'? I tried to move . . . can't move into some other bed. This is it. Not for the courts. Not for the parole board. Not for nobody. All I'm trying to do is survive and make good out of the dirty, nasty, unbelievable lifestyle that they gave me. I'm just trying to make something good out of that. It's like if you try and plant something in the concrete, if it grows and the rose petals got all kind of scratches and marks, you're not gonna say, 'Damn, look at all the scratches on the rose that grew from the concrete.' You're gonna say, 'Damn! A rose grew from the concrete?' Well that's the same thing with me. Folks should be sayin', 'Damn! He grew out of all that?' That's what they should see.

Sway: *Brother, you must be truly blessed to go through all these trials and tribulations you've been through and you're still maintaining. Even now they're still comin' after you. You got these demons and obstacles that keep comin' down harder and harder. It seems like every time you turn around, you got somebody knockin' on your door trying to take something from you . . . .*

Tupac: They come harder and harder. It's like every time I think this is it and I go all out to beat that and I win or I lose . . . I come into the next one and it's worse. It's like the twilight zone. It's like some evil, unstoppable shit that won't let me go. It's got its hands on me and it wants to see me fail. In my mind sometimes, when I'm drunk or I'm just laying down, I keep thinking to myself, 'Damn, is this true? Am I gonna fail? Am I supposed to fail? Should I just stop trying and give up?' But then I'm like, 'Naw, hold up, hold on, that's exactly what they're waiting on me to do.' They're waiting for me to give up. So now this is just a fun little game that I cry at sometime, that I laugh at sometime, that I smile at and have good times and bad times. But it's a game. It's the game of life . . . . Do I win or do I lose? I know one day they're gonna shut the game down but I gotta have as much fun and go around the board as many times as I can before it's my turn to leave . . . .

Sway: *How did you first get down with Suge Knight and Death Row?*

Tupac: I used to always see Suge. When they did the soundtrack for 'Murder Was the Case' and I was going through all those legal problems, he was like, 'Yo, give me a song, dog.' I gave him a song and I got the most I ever got for a song. It was damn near an album budget. I got something like $200,000 for one song and they didn't even use it. But I still got paid for everything I did for the soundtrack. I remember when he did it. He did it not because he was jocking me, but because he knew I was having crazy legal problems and I was a man. He had asked me to come to Death Row and I told him I wasn't ready. Instead of taking it personal he did that for me and I appreciated that. So when I was in jail, just sittin' there, I was gonna quit rappin' but then Puffy and Biggie came out in *Vibe* magazine and lied and twisted the facts. All I wanted to do was end everything and walk away from the shit. I wanted to get out the game. I'm trying to get out the game and they wanna dirty up my memory. They wanna dirty up everything I worked for. So instead of quittin' it made me wanna come back and be more relentless to destroy who used to be my comrades and homeboys. These guys were my closest click. I worked hard all my life as far as this music business to bring about East Coast/West Coast love and make everybody feel comfortable. I dreamed of the day when I could go to New York and feel comfortable and they could come out here and be comfortable. So when people ask me about this East Coast/West Coast thing, it's not silly at all . . . but you can't disrespect the love.

You can't disrespect the peace treaty. That's just like when the Indians made deals with the white dudes and they would just come and rape their women and shoot 'em up and leave . . . of course the Indians aren't gonna love white people no more.

They're gonna want to kick up some dust until people think about it and re-negotiate the terms of the treaty and that's where this East Coast/West Coast stuff is at right now. We gotta have this beef and these words and this dialogue until we can re-negotiate the terms of the treaty. I love the East Coast, I from the East Coast, but they have to understand you just can't be saying shit about us and think we're not gonna take it personally . . . . You just can't be calling us fakers and pretenders and non-creative and say we can't freestyle, and we just sit back and say, 'Naw, it's cool 'cause we love them because they started hip hop.' Hell no, we're gonna take it personal, just like a kid would when his bigger brother who ain't doing his shit steps to him. That's like a lit-

tle brother making lots of cash and the bigger brother comin' along and sayin', 'You owe it all to me.' That's wrong. Don't be mad because the little nigga is comin' up.

Sway: *Pac, you gave a lot of love back to some Bay Area artist like E-40, Rappin' 4Tay, Dru Down and the whole crew . . . talk about what made you decide to work with them.*

Tupac: Because I can't always be in the Bay. I know how the Bay is. The Bay is the type of place where if you ain't there they're gonna talk about you. I wanted them to know that I love you, I feel you and I'm gonna represent for you. I know I got a certain amount of acclaim so I bring the Bay with me . . . I know E-40 is what I was when I was with Digital Underground. He is the Bay right now, him and 4Tay. So I get them on my album to represent the Bay. It shows we still have love and we're still all good. By us being representatives we bring the Bay wherever we go. Rappin' 4Tay has always been raw to me and I like his style. When I was in jail I used to always listen to stuff, so when I got out we clicked and did the song. Now he's in jail and I gotta do what he did for me. When I was in jail he used to send out shout-outs and show support, so now I support 4Tay. Everybody pray for him and send letters. I hope the brother gets out of jail as soon as possible. [Rappin' 4Tay was released in July 1996.] You know it's a struggle for every young black man . . . . You know how it is, only God can judge us.

Sway: *Now is the East Coast/West Coast beef really both coasts? Or is it Bad Boy and Death Row?*

Tupac: It's not both coasts. What it is, is the people on the East Coast are real proud and real cultural and real strong like we are on the West Coast. What happen was Biggie came at a time just like Hitler did with the Germans. Biggie came at a time when they were open

'The American dream wasn't meant for me' – Tupac leaves court in 1994.

to somebody saying, 'We're the master race and these guys [West Coast] are nothing. They're pretenders and this is why we're not makin' it in the business. It's because of these guys. This is why we're not doing nothing.' So the East Coast really not hatin' us or knowing anything about us, have just been listening to their supposed-to-be leader. They were listening to the person who's supposed to be 'representing' for them . . . . They didn't know that what they were doing was ending our culture. We [West Coast] held it down for you all. That's how I felt. I was in tears. When LL [Cool J] was out there dancin' with women in silver suits, which I'm not mad at, because I might do that one day . . . . But when the East Coast was trying to be creative and test other boundaries we were holdin' it down with this hardcore shit. It might not have been what you [East Coast] wanted but it kept rap alive for years. It kept money comin' in. It let them [the world] notice us. So how could you [East Coast] look at us and say, 'You're not good enough'? We're from a broken home. Y'all [East Coast] didn't teach

us this, we ain't got no subways and graffiti. In spite of the gangs and all of that we still came up with this culture. I feel like we never got what we deserved. I took it personal because I'm from the East Coast and I know about that culture but I know about this [West Coast] culture because I was here when it was being put down . . . . So now I'm doing what the East Coast would've did if the West Coast did this to them . . . I'm riding, for my side. You're wrong. It's not right.

Recognize us. The only way the East Coast is gonna recognize us is for us to do it on record, by money, by sales and by representing. Just like KRS-One . . . when PM Dawn got on stage and he had been talking shit about him, what did KRS-One do? [He bum rushed him.] So why are people telling me I'm wrong for doing what I'm doing? They love KRS-One. He is hip hop, am I correct? I'm mad at Biggie and I'm rushin' the nigga. What's the problem? As soon as the East Coast separate themselves from Biggie we will do shows in the east. Everything is beautiful. But so far the East Coast has been with him. Everything I read, every letter I read, every interview I read, niggas keep saying, 'Fuck Tupac, Biggie Biggie this and Biggie Biggie that,' like he's representin' everyone from the East Coast. That's why I attack the way I do, I'm a general and I'm a smart general and I'm not gonna attack at no blind soldier. I'm gonna attack those who attack me. The only reason why people was mad was because I came out of jail and made this a reality. When I got out of jail the East Coast/West Coast shit was really started. 'California Love,' when I was singin' put it down, and now niggas is mad because money is fucked up, attitudes have changed, it's not as safe as it used to be. Niggas gotta think about their business and that's what I wanted to happen. Now let's go to the table. Let's talk. Let's make peace, let's work it out . . . let's give the community the money.

Sway: *So are you saying a conversation with Puffy and Biggie would . . . .*

Tupac: I wouldn't sit down and have a conversation with Puffy and Biggie, because that's like Scarface sitting down with the dude he's hoping to rule. They are not on my level, but I can sit down with the OGs and from there [back east], which we are doing. People need to know we're not beefing with the East Coast. We're about to start Death Row East with Eric B and all the OG niggas out there. We got Big Daddy Kane, Christopher Williams, we're trying to get Bobby Brown. We're trying to get the East Coast Death Row to be like the West Coast Death Row and make it major. We're not doing that until we get this business settled. Even while we're doing this we're trying to get Wu-Tang, I feel as though they represent the East Coast the way we represent the West Coast and I love them. If everybody's raps is what they really think then everybody should understand what I'm doing. It's gangsta shit. It's warrior shit, and it's all by the rules of the game. I'm calling for dialogue. I'm gathering attention for dialogue, which is what you do in a struggle for power.

Sway: *What's going on with Dre and how does that affect Death Row?*

Tupac: Dre is doing his own thing. It doesn't affect us. My take on what happened was that Snoop went on trial for murder for his life, somebody said Dre was in the car. The jury believed that we needed Dre to be able to say he wasn't there, once they would've saw that he wasn't there that would've saved Snoop's whole case. They would've saw that the witness was lying. Dre never showed up. He said he was too busy. That's how they told me. When they told me that I was like, no matter how dope he is, and Dre was one of my heroes in the music industry, if he's not down for his homeboys, I don't wanna be a part of him or around him. Plus I feel that what was done in the dark will come to light. There are secrets that everybody's gonna find out about, and you'll know why I did it. I swear to God y'all, we are living by the rules of the game.

Sway: *Hey Pac, why don't you talk about the project you are doing with Jodeci right now . . . ?*

Tupac: My next single is gonna be 'How Do You Want It?,' 'AmeriKKKa's Most Wanted,' 'Hit 'Em Up' and 'California Love,' the version people couldn't buy. 'Hit 'Em Up' is a song which is a classic hip hop record, meaning it's a straight battle record to all the Bad Boy staff. It's to Puffy, to Biggie, to Lil' Kim, to all of them.

Sway: *What about Mobb Deep?*

Tupac: My little homies is attacking them. That's why I'm not even addressing the Mobb Deep issue. They're not even on my level. I find it disrespectful that they would even think they can attack me or the West Coast . . . . So I don't even address those busta ass fakes. Please print that . . . . It is on and poppin'. If you don't see me rushin' them that means it's 'cause they bowed down. Those Mobb Deep fools, they don't want it. Chino XL, Mobb Deep, Bad Boy, Biggie, Lil' Ceasar, Junior Mafia, all of them is on our hit list and I'm getting them with my new click called the Outlawz. They're some Jersey dudes who are keeping that East Coast flava poppin'. It's some West Coast dudes, southern dudes, it's the epitome of what I represent. I got Big Syke from Thug Life . . . . We got 'How Do You Want It?' with Ron Hightower doing the directing with me and we got all porno stars. I got Nina Hartley from the Bay, and all the big time people. It's the dirtiest, nastiest video I've ever done. I got a *Playboy* version and a regular version. We got nudity. It's the most amazing video you'll ever see. We just did the video for 'AmeriKKKa's Most Wanted,' which is the classic diss video. We got 'Piggy' and 'Buffy' . . . . We're doing videos from *All Eyez on Me*, 'I Ain't Mad At Ya,' 'All About You.' The record company got all the money in the world so we're just gonna put it out . . . . When things get real slow, we'll release a home video with 'Ambitions of a Rider,' and a couple of the hardcore songs . . . I just did a remix to 'What's Your Phone Number?' with all new lyrics. We took that MC Lye beat from her new song she has out ['Keep On Movin' Up']. It's so freaky you won't believe it . . . I got a whole new album out . . . waiting for the soundtrack.

It's clean, all positive, all in the vein of songs like 'Keep Ya Head Up' and 'Brenda's Got a Baby,' it's that type of stuff. I just put out a hardcore double album, and next I'm gonna put out an introspective album. It'll be like a *Me Against the World Part Two*. That's what I think my fans are looking for . . . I'm gonna

'I loved my childhood, but I hated growing up poor, it made me very bitter.' – *Tupac*

show that I appreciate your support . . . .

Sway: *So you worked with Janet Jackson. I was wondering if you can hook me up with her number?*

Tupac: If anybody finds Janet, tell her I'm looking for her. That's why I said that shit in my song 'My Mind's Made Up,' but give me Janet. I feel like she got shit twisted and people gone and made her my enemy. She ain't my enemy, I ain't mad at her. I want her to know that. It ain't even like that. She met me at a time in my life when I was real immature. I was comin' up and going through a lot. Now she probably sees me in a whole different light. Maybe not and maybe she will. I want that opportunity. When I see Janet, I'm gonna try to make right where we made wrong.

Sway: *Let's talk on some other things, like your new movie and soundtrack you're working on.*

Tupac: We got a movie called *Gridlock'd* coming out which is a mainstream movie. It's me coming back into the theaters with Tim Roth from *Pulp Fiction*. I don't know who it is, but there's a big name female in the movie. I'm the music supervisor for the soundtrack. It's my first chance ever doing something like this . . . . We got Alanis Morrissette and all these other big name alternative groups. It's supposedly people I would never get with, I got them all on the soundtrack just to show what kind of range I got. I'll be putting that type of soundtrack out and then I'll be putting out a rap soundtrack. I'm gonna do it like a Tupac album with me doing a whole bunch of solo songs and Snoop on there doing some songs. This is just to show I have a business mind as well as a creative mind. I can make my way in this business besides rapping.

Sway: *What's the one thing you would like people to know about you?*

Tupac: Number one, when I diss y'all, meaning like when you come up to me and I'm not giving you the type of reaction that you think I should give you, it's not because I'm ungrateful . . . . It's because I'm nervous. I'm paranoid, I just got out of jail. I've been shot, cheated, lied [to] and framed and I just don't know how to deal with so many people giving me that much affection. I never had that in my life. So if I do that, don't take it personal. Try to understand it and see it for what it is. Now I understand what it's truly like to be a fine female who goes to a club and all the guys just rush you before you're ready to be rushed. Everyone is touching you before you're ready to get touched. So now I have a better understanding of what it's like to be a woman, I have a better understanding of fans not making you do things. I'm gonna do it because I love y'all, I do appreciate what you did. But if you make me do it, then I don't wanna do it. I don't care how many albums you bought. My fans to me are people who follow me, who are down for me, who understand me and no matter what people say, they know me . . . because they've followed me through my career.

A lot of people just bought my album, I buy albums all the time. I just buy them to listen to . . . . If you bought my album, you bought it for the music. You didn't buy it so when you see me, I just break down and start eating you out. I don't like that. Don't start extorting me for an autograph. I'm real. I give autographs when I want to . . . I wanna be in this game for a long time. I don't ever wanna hate the fans, that's what these other niggas do. They might give you autographs all the time, but they hate you. They never even look at you like people. I do look at you like people.

That's why I feel like I can look you in your eye and say, 'Yo, I don't feel like doing that right now, I don't feel like signing no autographs, and you should understand. I look at you like a human being. Let's kick it, let's not take pictures, let's kick it. Do that. I want some females to do that . . . . Every female wanna come up to me and show me how much they're not attracted to me. Do the opposite 'cause these ghetto girls, these minority women, they're the only women I can get 'cause everyone else is scared of me. Their parents tell them not to mess with me. Y'all can't fade me. Y'all can't turn on me. Don't change on me. Stay down for me, 'cause I stay down for you, and don't extort me unless you intend to do it forever.

Sway: *Five years from now, what do you see yourself doing?*

Tupac: I see myself having a job on Death Row . . . being the A&R person and an artist that drop an album like Paul McCartney every five years. Not that I'm like Paul McCartney but there's no rapper who ever did it so that's why I use him as an example . . . . But I wanna do it at leisure. My music will mean something and I'll drop deeper shit. I'll have my own production company which I'm close to right now . . . I'm doing my own movies. I have my own restaurant . . . which I got right now with Alanis or Suge or Snoop. I just wanna expand. I'm starting to put out some calendars for charity. I'm gonna start a little youth league in California so we can start playing some East Coast teams, some southern teams . . . I wanna have like a Pop Warner League except the rappers fund it and they're the head coaches. Have a league where you can get a big trophy with diamonds in it for a nigga to stay drug free and stay in school. That's the only way you can be on the team. We'll have fun and eat pizza and have the finest girls there and throw concerts at the end of the year. That's what mean I by giving back.

HAVE GUN WILL TRAVEL

by Ronin Ro

At Death Row Records, Snoop Doggy Dogg pitied his old friend Tupac's plight. In the past, label CEO Suge had wanted to sign Tupac to the label. 'But I kinda put the fuel to the flame and told Suge to put Tupac down with Death Row,' Snoop said. 'It's like an angel was talking to me when I told Suge, "We need 'Pac on Death Row."'

Suge agreed. Tupac was having trouble with Puffy. Now would be a good time to offer Tupac a contract. Suge made his offer. Behind bars, Tupac accepted. His friends urged him not to sign, but Tupac desperately wanted to be free. In the past, he had said, 'If I have to go to jail, I don't even want to be living. I just want to cease to exist for however long they have me there, and then when I come out, I'll be reborn, you know what I'm saying?'

During a visit before Suge arrived in upstate New York, Tupac's old friend Watani Tyehimba urged him not to sign with the controversial label. Tupac hugged him, wept openly. 'I know I'm selling my soul to the devil,' he said. 'At that point,' his mother, Afeni Shakur, claimed, 'I don't think he had any choice but to sign that contract.' This was not entirely true: Tupac could have decided to refuse Suge's offer and serve his time in prison – just like any other inmate.

Interscope, supportive of Tupac's decision to sign with Death Row, granted him a 'verbal release.' Suge's attorney, David Kenner, drafted a crude, handwritten three-page contract. Tupac scribbled his signature. Beneath it, Suge countersigned.

On October 12, 1995, Suge and Kenner chartered a private jet and flew to upstate New York. As their white limousine cruised through a small economically depressed white town, drawing stares from locals in old jeans and baseball caps, Tupac prepared to leave Dannemora. He walked out of the gray prison, past hostile guards and inmates,

posed for a photo near the limousine, then quickly entered the vehicle. In the photo he looked gaunt. His stare was tentative and weak. The last few years had been rough ones, beating a limo driver in Los Angeles, attacking the Hughes brothers on the set of a video, swinging a bat at a rapper onstage at a concert in Michigan, being punched in the eye by a Crip in a convenience store, shooting two drunk off-duty cops in Atlanta, being accused of rape in New York, getting robbed and shot five times in the head and groin in Times Square, serving time in Riker's Island, then Dannemora. But the next year would be even worse. It would also be his last.

When he entered the white limo, Tupac's last album, *Me Against the World*, was still on the nation's pop album chart, lingering at No. 108 after 26 weeks. During the flight to Los Angeles and studio sessions that night, Tupac believed Suge Knight had been solely responsible for posting $1.4 million bond. Despite the fact that he had provided only $250,000 – with Interscope and Time Warner paying the difference – Suge took sole credit for Tupac's release. 'Whether the odds are in your favor or appear to be stacked against you,' he said the next day, 'the Death Row family sticks with you.'

Upon signing, Tupac vowed to make Death Row the biggest label in the world. Even bigger than Snoop had made it. 'Not stepping on Snoop's toes,' he said, 'he did a lot of work. Him, Dogg Pound, Nate Dogg, Dre, all of them. They made Death Row what it is today. I'm gonna take it to the next level.'

'I saw him right when he got out of jail,' said producer E Swift of the California rap trio Tha Alkaholiks. 'Every time I saw him he was all love. He was so happy to be out, free. That was all he could talk about: "Man, I'm out, I'm out! I'm happy to be alive!" He was

65

just living for the moment.'

Suge Knight, meanwhile, knew Tupac's arrival at Death Row would change the label. 'It gave them a much more public profile,' said author Brian Cross. 'Snoop and Dre would always get press. But now there were three public stars: And at that point, with the benefit of Tupac becoming his running buddy, Suge was starting to get press. Suddenly the lights were shining on Suge and he became a player in the whole thing.'

From the beginning, however, Tupac could not escape accusations that he signed to Death Row for protection. National music magazines had publicized his feud with Bad Boy, and his accusations that people connected with that label had stalked him on the East Coast. From the macho image they had promoted in his early days, when he shot off-duty white police officers, reporters now focused on the fact that Tupac had feared for his life; he had been robbed; he had lost a testicle and been left with nightmares and persistent headaches; he was rumored to have been sodomized in a New York prison. They also wrote articles emphasizing how Suge was a force powerful enough to repel any would-be assassin: He was known for brutalizing his competition and granting enemies no leniency. If anyone could keep ruthless drug dealers from killing him, reporters stressed, it was Suge Knight and his sociopathic friends in the brutal Tree Top Pirus street gang. And Tupac, they inferred, was well aware of this.

'There's nobody in the business strong enough to scare me,' Tupac claimed. 'I'm with Death Row 'cause they not scared either. When I was in jail, Suge was the only one who used to see me. Nigga used to fly a private plane all the way to New York and spend time with me. He got his lawyer to look into all my cases. Suge supported me, whatever I needed. When I got out of jail, he had a private plane for me, a limo, five police officers for security. I said, "I need a house for my moms."'

Much as Tupac supported the label, ini-tially, former-Black Panther Afeni Shakur cheer-led for generous black music mogul Suge Knight. In the past, said Tupac's aunt Yaasmyn Fula, Afeni and her brood 'lived lives of scarcity, worrying about the next meal, worrying about how to pay the rent.'

When Suge signed her son, he had also bought Afeni a home. When the Shakur family came to town, he put them up at the luxurious Westwood Marquis and never complained about the huge bills they ran up. 'Death Row in the beginning treated us much better than Interscope had,' Afeni confirmed.

By now, however, ''Pac felt he was cursed with this dysfunctional family although he loved them,' his aunt Yaasmyn later told *The New Yorker*. 'And as his success grew, especially in the last year, this presence grew. They were *always* there.'

Since childhood, Tupac had suffered feelings of inadequacy: His cousins used to tease him about his effeminate facial features; he felt 'unmanly,' he said. Free from prison, Tupac was now expected to return to the role he willingly abandoned during his incarceration; he was expected to record 'macho' gangsta rap.

Tupac regularly spent nineteen hours at a time in the studio. Though he claimed to have quit smoking and drinking, he soon picked up where he left off. High on marijuana and drunk on cheap booze, he worked on his next album. 'He was released on Thursday,' Afeni Shakur reported. 'By Thursday night he was in the studio. By Friday he had seven songs from that double CD completed.'

Like Snoop, Tupac was working to pay off legal fees Death Row had provided. To ensure that Tupac's album would sell, Suge provided Tupac with tracks that Dr. Dre had originally planned to use on his *Helter Skelter* album with Ice Cube. Suge owned every master tape used by Death Row musicians. He located a song featuring Dre and Ice Cube rhyming over a snazzy Dre production (their collaboration with funk musician George Clinton, 'You Can't See Me.') Without permission, Suge erased their vocals and allowed Tupac to record a generic profanity-ridden gangsta rap.

Then Suge called Johnny Jackson (producer of 'Pour Out a Little Liquor') into the studio. 'We were very prolific,' Jackson explained. 'We'd put down four to five songs a day. I saw him work with other producers, and if they took too long to lay down the music, he'd get upset. He'd say, "You're not moving fast enough. I need you to pick up the pace." So when me and him got together for *All Eyez on Me*, we were going at it like mad scientists.

'A typical day would go like this,' Jackson continued. 'After I'd been there laying down the tracks for an hour or two, he'd come in, sit right down, and write three verses in fifteen or twenty minutes. Then he'd go into the booth and deliver the vocal – and it was off to the next track. I didn't realize a rapper could write the lyrics and deliver the vocals as fast as he could. That really amazed me.'

At the time, Biggie Smalls's wife was in town on business. A caramel-colored woman with bleached-blonde hair, Faith Evans was born in Lakeland, Florida, in 1973. A year after her birth, she moved to her grandparents' home in Newark, New Jersey. 'My mama used to sing with a white rock band,' she remembered. 'I don't know the name of it, but she used to take me to her shows sometime.' By the age of two, Faith was singing at the Emanuel Baptist Church. An honor student at University High School, she received a scholarship to Fordham University. In 1993 she decided to begin writing songs.

Before marrying Biggie, she had been a songwriter for Mary J. Blige, Soul for Real, and Usher. Nine days after they met at a Bad Boy photo shoot on August 4, 1994, they became man and wife. 'I can't explain it,' Biggie said. 'I just knew Faith was different. I wanted her locked down.' But Faith had to deal with people assuming she was out for Biggie's money despite her songwriting credits. 'Hello?' she once said. 'I was already doing my own thing.' A week after the wedding, she bought Biggie a green Land Cruiser. 'Then he got a burgundy one,' writer dream hampton recalled. 'Then a Lexus. Then an SL.'

They moved into a spacious apartment off Myrtle Street in Brooklyn, then Biggie went on tour. Faith felt terrible but focused on recording her solo album. When Biggie returned to Brooklyn, he leaped into recording an album for his protégés, Junior M.A.F.I.A. 'These are my peoples.'

Biggie said of the group. 'I grew up with them and I know how it is to come from the Ave. I wasn't going to give up the Ave. and leave my niggas out there.'

A member of the group, Lil' Kim, said she loved Biggie to death. 'And I mean that literally. Everybody knows. It's not a secret. I love him.'

As Biggie spent time with Kim, recording her for Junior M.A.F.I.A.'s album *Conspiracy*, Faith became unhappy. 'A few months after our anniversary,' she told *Vibe*, 'it seemed like he was getting caught up in all that "big poppa" stuff. But I couldn't see myself being without him. He was real . . . real . . . *real*.'

While Biggie toured with Kim's group, his storybook marriage to Faith Evans suffered. After a show in Virginia, a telephone conversation with Faith erupted into an argument, and Biggie hung up on her. She kept trying to call back, but he refused to answer the telephone. That night his friends invited female groupies over. One was left out, Biggie explained, so he let her sleep in his room. 'It was some completely innocent shit. We weren't fucking.' At eight the next morning, someone knocked on the door. Big remained in bed while his female guest went to answer. ''Who is it?' she asked. A winsome voice replied, 'housekeeping.'

'She opened the door,' Big remembered, 'and Faith beat the shit out of her. Oh, my God. Punched homegirl in the face about 30 times, then got on the next flight back to New York.' It was like a scene from *Casino*. The vengeful wife strikes back. Biggie was nervous, he rushed to the airport. ''Cause I wasn't gonna leave her buck willing like that. The girl was mad cool and I felt horrible, but fuck that. I got on that plane.'

Despite his marriage, Junior M.A.F.I.A. member Lil' Kim began a campaign to get Biggie back. 'The whole thing between me and Faith,' Kim told *Rappages*: 'We don't have to be friends, but it don't need to be no beef. "I feel your pain, but you got to feel mine. I've been there way before you. Imagine what I was going through. Imagine how I felt when y'all two got married."

In Los Angeles shortly after Tupac's release from prison in October 1995, Faith kept seeing Tupac at parties. Despite the fact that Tupac had accused her husband of trying to have him killed, Faith Evans felt Tupac was 'mad cool.' She said, 'I saw him at a couple of parties and we was chillin', havin' drinks, him and my friends. And I knew Biggie always said he had mad love for Tupac.'

When Tupac asked her to appear on a song, Faith agreed – pending her record company's, Bad Boy's, approval. Tupac encouraged her to record a vocal over one of his new beats. Even though Death Row Records and Bad Boy were literally at war, she complied, then returned to New York. Months later, as Death Row continued to express nothing but hate for Bad Boy, Faith's friends began to tell her they had heard her performance on Tupac's new song, 'Wonda Why They Call U Bytch.' Alarmed by the title, Faith was also confused. How could Death Row Records release the song when clearance forms hadn't been finalized? Bad Boy made inquiries, and Death Row insisted it wasn't Faith. Everyone was hearing Death Row's own singer Jewel, they claimed. Faith did not suspect that her associating with the maniacal Tupac would be used as ammuni-tion against her husband and record label.

As Death Row's one-sided feud against Bad Boy continued, Bad Boy CEO Sean 'Puffy' Combs continued to deny involvement in Tupac's shooting at the Quad Recording Studio, and Jake Robles's murder in Atlanta. In doing so, however, he revealed that he knew who shot Tupac. 'He ain't mad at the niggas that shot him,' Puffy said publicly, 'he knows where they're at. He knows who shot him. If you ask him, he knows, and everybody in the street knows, and he's not stepping to them, because he knows that he's not gonna get away with that shit. To me, that's some real sucker shit.'

Soon, the national media reported on the feud. But Suge tried to clarify that the battle was not between African Americans on the East and West coasts. It was 'ghetto niggas and phony niggas.' And Puffy, he said: 'That's a phony nigga. He's frontin', tryin to be somethin' he ain't. Here's the whole thang with Puffy: They say shit to make themselves bigger. I ain't never did no interview sayin' shit about people. By sayin' shit about Death Row in magazines, they tryin' to put themselves on our level, and it ain't no muthafuckin' comparison.'

The ideal solution, Suge felt, would be a boxing event that would benefit various inner-city charity organizations. 'Puffy, get yo' muthafuckin' ass in the ring and fight Tupac,' Suge roared. 'Look at Puffy's body! Who can he whup? How you gon' talk shit and be in a little boy's body? And I'll beat Biggie's ass all over the ring! We can do it in Vegas and give the money to the ghetto.'

Puffy tried to make peace. 'I'm not a gangsta and I don't have no rivalry with no person in this industry whatsoever. The whole shit is stupid – tryin' to make an East Coast/West Coast war.'

Dr. Dre watched from the sidelines. 'If it keeps going this way,' he predicted, 'pretty soon niggaz from the East Coast ain't gonna be able to come out here and vice versa.'

A BLACK DE NIRO?

PART THREE

KING OF STAGE
by Joshua Rubin

The mist descends quietly on a rainy Marin County evening, while just over the hill at Tamalpais High School, the audience grows quiet. The curtains part, and the lights begin to fade up a production of Chekhov's *The Boor*, a Russian farce about a landowner who becomes so frustrated with the stupid widow he's trying to seduce that he challenges her to a duel. The audience titters in anticipation as the young black actor playing the lead role of Smiroff swaggers onto the stage. He leads the audience into hysterics, and then deeper, into awareness and self-reflection, like a consummate preacher leading his congregation, articulate and confident. And if, at the end of the play, a curious theatergoer were to flip open the program to find the name of that talented young actor, they would not be nearly as surprised as we would be now, to find in small bold letters: Tupac Amaru Shakur.

The image of Tupac that most Americans recall comes from his music, which was dark and honest, hot with revolution and grounded in stories of death and despair. His career coincided with the birth of gangsta rap, and most critics focus on the violence surrounding his final years with Death Row, the label run by Marion 'Suge' Knight like a bad *Sopranos* episode. And while many people are aware that Tupac made some films, they certainly don't view it as anything more than an extension of his rap career.

But few people realize that Tupac was a classically trained actor, who had performed Shakespeare and Chekhov and attended the Baltimore School of the Performing Arts. Tupac was filming 1992's critically lauded *Juice* at the same time as he was recording his first album, *2Pacalypse Now*, and it was the double whammy of this double debut that blasted 'Pac into the American consciousness, setting him on a two-pronged career path. He made six films – *Juice* (1992), *Poetic Justice* (1993), *Above the Rim*

(1994), *Bullet* (1996), *Gridlock'd* (1997), and *Gang Related* (1997) – and they range in quality from the sublime to the awful. But a careful look at the stories behind 'Pac's filmography reveals that from his childhood to his early death, 'Pac often considered himself an actor first – and a rapper second.

'It's kind of interesting, considering how people generally think of him,' said Tim Roth, the British actor who co-starred with him in *Gridlock'd*, 'Pac's most mature film. 'If he'd played his cards right, he could have gone on to be a very established actor.'

''Pac was going to be my Robert De Niro,' confided John Singleton, who directed Tupac in his biggest studio film, *Poetic Justice* with Janet Jackson. He added with a laugh: 'I [once said] to Tupac: "You know what, you should just fuck all this music shit."'

Back when 'Pac was alive and kicking up shit, Nelson George, the acclaimed cultural critic, used to write: 'If he survives his twenties, Shakur could one day emerge as a true movie star.' Recently, in an e-mail, he broke it down: 'Whatever he did wrong off screen, in *Juice* and *Poetic Justice* there's a charisma, confidence and ease that few have had. I'm not sure if he'd ever have become as big as Will Smith, but he had a chance to be a Robert De Niro, and create a catalogue of troubled (young) men no other African-American actor could have matched. His movie work is crucial to his mythology.'

When you've seen Tupac on screen, you've seen a man of obvious sensitivity and heart. His feline, almost feminine eyes revealed depths of soulfulness that contradicted the media's often demonized portrait of him, and his own pose as the epitome of 'Thug Life' – the phrase tattooed across his belly. As Tupac's public image got harder and harder, his film roles actually got softer and more introspective, and by the end, it seemed he was attempting to expand out of a role that he had built out of proportion.

So, it's hard not to ask, how could Tupac be both a sensitive artist and a thugged-out G? And why is it that someone with such artfulness and talent inside him couldn't escape the pitfalls of the gangsta lifestyle?

'I got a lot to do. A lot I need to get done.' Tupac was twelve years old when he made his acting debut in *Raisin in the Sun*, Lorraine Hansberry's play about a black Chicago family. It was a production by the Harlem theater group, the 127th Street Ensemble, and when they performed for Jesse Jackson at a benefit at the Apollo Theater, little 'Pac got bit hard by the acting bug. He had always been geared toward the arts by his intellectual, Black Panther Party mother, Afeni, but now 'Pac had found his calling. He wrote in a handwritten letter to the troupe's director, Ernie McKlintock: 'Ernie, I'm available for acting. I can act! I was leader of my drama club last year.'

Two years later, after moving to Baltimore, he was accepted to the city's prestigious School of the Arts. Following a string of public schools where his creative impulses were never particularly valued, he was suddenly in a place that put enormous value on his impulses, his imagination. He was surrounded by artists of all types and colors, he studied dance and voice, and started rapping there, under the name MC New York. '[Tupac] could have done quite a good Hamlet,' claims Richard Pilcher, who taught Shakespeare to him. 'He really had a connection – it's very obvious now – with the words and the rhythm of the sounds.'

He got into seeing musicals like *Les Misérables*, and took classes in improv and method acting, which fascinated him. Donald Hicken, the teacher who would become Tupac's mentor, remembers watching 'Pac and a classmate perform a scene from Sam Shepard's *Fool for Love*, when he realized by the smell that they were drinking from a real bottle of tequila. When he stepped up on stage and confronted them, Tupac responded: 'Well, yeah, they drink

tequila in the scene – before they pull the gun out.' Then Hicken glanced down and gasped: 'My God, you've got a gun!' 'Pac shrugged and smiled. He was just keepin' it real. Hicken ordered the boys to come back the next day with iced tea and a water pistol.

'He was really very charismatic, even as a young kid,' remembers Pilcher. 'I think he sorta went through the ballet department – that is, the girls of the ballet department.' Donald Hicken remembers often seeing Tupac with Jada Pinkett, his best friend at BSA, and later a girlfriend, sitting in a circle of students on the floor during homeroom, dropping rhymes they had written the night before, tapping out rhythms on the tile. 'That school was saving me, you know what I'm saying?' Tupac once told a journalist.

But, in the middle of his junior year, Tupac showed up at Hicken's office and before he could speak, he burst into tears. His mother had told him they were moving to the West Coast. 'He was just heartbroken,' said Hicken. Marin City, north of San Francisco, was no West Coast paradise, just another depressed ghetto. But 'Pac managed to find himself a school there with a good theater program, Tamalpais High. Tupac was already such a well-trained actor, remembers Dan Caldwell, who taught there, that he was able to go directly into the advanced program. It was at Tam that Tupac performed in the Chekhov play, as well as creating a 1990s version of *Macbeth*, writing new rap lyrics to go with Shakespeare's. '[The performance] was highly emotional, people really crying,' remembers Caldwell. 'It had a profound effect on the people who did the project with him.'

'Pac was working on a piece about Martin Luther King, when the Bay Area rap group Digital Underground heard his demo tape and invited him to be a roadie and sometime dancer in their shows. It meant dropping out of school, and it wasn't the work as an actor he'd been training for, but he was going to get paid. And as John Singleton later said about him, '[He was into] anything that could make him come up.' As it turned out, his stint with DU led to his first shot at a film role, when he tagged along with DU's Money B to a New York audition for *Juice*, the first film by Spike Lee's longtime cinematographer Ernest R. Dickerson.

There were about 200 kids trying out for four parts, and after Money B had gone in, Tupac strode up to the film's producer and said, 'Man, I can do this shit.' They gave the cocky kid a chance, and he made it through round after round, over six weeks of auditions. Khalil Kain, the actor who played Raheem in the film, remembers: ''Pac was the cat that kinda set the tone for the rest of us. 'Cause he was going for it, just becoming that part [of Bishop, the film's loose cannon]. He acted like a complete savage. He was loud and obnoxious. It's like, you put eight guys in a room, somebody's going to be the alpha dog, and 'Pac had all the cats intimidated.'

'Bishop wasn't even as much a threat on paper until 'Pac brought that character to life. . .' said Jermaine Hopkins, who played the character of Steel. 'A lot of people have said about 'Pac that after playing that character in *Juice*, he started acting like that. But he played that role to get that role. He was that nigga in the audition, for real.'

Once in, Tupac maintained that intensity throughout the entire shoot. He was always on. Always moving, always jumping, always antsy to get to the next thing. 'He was a handful,' recalls Neal Moritz, one of the film's producers. 'But, he was a good handful. He was outspoken, had a lot to say, and questioned a lot of things.'

'Pac's biggest problems on the film were issues that would stay with him the rest of his career. He was accustomed to the pacing of theater, and he hated to do more than one take of a scene. After that he got self-conscious of his acting, and he would scream when they had to do a scene over and over.

He was also starting to piss people off by being late for his calls, smoking copious amounts of ganja, and taking off for the night, seemingly, whenever he felt like it. But Hopkins discovered that 'Pac was actually spending every single night and weekend in the studio, working on his first record. 'It done been times where 'Pac say, "OK, I gotta be in the studio by a certain time." And if they don't finish shooting, he would just walk off the set.'

'Pac felt his life really starting, and he became possessed by a need to be constantly working. 'He never stopped creating,' said Kain. 'I remember him telling me, when we finished *Juice*: "Please. Give me two years. I'm going to be a millionaire." And he did it.'

'He didn't sleep,' Tim Roth said, about working with Tupac on *Gridlock'd* in 1997. 'I got pissed at him that he'd come in tired all the time, because he'd have been up all night writing, shooting videos on the weekends and recording. There's only 24 hours in a day, and he'd use them all.'

'Tupac had realized that it takes a tremendous amount of effort to produce exemplary work,' said Donald Hicken, his mentor from the Baltimore School of the Arts, who believes 'Pac learned his workaholic tendencies there. 'When you're in a conservatory environment like BSA, it's like, everybody here was the hottest kid in their middle school. So, you're not singled out because you're gifted. You're singled out because you work hard. And he really got that.'

Preston Holmes, a longtime friend of the Shakur family, and a producer on both *Juice* and *Gridlock'd*, said: 'I'll never forget going to see him on the set of a music video, late at night before the first day of principal photography on *Gridlock'd*. His call was something like 6 a.m., and I said to him, "Why are you doing this? This is going to be very tough." And he said, "I got a lot to do. A lot I need to get done . . . ."'

'I look at Pac's life and the things he created, and I feel lazy,' said *Juice*'s Khalil Kain. 'Look at how old he was when he died. He was 25. 25!? That's crazy. But look how much he created in his 25 years. He did more than the average person will do in three lifetimes.' Kain has a tattoo running the length of his left thigh, which says Bishop inside a cross. It's a reminder of what's possible. 'And I'm not the only one. There's a whole bunch of cats, and it's not like we talked about it. I know Treach got a tat for 'Pac, I know Omar [Epps] got a tat for 'Pac.'

From the Golden Gate to the Apple State, the streets are filled with kids who see Tupac's prolific and multifaceted success as proof that anyone can find a way up. 'Honestly, the man is a martyr,' said Kain. 'He told me all the time that he was gonna be taken out. I'd just tell him to shut the fuck up, stop talking like that. But he knew the power in that. And if he only motivated one person, and that person is me, and he damn sure did, it was worth it to him. And there are hundreds of thousands of young black men, just like me, who are completely inspired by that young man.'

'They're about to see a real new nigga come in Hollywood.' John Singleton remembers first seeing Tupac on a BET interview in December of 1991. 'He was just railing on everybody in Hollywood. He talked about Quincy Jones, and Spike and all these people, talking about how fake-ass these muthafuckas are, and how they're about to see a real new nigga come in Hollywood. And I was like, man, I gotta work with him.' So they got together, and Singleton brought up *Poetic Justice*, and told him, 'I'm looking for somebody who just be a real muthafucka around Janet Jackson.'

Tupac showed up to the audition with a whole entourage, clearly high, and his performance was way over the top. Perhaps they should have taken this as a warning of how real 'Pac could be. But according to Steve Nicolaides, one of the film's producers, 'We cast him because he was a charismatic, fascinating guy, who had the look of a lover, but also had a kind of dangerous edge underneath. Which is the curse and the charm of Tupac Shakur.'

That dichotomy would characterize 'Pac's entire run on the Singleton shoot. Tupac wasn't yet a star, he didn't even have enough marquee value to get his name on the movie poster. But that didn't stop him from trying to act like a star. The rumors of non-stop blunt smoking and hoes did as much to begin building Tupac's mythology as his portrayal of Lucky, the film's soulful postman.

'We started shooting in Los Angeles, and everything was pretty good,' said Nicolaides. 'Then we went on the road, just like the movie. And the closer we got to Oakland, [to Tupac's home, and his homeboys], the more rock star-ish the behavior became.'

'There was always different women coming on the set, he was smoking pot excessively, never showin' up on time,' said Joe Torry, who played Chicago in the film. 'They caught him fucking in the trailer.' One time he snapped and started chasing after this extra that kept calling him 6Pac, right in front of a bunch of old grandmothers in the park. 'They had to stop production for a minute.'

'You know who broke up the fight?' added Singleton. 'Maya Angelou. Maya Angelou jumped, and she was like, "Dear boy. No. Not now. No." 'Pac just chilled, just went over and sat with Angelou for an hour. Now that was deep.'

There seems to have been no love lost between Tupac and Janet, who were barely cordial with each other. There's a longstanding rumor from those days that Janet refused to do any kissing scenes with him unless he took an AIDS test. Tupac, apparently, was insulted. 'I said, "If I can make love to Janet Jackson, I'll take four AIDS tests,"' he told MTV. '"Otherwise, get the fuck out of my trailer."'

Singleton laughed the story off, protecting the honor of his departed friend. He claimed that 'Pac and Janet and him came up with the story as a joke, and spread the controversy just for publicity. But others have come forward to confirm what happened. 'First of all, John's not that clever,'

Tupac with co-star Janet Jackson on the set of Poetic Justice.

said another of the film's producers. 'Janet could have faked it, but I don't think she's that good an actress. And, in terms of concocting a controversy, well, it never went anywhere.'

'People wonder why 'Pac had this beef with Janet, but it didn't start out like that,' said Joe Torry. 'At the beginning, she would have us all over to her house in Malibu, ride the jet skis.' But on the road, Tupac's lifestyle became hedonistic. 'He was bangin' a lot of girls and he had a little rumor about having a dirty dick. Janet had already caught a cold from kissing Q-Tip in the first scene. So it was really Janet's people who were being careful, just protecting their ass.'

But this was after weeks of caravanning on the road together, getting tired of each other, and Janet, who had her own travel situation, had basically stopped socializing with the rest of the cast. 'I think 'Pac really looked at it like, "Oh, OK, you superstar, you got your own trailer, you can't ride with us." He felt like she was demanding special privileges, so he need some too.' So he started

making scenes, showing up hours late, or not showing up at all.

Singleton said that the only time he ever had a true beef with 'Pac was when they were filming in Simi Valley during the L.A. riots. 'He wanted to go back down, and I wasn't happenin' to it. So he lied to me, and went down anyway. Drove up and down Wilshire Boulevard, shooting out car windows.' Singleton laughed ruefully before adding: 'He was a wildcat. But he was twenty years old, he was making a movie with Janet Jackson, and three years previously he had been practically homeless. Of course he was going to act up. He was a kid. All the weed he can smoke, every girl wants to give him some pussy, every cat wants to be cool with him, you think you wouldn't lose your mind?'

And even as Tupac's behavior grew worse, Singleton pointed out, he continued to turn in one of his most honest performances. There's a shockingly emotional scene near the end of the film where Lucky explores the DJ equipment of a cousin who's been murdered, a room full of stunted dreams, and slowly he begins to sob. Singleton remembered being furious at Tupac for showing up six hours late that day, but then 'Pac went onto the set, and just broke down, tears flowing – in one take.

'I [never] knew that his education in the theater was as dope as it was,' said Tony. 'He never let on, he just made it look effortless. But he was a serious actor.'

'The tragedy of Tupac is that he could never come to terms with the fact that he was an artist and not a gangsta,' figured Nicolaides, who noticed during 'Pac's fight scene with Torry that he threw punches like someone who'd never been in a fight. 'He so diligently and seriously wanted to be a thug. He so wanted to be hard. And he so wasn't.'

It points to one of the essential ironies of 'Pac's life that when he was nominated for an NAACP Image award for his sensitive performance in *Poetic Justice*, in January of 1994, the National Political Congress of Black Women boycotted the NAACP, claiming Tupac promoted wholesale sexism and misogyny in his music. 'I suspect the nomination did more damage to his image than it did to the NAACP's, though,' wrote Elmer Smith in a syndicated editorial, referring to Tupac's growing legions of fans, six months after the release of his second album, *Strictly for My N.I.G.G.A.Z.* But while no one denies that 'Pac dropped some of the nastiest bitch and hoe lyrics, he's also the guy who wrote 'Dear Mama,' forever etching him in the hearts of women everywhere.

'One of the concepts American society has a hard time grasping is the one called "dichotomy,"' Nelson George explained to me. 'The idea that someone can feel deeply two different and often conflicting modes of

'We kissed and we said goodbye – and he was dead five days later.' – Lela Rochon

living bothers us. We want things as simple as a tabloid newspaper. The truth is, we all are way more complex than we give ourselves credit for. Tupac couldn't escape the gangsta lifestyle because it expressed an angry need to lash out that was an essential part of his character. The dichotomy of Tupac is that he was a gangsta with a deeply artistic soul.'

Preston Holmes, the producer who knew Tupac for much of his life, added: 'He often referred to himself as someone with conflicting personalities, but that's true of all of us. The difference is that Tupac put it all out there for us. There's a quote of his where he talked about being so confident in who he is, "That y'all can watch me do what I do. Watch me live, watch me cry . . . and watch me die." Where the rest of us find all kinds of ways to disguise those parts of us that we find unappealing, he accepted everything about who he was, and had no qualms about presenting it to the world.'

'This isn't all there is for you. There's more for you to do . . .' It was during the filming of the 1994 basketball flick *Above the Rim* that Tupac's troubles with the law started. Singleton described hanging out with him in New York, the weekend he came back from the incident in Atlanta (he was accused of shooting at two off-duty cops who'd been harassing him). He was eventually cleared of that charge, but in the media you're guilty until proven innocent, and they pounced on this example of the Gangsta Rapper practicing the violence he preaches. Singleton remembered saying to him, 'Listen, Dan Quayle is already talking about your music, and then this thing happens. You're going to have to just put yourself on lockdown. Get with one girl, and just stay out of sight, 'cause they're going to come after you.' And then a week later, a twenty-year-old girl who'd given Tupac head on the dance floor at Nell's nightclub, accused him of sexual assault. The media crucified him. 'I always looked at that time as the turning point in his life.'

By the end of 1993, when Singleton was beginning his next movie, *Higher Learning*, executives at Sony strong-armed him into dropping Tupac from the cast – even though the lead role had been written for him. 'Pac had become too risky to insure, and the studio was scared off. Of all the calamities befalling Tupac then, this was probably the most devastating.

'And I was pissed,' said Singleton. 'This was messing with our plans. If 'Pac hadn't gotten in trouble, he would've been the lead in *Higher Learning*, he probably would've been *Shaft*, and he would've been the lead in *Baby Boy*. I mean, this is the person I wanted to work with as an actor. 'Cause he came from an arts background, but he also had a knowledge of the street.'

But few people, if any, knew of Tupac's arts background by this point. He was now getting cast as the big gangsta – in *Above the Rim* and his next film *Bullet* – not because of his acting ability, but because he was 2Pac. He'd blown up super-nova, but it was becoming a one-pitch performance. 'Movies have the ability to either reinforce, or contradict a rapper's persona,' said Jeff Pollack, who directed *Above the Rim*. 'And I don't think Tupac did anything in *Above the Rim* that was contradictory to the persona he'd been creating through his music.'

Periodically over the years, Tupac would go back to the Baltimore School of the Arts to talk with Donald Hicken, someone he came to rely on as a grounding element in his life. Hicken remembers their last conversation, in the weeks before Tupac served his eight months in jail for the sexual assault case – which, like Bill Clinton's sex scandal, he was deemed not responsible for but guilty of.

'I just said to him, "Look, this isn't all there is for you. There's more for you to do that's also important,"' Hicken recalled. 'He was such a talented actor, and Hollywood was putting him in a box because of his hip hop persona – making him play the same characters over and over again, like a performing seal. I was trying to encourage him to look for projects that would show his diversity. He didn't have to just play a gangsta.'

When he was bailed out of jail and practically indentured by Death Row's 'Suge' Knight in 1995, Tupac began work on his fifth album, *All Eyez on Me*. But he also immediately began looking for parts that would allow him to get serious about acting again. 'He sort of hounded me down,' described Vondie Curtis-Hall, who wrote and directed *Gridlock'd*, admitting that Tupac was not the first choice for his grimly humorous independent film about two addicts trying to kick. 'I'd wanted an Actor in the role. I'd been talking to Larry Fishburne. But then Preston Holmes, who had known 'Pac since he was a kid, said, "You gotta meet Tupac, he's completely different than the stuff you hear." I said no. But he ended up slipping the script to 'Pac anyway, and suddenly he was calling me nonstop and begging, "At least sit and talk with me."'

He was staying at the Peninsula in LA, under the name Welcome Homey. They met there, and though 'Pac had just gotten out of jail, he managed to conjure all the confidence and tenacity he'd once depended on to win him his first part in *Juice*. Curtis-Hall was impressed. 'He was just really smart and passionate. And there were things he needed to prove, that A) he was responsible, otherwise nobody in Hollywood would touch him and B) that he was an actor.'

Curtis-Hall called Tim Roth to tell him he was casting Tupac, but Roth called back, after friends had warned him: 'Don't do a movie with that fucking guy. You'll get shot on the set.' But the director sat them down at Café des Artistes, in Los Angeles, and they smoked a couple packs of cigarettes together. 'We started talking about acting,' remembered Roth, 'about the part and the character, and he just really . . . hit it.'

The irony of 'Pac's next and last role, as an undercover cop in *Gang Related*, was not lost on him. But he was not only trying to stir up his public image, he viewed acting as a career to land in when he'd eased his way out of Death Row's grip. Jim Kouf, who directed Tupac in *Gang Related*, said: 'He was wanting to focus on his film career because he knew that he could control that part of his life.'

In the hectic and violent last year of his life, Tupac began having a bodyguard with him 24-7. Kouf realized the seriousness of Tupac's situation one night, filming in East L.A., when he saw him blow up at his bodyguard. 'He really expected that somebody was going to drive by and shoot him, right on the set.'

'He had been in so much trouble, I just thought that if we didn't finish the movie, it wouldn't surprise me,' said Lela Rochon, who co-starred in *Gang Related*. 'I told him to his face, I was scared to hang out with him. I just said, "Oh no, there are people that don't like you."

'He was *so* trying to make an effort to change. He wanted to be a movie star, and he had the possibility and the opportunity to be the young, black movie star that we really, still, don't have. I can't even begin to tell you the sorrow and the grief and how bad we felt, when we kissed and we said goodbye – and he was dead five days later.'

'Just be . . . ' The way director Jim Kouf describes it, 'Pac's greatest difficulty as a film actor stayed a consistent pattern from the days of *Juice*. He was a classically trained theater actor, and he could never get used to the rhythm of having to produce real emotions for the same scene again and again. 'He was honest about it. He said, "After the first two takes, I can feel myself acting. I don't

think I'm as good,"' recalled Kouf.

'It drives you nuts. Absolutely. But that's part of the job,' agrees Roth. 'Sometimes you feel you've got it, and the other actor doesn't. But, you just have to bite it and keep doing it, until you all get to the point where it's happening.'

'About a week into the shoot, we got to the first scene where it was just about sitting and being,' describes Curtis-Hall. 'In those first couple takes, 'Pac didn't go as deep as we needed to go. Tim wasn't going to hit it for another three or four takes, and we needed to do eight or nine or ten. And 'Pac just got frustrated, and went off to his trailer, and just sat there.'

The scene they were shooting was an early one, where Tupac and Tim's characters are sitting by the hospital bed of Thandie Newton, who is dying of an overdose. Tupac has sort of an epiphany, and the two make the decision to change their lives and kick their habit. It's also the scene in which 'Pac had to utter the oft-quoted line: 'Do you ever feel like your time is running out?' The repetition of the scene was certainly hitting buttons deep down for 'Pac, who always wanted to keep moving, get to the next thing, do everything before his time ran out. These words were becoming deeply personal.

'It was tough [for him], just to be able to trust and be there,' said Curtis-Hall. 'And it really took going into the trailer with 'Pac and smoking a joint, just kicking back and going: "Hey. It's gonna be alright."' Curtis-Hall laughed warmly in his deep baritone as he remembered 'Pac nodding his head and really listening. And he said to him: 'Don't worry about how it's going to come off. Don't worry about presentation. Just let's be.'

'And after that,' said Curtis-Hall, who only later realized how important the moment was, 'he [began to] feel safe. He knew that, no matter what happened, it was going to be good, and he didn't have to prove anything. He just had to be.'

CONVERSATIONS WITH TUPAC

by Veronica Chambers

I first met Tupac Shakur almost five years ago, when John Singleton invited me to do a behind-the-scenes book for his second movie, *Poetic Justice*. It was early on in pre-production when Tupac was cast, and we were on a location scout. A production assistant was driving the van; John and Tupac were sitting up front, and I sat behind them. It was the end of the day, and we were all talking about John's recent Academy Award nominations for *Boyz N the Hood*. Tupac was so clearly enamored of John, discussing scene after scene – what he thought made the movie so special, why he was so excited to be starring in John's second film.

We started talking about the music in the film, and instead of talking about the rap songs, Tupac brought up the scene where Furious Styles, played by Laurence Fishbume, is taking custody of young Tre for the first time. He takes his son to the beach, and as they drive home in their old Seventies-model car, a song comes on the radio. The song is 'O-o-h Child,' and the music provides the dissolve from Tre's youth to his teenage years in the 'hood. All of a sudden, Tupac started singing the song: 'O-o-h child, things are goin' to get easier / O-o-h child, things will get brighter / Someday, we'll walk in the rays of the beautiful sun / Someday, when the world is much brighter . . . . '

Tupac turned to John and said, 'I loved that song, man. That shit meant a lot to me.' And it did. In many ways, Tupac exemplified a generation of men who grew up without fathers. Later, he would try to blame his criminal activity on that very fact.

'You've never seen a young black male grow up, but now you have to watch, and you have to help, because my father is not alive, ' he told me. 'This system took him, so it's up to everybody else to raise me.'

If Singleton envied Tupac's rawness, Tupac envied Singleton's stable family life.

'John had a father that cared, but I didn't have one,' Tupac told me, his voice thick with longing. 'He knew that part of my pain, because he know how hard it is to grow up without [a father].'

That day, on the location scout, Tupac asked John why he hadn't put 'O-o-h Child' on the movie soundtrack. John said there had been a problem getting rights and clearances, but two years later Tupac used a sample of the song for his inspirational ode to black women, 'Keep Ya Head Up.' Hearing the song now always makes me think of Tupac, singing it *a cappella*.

As happy as he was to make a movie with John Singleton, Tupac had a hard time following rules. Half the time, there were no problems at all, but it wasn't unusual for Tupac to get high in his trailer, to be hours late to the set in the morning, or to get pissed off for what seemed like no reason at all. Once, toward the end of the shoot, Tupac was told he could have a day off. That morning, the producers decided that they would shoot publicity stills and called Tupac to the set. He arrived with his homeboys and began screaming, 'I can't take this shit. Y'all treat a nigga like a slave.' He stormed off to his trailer and promptly punched in a window. It certainly wasn't the first time a star has had a fit on a set. But Tupac was a young black male with more than a little street credibility. (I often heard talk that he kept a gun on set, though I never saw one.) At the time, nobody knew how far he was willing to take his mantras about living a 'thug life.' There was indignation on the set about being blasted by some young punk, but there was also fear: fear both *of* Tupac and *for* Tupac. I believe this was a pattern of concern that those around him felt right up until his death.

The last weeks of the *Poetic Justice* production were shot in Oakland. Although

Tupac in his role of Lucky, from John Singleton's romantic drama Poetic Justice *(1993).*

Tupac endured a nomadic childhood, living in Harlem, the Bronx, and Baltimore, Oakland was where he passed his teen years. His homies there were the last to know him before he made his way into show business – first as a dancer for Digital Underground, then as a featured rapper with the group, and eventually as a solo rapper. The shoot in Oakland was difficult for a number of reasons. It was the end of a long fourteen-week production that had worn everybody out. Singleton was shooting mostly night scenes, which meant the crew didn't start until 6 p.m. and didn't finish until dawn. Not ideal working conditions under any circumstances, but especially if you're shooting in the 'hood. I remember feeling nervous for Tupac. The production assistants had a hard time keeping people away from the set – there was no real security force – and everybody and his dog claimed to be a friend of Tupac's.

There was always a group of tough-looking guys calling out, ''Pac, 'Pac.' Sometimes they interrupted shooting, and it was worse if they actually caught Tupac's eye and knew that he saw them. 'Don't pretend that you don't know me, nigga!' they would threaten. 'Nigga's a movie star and can't speak to nobody.'

Tupac had more patience with these guys than with anyone else. 'Yo, man, it's good to see you,' he would say, never raising his voice. 'But a brother's trying to work. I'm just trying to make that paper, same as you.' But even after he'd come over, acknowledged them, rapped a little with them, the guys would keep yelling. 'Fuck you, nigga,' they would say, trying to provoke a fight and look hard in front of their friends.

To his homies around the way, standing in front of a movie camera and a crew of 50 people, talking to Janet Jackson, wasn't work. They felt that they knew Tupac, knew that he was no different from them and felt it was their sworn duty to remind him of that.

I asked Tupac about the young men who would harass him on set. 'The young bucks are *gonna* be jealous,' he said as if it couldn't be helped. 'Some older people, too. They got mad because I used to be their gofer. They used to run me to the store. They're sitting there knowing they used to give me money to go to the store, and now I've got their whole family taking pictures with me. That's an animosity that nothing I can do can kill, because that's poverty shit and I can understand.'

Dana Smith was a friend of Tupac's from Baltimore. They met in the eighth grade at Rolling Park Junior High School. Tupac arranged for him to be his assistant on the set. He saw the danger Tupac was in in places like Oakland but insisted that Tupac couldn't avoid the danger, that he needed to keep up 'his street mentality' to handle it.

'People get jealous,' Dana told me. 'They see Tupac as a young brother coming up from nothing to something. They're like, "Damn, how did he do that? He was homeless a while ago . . . " Tupac could try to stay out of trouble, stay in the hotel, but that's not real. If he did that, people would call him snobby. You can't get away from the street. That's where you're from. You've got to give that love back.'

Even then, everybody was always talking about the possibility of Tupac's death. 'Being a young black male,' Dana said, 'he's already reached his life expectancy – 21.'

Afeni Shakur, Tupac's mother and a former radical activist, told me that she constantly feared for her son's life. 'It's funny, because I never believed he would live,' she said. She spent most of her pregnancy in jail, preparing her own defense as a member of the famed New York 21 Black Panthers. (Afeni was married to fellow Panther Lumumba Abdul Shakur.) 'Every five years, I'd be just amazed that he made it to five, he made it to ten, he made it to fifteen.' A beautiful woman who blessed her son with her own clear, dark skin and large, bright eyes, Afeni clenched her hands as she spoke. 'I had a million miscarriages, you know,' she said. 'This child stayed in my womb through the worst possible conditions. I had to get a

court order to get an egg to eat every day. I had to get a court order to get a glass of milk every day – you know what I'm saying? I lost weight, but he gained weight. He was born one month and three days after we were acquitted. I had not been able to carry a child. Then this child comes and hangs on and really fights for his life.'

At the time we last spoke, three years ago, Tupac and Afeni Shakur were living in the San Fernando Valley in a pretty blue-and-white house on a quiet tree-lined street. Tupac teased his mother about showing me family pictures. 'I will be suing my mother for giving away those pictures,' he said, holding his mother in a loving embrace. 'You've got the information when I take this to court – I did not give her permission.'

He also spoke with pride about growing up the son of a Black Panther. 'Everybody else's mother was just a regular mother, but my mother was Afeni – you know what I'm saying?' He turned to his mother and gave her the same cool appraisal that a homie would give an older G in the 'hood. 'My mother had a strong reputation. It was just like having a daddy because she had a rep. Motherfuckers get roasted if you fuck with Afeni or her children. Couldn't nobody touch us.'

Watching Tupac with his mother or his younger sister revealed a side of him that the media rarely portrayed. Gangsta rapper or no, at the end of the day, he was somebody's son, somebody's brother, somebody's cousin.

With other women, Tupac sometimes had problems, leading to his conviction for sexual assault in 1994. He was always proud, however, of never having fathered a child out of wedlock. 'Procreation is so much about ego,' he'd muse. 'Everybody wants to have a junior. But I could care less about having a junior to tell, "I got fucked by America and you're about to get fucked, too." Until we get a world where I feel like a first-class citizen, I can't have a child. 'Cause my child has to be a first-class citizen, and

I'm not having no white babies.

'There's no way around it unless I want to turn white, turn my back on what's really going on in America,' Tupac insisted. 'I either will be in jail or dead or be so fucking stressed out from not going to jail or dying or on crack that I'd just pop a vessel,' he said. 'I'll just die from a heart attack. All the deaths are not going to be from the police killing you.'

I asked him if he didn't think that staying in the Valley, instead of going out and instigating all the trouble he did, would make him live longer. He looked at me as if I were crazy. 'It would be an honor to die in the 'hood,' he said solemnly; as if he were reciting the Pledge of Allegiance. 'Don't let me die in Saudi Arabia. These motherfuckers are rushing with a flag to die on foreign soil, fighting for motherfuckers that don't care about us. I'd rather die in the 'hood, where I get my love. I'm not saying I want to die, but if I got to die, let me die in the line of duty; the duty of the 'hood.'

Of all the rumors and conspiracy theories I've heard since Tupac died, only one has reverberated inside my head. 'I've heard that Tupac isn't really dead,' a friend said. 'Why did they cremate the body right away In Las Vegas, where they had no family or friends?'

I shrugged. I make it a point never to argue down conspiracy theories.

'What I heard is that Afeni has had Tupac's identity changed and shipped him to Cuba.'

As I listened to my friend, what surprised me was how my heart leaped at the thought of Tupac alive.

That night, I had what was surely one of hundreds of dreams that people across America have had about Tupac. In the dream, I am walking down a street in Havana. The air is thick with the perfume of strong black coffee, and black men in starched white shirts play dominoes on the street. The walls are pastel pink, white, and green, the paint is peeling, the mortar is crumbling. Only the high arches in the doorways and the spiraling staircases that center

the apartment buildings are indications of this city's glorious past.

I walk down a hallway, past overcrowded apartments with no curtains because in Fidel's Cuba, no one has anything to hide.

'*Estás buscando el negro?*' a woman asks me, a grandmother who I'm sure is a Fidel spy.

'Yes,' I answer in pitch-perfect Spanish. 'I am looking for the black guy. He's my brother.'

She points me to the last door on the floor. I make my way into a tiny studio that is decorated with orange and green crushed-velvet furniture – classy stuff if it were still 1959. Afeni is there. Tupac is there, but he looks nothing like Tupac. I know him only by his voice.

He is asking for a CD player. He wants some rap CDs. His mother explains that such music will give him away. She prompts him to listen to his Spanish tapes; he may never go home, so he must learn the language. She directs him to a large stack of books – books about Che Guevara, about Fidel, about Latin-American history. She tells him that his life has been saved for only one purpose – to aid the revolution he was born into.

'Y'all don't give a nigga much of a choice,' he says, looking around the tiny room and smiling at the woman who has loved him better and more wisely than he ever loved himself. He goes over to the window and looks out, thinking, as he always does, that if he stares hard enough, he can see past the *calles* of Cuba to his beloved 'hood, where on the corner, someone is playing c-low and someone is smoking crack and someone is playing a Tupac song and someone is laughing and someone is crying. But he can't see any of it, not really. And as each day goes by, it's that much harder to conjure the 'hood in his mind. He sits down, puts his feet up on the table, opens a book, and begins to read.

JUICE

review by Roger Ebert

There's a scene in *Grand Canyon*, a film released shortly before *Juice*, that's like a setup for the second movie's whole tragic story. In the earlier film, an older black man confronts a group of young punks on the street. One punk has a gun. He asks the older man, 'Do you respect me, or do you respect my gun?' The answer is: 'You don't have that gun, there's no way we're having this conversation.' That is a dangerous answer, but an honest one, and *Juice* is like a mirror image of the *Grand Canyon* scene; it tells the story of the young men – how they got into a criminal situation, and how they got the gun. It tells one of those stories with the quality of a nightmare, in which foolish young men try to out-macho one another until they get trapped in a violent situation which will forever alter their lives.

"Pac was going to be my Robert De Niro.' – John Singleton

The movie was directed and co-written by Ernest Dickerson, the cinematographer on Spike Lee's films, and like Lee's *Do the Right Thing* it is filled with details of the daily life, fashions, music and language of a black neighborhood. It introduces its four central characters as they get up in the morning and venture out from poor but supportive homes into New York streets where, as they perceive it, the person with a gun commands respect. At first the movie seems meandering, following these young men through their daily routines, listening to their talk, looking at the street life in their neighborhood, watching the ambition of one nicknamed Q (Omar Epps), who dreams of being a disc jockey in a club.

Then the focus tightens, as everything turns wrong, when Bishop (Tupac Shakur) gets his hands on a gun and decides the four of them should stick up the corner store. There is a sense in which the existence of the gun leads to the necessity of using it; without the cheap handgun, there would be no crime, and lives would be saved. Q doesn't want anything to do with the stickup; his mind is focused on a DJ contest at a local club. But Bishop has the stronger personality, and badgers them all into coming along.

The best shot in the movie takes place in a club where Q has just done a successful gig as a DJ, and is filled with joy, until he sees the unsmiling faces of his friends in the crowd, and realizes he has to leave, now, and commit the stickup. What happens next depends too much on surprise for me to reveal it, but the movie generates a real tension in its closing passages, as it shows its characters trapped in a plot that seems to be unfolding according to its own merciless logic.

Much of the strength of the film comes from the actors, Epps, Shakur, Khalil Kain as Raheem, whose enthusiasm for the stickup ends tragically, and Jermaine Hopkins as Steel, a pudgy innocent.

They are able to make us know their characters, which is important if *Juice* is to be more than just a morality play. It is also interesting the way Dickerson's story makes them – and the street culture of cheap handguns – the instruments of their own downfall.

83

'Pac faces up to the grim realities of street life as Bishop in Juice *(1992).*

There are a lot of cops in the movie, but for a change they are seen not as villains but as street troops in the fight against crime.

It's a common criticism of cinematographers that when they direct their own films, they pay too much attention to style, not enough to the story. The scene-setting opening moments of *Juice* seem almost too picturesque, but then we feel the underlying logic of the story, and Dickerson finds a rhythm that uses the visuals instead of just flaunting them. *Juice*, like *Boyz N the Hood* and *Straight Out of Brooklyn*, is like a reaction to years of movies that have glamorized urban violence. There is a real terror in the faces of these kids as they realize that people have died, that guns kill, that your life can be ruined, or over, in an instant.

POETIC JUSTICE

review by Roger Ebert

Poetic Justice is described as the second of three films John Singleton plans to make about the South Central neighborhood in Los Angeles.

His first, *Boyz N the Hood*, showed a young black man growing up in an atmosphere of street violence, but encouraged by his father to stand aside from the gangs and shootings and place a higher worth on his life. At the end of the film, the hero's friend was shot dead. Now comes a film told from the point of view of a young woman in the same neighborhood – Justice, played by Janet Jackson. At the beginning of the film she's on a date at a drive-in theater with her boyfriend. Words are exchanged at the refreshment stand, egos are wounded, and before long her boyfriend is shot dead. (One of the realities in both films is the desperation of a community where self-respect is so precarious that small insults can become capital offenses.)

Justice emerges from mourning determined to go it alone. What's the use of committing her heart to a man who will simply get himself killed in another stupid incident? She works in a beauty shop, where one day a mailman (Tupac Shakur) comes in and starts making soft talk. She leads him on and then lets him down with a mean trick. But the tables are turned when her friend Simone (Khandi Alexander) invites her to go along on a trip to Oakland. Her boyfriend has a friend who works for the post office and will let them ride along in a mail truck. Of course, the friend is Shakur.

Unlike *Boyz*, which was fairly strongly plotted, *Poetic Justice* unwinds like a road picture from the early 1970s, in which the characters are introduced and then set off on a trip that becomes a journey of discovery. By the end of the film, Justice will have learned to trust and love again, and Shakur will have learned how to listen to a woman. And all of the characters – who in one way or another lack families – will begin to get a feeling for the larger African-American family to which they belong.

The scene where that takes place is one of the best in the film.

The mail truck takes them down back roads until they stumble across the Johnson Family Picnic, a sprawling, populous affair where not all of the cousins even know each other. That makes an ideal opportunity for the four travelers to wander in and get a free meal. But along the way they're also embraced by one of the cousins, and hear some words of wisdom from another one (the poet, Maya Angelou).

It is Angelou's poetry we hear on the sound track of the movie; Justice is a poet, and we are told it is hers. She has aspirations and sensitivities, and as played by Jackson she emerges as a sweet, smart woman who is growing up to be a good person.

Her romance with Shakur is touching precisely because it doesn't take place in a world of innocence and naiveté; because they both know the risks of love, their gradual acceptance of each other is convincing.

Boyz N the Hood was one of the most powerful and influential films of its time, in 1991. *Poetic Justice* is not its equal, but does not aspire to be; it is a softer, gentler film, more of a romance than a commentary on social conditions. Janet Jackson provides a lovable center for it, and by the time it's over we can see more clearly how *Boyz* presented only part of the South Central reality.

Yes, things are hard. But they aren't impossible. Sometimes they're wonderful. And sometimes you can find someone to share them with.

ABOVE THE RIM

review by Chris Hicks

Sort of a combination of *Boyz N the Hood* and *Hoosiers*, *Above the Rim* is the predictable story of a young inner-city basketball player who is tempted by street evils before deciding to win the big game for friends and family. Despite obvious weaknesses, however, the film gets a huge boost from several excellent performances.

Duane Martin is appealing in the lead as a young high school basketball star who grandstands at his team's expense, showing off for a Georgetown University scout. His coach (David Bailey) is frustrated, his mother (Tonya Pinkins) is beginning to worry and the new school security guard (Leon) sees a lot of himself in the lad.

Soon, a smooth-talking drug dealer (Tupac Shakur) is promising Martin money, cars and women if he'll leave the high school team and play for his team in a neighborhood basketball shootout, on which he plans to bet a lot of money.

Recognizing that the chip on his shoulder is hindering his Georgetown chances and attracted by the lure of wealth, power and local fame, Martin goes over to Shakur's camp – urged on by an ex-con friend (Marlon Wayans, providing comic relief). But it isn't long before he realizes he's made a deal with the devil.

Meanwhile, the coach, his mother and Leon all attempt to reach out to him, but Martin will have none of it. By the time we get to the shootout, however, it's apparent that Martin will change camps and help his coach's team defeat the evil Shakur.

The soap opera machinations are by-the-numbers stuff, with an odd undercurrent involving Leon's character. He broods because his best friend died by jumping up at a basketball backboard and falling over the ledge of a tall building. Since when are basketball hoops on building ledges?

The film is shaken up a bit by edgy footage during the final basketball game and a violent climactic twist. In fact, there are a couple of violent climaxes – which prove to be two too many.

But the real saving grace here is several performances that are hard to shake, from the brooding Leon, who develops a stoic presence that helps us feel his character's pain, to the strict but helpless Pinkins, who is forced to work long hours and can't spend the time necessary to watch over her son. And Martin shows a solid range of emotion in the lead role. But the scene-stealer is Shakur, who has a genuine screen presence. His off-screen problems (allegations of rape and gunplay) are well-documented, but judging by his performances here and in *Juice* and *Poetic Justice*, he has a solid career ahead – if he doesn't blow it.

> 'The scene-stealer is Shakur, who has a genuine screen presence ... he has a solid career ahead – if he doesn't blow it.'
> – Chris Hicks

GOT YOUR BACK

by Frank Alexander

I couldn't count the number of hoochies 'Pac slept with while I was working with him. I don't have enough fingers and toes, because it would have to be in the three digits. Suffice it to say, if you were a groupie and you wanted a piece of 'Pac, chances are, you'd get it. He'd didn't disappoint many fans. Every single video we worked on, he fucked many women on the set. He fucked the extras, the leads, you name it. And we did a lot of videos. As far as movies, it's the same story. In Italy, he fucked three women over there. On the 'How Do U Want It' video, he fucked women all that day, and then he had a sex party the last night. Ron Hightower, the porn director, threw an after-party that was really an orgy. He snuck out under a table and went to the party, he didn't want any security that night. Suge, Norris, Roy – shit, nearly every Death Row employee called me that night looking for him. I knew where he was, and it looked as if he had company, so to speak.

One thing's for sure, Death Row knew how to party. They had orgy parties, sex parties, after-hours shit, postproduction wrap parties – D.R. was all about California Love. The more, the merrier.

Let's just break it down for you. Women threw themselves at 'Pac, and he wasn't dodging.

Tupac wasn't prejudiced when it came to women. He loved them all. People often stepped to him and said, ''Pac, you should only be with black women, because you're a strong black male and you stand for something.' Clearly it was Suge's concern, Reggie was just the messenger.

Reggie used to complain to me. 'What's up with 'Pac, he's got all these white girls in his videos? It don't look good.'

He was particularly concerned about 'How Do U Want It.'

I said, 'Why don't you just ask him, Reggie?'

'You the closest to him, that's why I'm asking you.'

'Hey,' I said. 'That's just what he likes. That's what he wants.'

Tupac loved women, period. I don't care if they were black, white, Mexican, Puerto Rican, Chinese, Japanese, it did not matter. He liked pussy. Yeah, he liked paper, meaning he liked cash, he liked his weed, but the one other thing he couldn't live without was pussy. Above my fireplace, I have a signed collage of Death Row photos, and on it, Tupac wrote to me: *To my road dog, big swoe-ass Frank, let's get paper and women – Tupac.*

90 percent of the time, that's what he was thinking about. He fucked uncountable women when we were on tour. Brother had stamina. They'd get 'em backstage, after his homies would single them out from the front. Everybody had their own dressing room. It was all laid out. This was in January, and it was Tha Dogg Pound and Tupac. If you went back into the dressing room, and you started partying, smoking pot and doing what they do, you gonna get fucked. You didn't go into that room and not come out unfucked if you're a woman.

Every single video shoot, Tupac fucked at least two women or more. On 'How Do U Want It,' he fucked so many women he passed out. I couldn't get him to wake up because he was so exhausted. That video shoot was legendary. First off, if you listen to the words of the song, it's all about a baller, a player, who's out macking a bitch. It's about a man who could have any woman he wants and he's talking to the woman he's with that night, asking her how she wants it. At one point in the song, he says, *'Is it cool to fuck? 'Cause I'm not here to talk.'*

Leslie remembers him saying that for

real when they were on tour with him in Cleveland. He had one of his homies bring these two black girls backstage, and on their way to the hotel, he interviewed them.

'One was on the right of him and one was on the left,' says Leslie. 'I heard him say, "So, both of y'all want to come back to my hotel room with me?" They nodded. He said, "But I'm still confused, it's two of you guys . . . . "

'One took him by the chin and kissed him on the lips. When she was finished, the other woman bent over and also kissed him on the lips. 'Oh, it's like that,' he said. They both started giggling. He said, 'We gonna fuck.' They both looked at him and smiled and started giggling. 'Yeah . . . ' He said, 'Okay, you know I got to clear that out, because my black ass ain't going back to jail.'

Both Les and I find it hard to believe Tupac raped anybody. After spending a lot of time with Tupac, I also don't believe he was on some trip where he got off on sexual abuse. The fact is, he got off on women, and they got off on him, and it's difficult to believe he hurt anybody. The truth is, he loved the fuck out of the women. For the most part, the groupies made the approach. They were the ones trying to meet him and get with him. They had their own things in mind. When I think about the charges that got him sent to Riker's, it's like, Why rob a bank, if you have millions?

Tupac's friend, Mike Tyson, hadn't lost his sexual appetite, either, despite his own sexual assault conviction. Tupac and Mike had become close friends ever since Mike sent 'Pac a letter in prison. He happened to be with us when we were in Cleveland and all it took was a nod for Suge to hook his shit up. Usually, women who hung out around the Death Row camp knew what was up and were just as freaky as the men.

This is how buck-wild things were around there.

During the end of Tupac's set, Tyson came on the stage and asked Les about one of 'Pac's background dancers. Les ended up mentioning to Suge that Mike liked the dancer, and Suge told her to go get busy. She finished the show and everyone started walking to the back dressing room.

Someone asked where Mike was, and one of the security guards said he's in Tha Dogg Pound's dressing room with this particular dancer, who we all knew.

I was right outside the door because I was working with Tha Dogg Pound at the time, and I was talking to a member of Mike's entourage when she came out of there about 25 minutes later, with lipstick all over her face.

I know most of you have probably only seen the 'G-rated' version of the 'How Do U Want It' video, which is little more than watching a Tupac concert, but there's an X-rated one, too, with topless women everywhere, dancing erotically and spilling champagne on their titties; while Tupac plays with one, another woman's coming up from behind working him. Even the video seems G-rated compared to what really went down that day.

Oh my God, trip off this. The shoot took place over two days, at a club in Hollywood called the Love Lounge. There's a gym downstairs and people were trippin', watching all these porn stars come and go. Most of the girls were either strippers or triple-X stars, straight up. It was a closed set and the producer made everyone take their clothes off. He stripped down, too, and was walking around only in his socks. The freak was on.

Tupac fucked this one chick first. We were all in the trailer listening. When he was done with her, he shot a couple of scenes, finished doing that, and he put his hands around this other girl while another chick was watching – she told me she *really* liked 'Pac. He was doing it in front of her friend, and they were all getting off on it.

The trailer was rockin'. I was sitting on one end of the trailer, and they were in the back, but you could hear the noises and by the time I looked up, another girl had crawled in with them, and he fucked her, too. He came out of the trailer with a shit-

East meets West – Tupac hooks up with Sean 'P Diddy' Combs.

eating grin. He knew all of the girls were friends, because he'd flown them in from Las Vegas. You gotta see these girls, these are some fine fucking girls. This wasn't your run-of-the-mill porn skank – they were fine women. Three times, he walked out of the trailer, shot a scene, got something to eat, came back and started fuckin'.

Now check this out. When he left the trailer for a third time, he made his way out to the set but not without stopping and finger-fuckin' every porn star who was there that day. One star in particular, this woman named Nina Hartley, took his hand and was showing him how to play with a woman's pussy prop-er. So he tested out Nina's suggestions on any woman who wanted it. The fact is, most of them wanted it. He'd handpicked the women who were on the shoot (no pun intended). A lot of the women were from New York, and they'd flown out specially to be in the video. He didn't fuck around with no dogs, and if you can get your hands on a copy of the X-rated version, you'll see what I'm talking about. It aired on the Playboy Channel,

because it was made for Playboy.

A couple weeks later, we shot the concert version, and he fucked two more chicks from that production. I saw one of the women walking into the trailer, she had her makeup all on and looked all done-up. I looked at Kevin and we both said, 'Uh-oh.' By the time she came out, her lips were all fucked-up. Makeup was everywhere.

Now you know Tupac loved women, but do you know why women loved Tupac? The obvious reasons are his talent, his looks, and his charisma. But he also had a secret arsenal. I may as well spell it out.

Tupac had a fuckin' horse cock.

The only reason I know this is, at one of Death Row's infamous sex parties, Suge, who flew in bitches from everywhere, brought in 40 women from Atlanta. Forty black girls. 4-0. He flew them into Las Vegas. Tupac and I flew in to meet up with them. This was the first time I got to fly first-class with 'Pac, and it was cool. The limo picked us up, and we went straight to Suge's house. He'd had a party the week before that Tupac didn't go to. That time Suge had flown in women from Ohio. By the time we got to Suge's house, there were maybe four or five still there, cleaning Suge's house. The place was spotless, which was cool because later that night, the front door came open and women started walking in like there was no tomorrow. They just kept coming and coming, and limos kept pulling up with women getting out. I thought to myself, *Damn! These niggas know how to pah-tay!*

The party was catered with the best soul food around, smothered pork chops and smothered chicken, fried chicken, barbecued ribs, collard greens, black-eye peas and rice, cornbread, sweet potato yams, macaroni and cheese, and always more food to go around than what we could eat. One thing I can say about Death Row is we always ate good. Suge hooked it up.

On that night, though, people had other things on their mind. As soon as women start showing up, right away, and I mean right away, the pot gets laid out. Liquor, everywhere, just laid out. People got festive real quick.

At one point, I looked around for Tupac and someone told me he was in another room of the house. I was kickin' it by the television and I was fuckin' around with the remote. I started switching channels. Turned out I grabbed the wrong remote, because when I began flippin' channels, I got a view of one of the bedrooms. Nobody knew this, not even Suge, but one of the bedrooms had a camera in it. 'Pac was in that room with this chick. He'd hooked up with this light-skinned sister, who had short hair and

looked like she might be part Asian. As usual, she was fine. He had her all night, he didn't fuck with any of the other girls.

When I hit on this channel accidentally, I could see Tupac with this girl. I only saw what was happening for a split second. I turned it off right away because I didn't want to invade the brotha's privacy. It wouldn't look cool if a bunch of people were sitting around watching Tupac fuck this bitch.

Later on when Suge showed up, I told him about it. He said, 'I don't have any cameras in the bedroom.' I showed him the channel and there was nobody in there at the time, and Suge flipped: 'No shit! I got fuckin' cameras in the bedroom?' Everybody started laughing when I told them 'Pac had been in there.

"'Pac represents something that is heroic and tragic, not just for black society, but for American society.' — *Mos Def*

By this time, 'Pac was already in the shower in what we called 'the Red Room,' which was Suge's master suite. I walked in, fully clothed, of course – I wasn't a participant. There were a bunch of people in the room and when 'Pac walked out, he was butt-ass naked and you could see his dick. 'Pac was chasing this one big muscular bitch with his dick, and ask anybody who was there, brotha had a big dick.

It wasn't like he was trying to hide anything. Since all the women were either dressed in scandalous bikinis or shorts or were walking around nude, they were participating in the orgy that was going on. There wasn't any raping or anything illegal happening. It was consensual sex among adults. Fuckin' went on all night long. It was one big fuck-fest, put on as only Death Row knew how.

There was another one after one of the

Tyson fights. The night he fought Frank Bruno. This time, he rented a house out for the occasion. His place wasn't ready yet. It was a house next door to Mike Tyson's. Tyson was invited but he didn't come, and there were even more bitches than the last time.

I'd seen Tupac with some amazing-looking women, women who looked like they should be with a husband. I watched him dog them out, over and over again. Women threw themselves at 'Pac and he chose what he wanted and threw the rest back. Brotha didn't just fuck something walking. They definitely had to have a look about them. He favored tits and ass, didn't matter if they were short or tall.

I only remember one time questioning a woman he picked up once. She was this white chick and she wasn't anything spectacular. I asked him, 'Man, what are you doing with this bitch?' And he said he had nothing better to do that night. It was after a video shoot. The next morning, when I picked him up, she was there, wearing the same clothes she had the day before. Get this, we see the girl out again at another shoot a few weeks later, and she's wearing the same outfit, again.

I thought, *This is a scandalous girl right here*.

Sometimes his sexual encounters were more innocent. Leslie remembers an incident that took place with only a kiss. He was riding to the Century Club in a limo with the Outlaws and 'Pac, and 'Pac was clowning him.

'I was listening to these fools, and laughing in my head because they were funny, and 'Pac turns to me and says, "Leslie, man, why you always quiet? Why you ain't got nothin' to say?" I said, "I'm just listening to y'all."

'So he goes off on this routine to the Outlaws, that he's Leslie's bodyguard. He works for me, I don't work for him. We get to the club, and there's this beautiful Latin female. She was so beautiful, I can't emphasize it enough. She was waiting for the valet to bring her car, and she turns to look at Tupac. They locked eyes and she said, "Excuse me, Tupac?" He turned to look at her and he said, "Yes?"

'"Can I ask you something?"

'He said, "Go ahead." And she said, "But it's kind of personal."

'She then motioned with her finger for him to come to her. Tupac walked toward her and she leaned over and whispered in his ear, "Can I have a kiss?"

'He backs up and looks at her, with a look like, Damn, I don't even know you. And she just smiled at him, she was super sexy and she knew it. He leaned over and gave her a kiss on the cheek and then proceeds to walk back to the club.

'She said, "Wait a minute, Tupac . . . come here." He turns again to look at her with a funny look, and walks back in her direction. Again, she leans over and whispers in his ear, "I mean a kiss on the lips, something to remember you by."

'He looks at her and slowly leans in to give her a kiss on the lips. They locked lips for a moment, and then he backs away. "Thank you, Tupac," she says with a sigh. Now, he turns to again walk toward the club, and I looked at him and said, "Yo 'Pac. You're fired."'

BULLET

review by Micah Robinson

You ever find yourself looking at a DVD box as you're viewing a movie, and the box tells you how the DVD contains this 'gripping' or 'gritty' drama, and you think to yourself, 'Man, when I get done watching this slightly above average film I'm looking at now, it's gonna be sweet to finally see the movie that the box describes! I bet it'll come on as soon as this flick finishes!'?

That ever happen to you? It does to me every so often. I guess I kind of hope in vain that with an average film, the 'extras' will include a completely re-shot, acted and edited version of the film that lives up to the superlative description on the box. The first DVD company that does that is going places, I tell you . . . .

I had no such luck with *Bullet*. It's not that the film is that bad. It's not really bad at all. But when you read about the 'gritty urban thriller' that's 'a stylish mix of brutality and revenge,' this is probably not the film you would envision. By setting, it is urban and there is some gory brutality here and there, though it's so poorly done, you'll laugh more than anything else. But the 'style,' 'grit,' 'thriller' and 'revenge' parts are few and far between.

The marketing of the film hinges around two people, Mickey Rourke and Tupac Shakur, both of whom were at interesting points of their lives when this film was originally released. Mickey Rourke had pretty much fallen out of Hollywood favor and was physically bulked up from his new career in boxing. Tupac Shakur, on the other hand, was disintegrating in a box somewhere due to having died some months earlier. Much like his posthumous musical output, the guy had a full three unreleased films in the can at the time of his death, and if Suge Knight ran a film production company back then, they'd probably all have sequels using the

outtakes and deleted scenes.

In this film, they're cast as bitter rivals. Rourke plays the protagonist, Butch 'Bullet' Stein, a Jewish thug just released from the 'big house' and returning home to a somewhat quiet family life in the suburbs. He was a promising baseball prospect in college at one point, but the lure of the streets was too much and his life was derailed. Now, all he has are his brothers, a sensitive artistic type who just hangs around his thug brother because he loves him (Adrien Brody) and a schizophrenic combat vet who's not quite as mad as he seems (Ted Levine), plus his best friend Lester (John Enos III), a man as narcissistic, psychotic, and latently homosexual as *American Psycho*'s Patrick Bateman, but without even half of the intelligence.

As soon as Bullet hits the 'hood, he robs some preppies looking to score some drugs and blinds their dealer knowing that they're all associated with hood kingpin Tank (Shakur), a fellow thug whose left eye was taken out by Bullet in the stir some months earlier. The confrontation is set, and the film is a countdown to the inevitable. The only problem is that this is all established about ten minutes into the film. The other 85 minutes are the screenwriters desperately trying to think of entertaining ways to prolong a conflict that should naturally be settled in about five minutes.

Tank and Bullet have a couple of confrontations, but for some odd reason, despite being in control of a lot more firepower and men, Tank keeps letting Bullet off the hook. Ostensibly, it's because the two respect each other for being survivors as much as they hate each other for being adversaries. But while that may be true, it's self-sabotaging because when the film finally does resolve their beef in the last couple of minutes, it does it in a way that could and

Tupac with Bullet *co-star Mickey Rourke at a function held in honor of the actor, November 1994.*

should have happened much earlier.

Bullet has some stock archetypes, but they're occupied by very powerful actors. Whatever jokes you can conjure about Rourke's career choices, he has always been someone who's the most visually interesting person in almost any shot he's in. The guy just has that certain thing about him that makes him fun to watch. It's no surprise that the character of Bullet isn't significantly different to many of the other tough guys he's played, but it is nice to see little character moments like Bullet's 'limp' night with a hot Hispanic girl and his banter with his friends adding dimension and texture to the character. You know the film can't end well for him no matter how it turns out, but you care anyway.

Shakur, though given a lot less screen time, is no less a force. He had barely dipped his toes in the waters of theatrical acting when he died, but he was a natural performer from the first time a camera ever caught him on film. As written, Tank would be a pretty boring 'hood thug,' but as he surveys his 'kingdom' from behind the doors of his tinted black Cadillac cruising the streets, he really gives an eerily regal vibe to the character. The supporting players fall in just as well, with the exception of Bullet's shrill and one-note Jewish parents, who – to be fair – were directly taken from the real life experience of writer Bruce Rubenstein.

Bullet isn't the sort of film you watch because it's a great film. It's the sort of film you watch when you want to see two guys shine in underrated, little-seen roles. The great film whose description keeps popping up on DVD boxes is out there, but it'll take a while to find it. This'll keep you company in the interim.

REBEL FOR THE HELL OF IT

by Armond White

Against the many negative images of Tupac, there are those he actually approved in numerous music videos. Stephanie James remembers watching video tapes of *Black Caesar* and *Superfly* with Tupac in Baltimore: 'Superfly was funny but it didn't mean as much to him as *Black Caesar*, cuz that had a black man thinking up ways to control his neighborhood and his destiny. Like in *Shaft*. Tupac liked those because the heroes took control.'

TV pundits Siskel and Ebert once registered surprise that rappers made such good actors, but role-playing is a large part of what any recording artist does. It's especially important to rap stars. Tupac, looking for more acceptance, delighted: 'Yeah, I like that people come to me and go, "*you* did a good job," when all my career it's been you guys this or that. I love it that somebody came and say, "Tupac, you a great actor, you did a great part." So now I want to do that even more and do other parts and do better parts. I want to do *Terminator 2* roles, something different so people can really see the diversity, cuz even now people, I think some people goin', "Now wait a minute, that's just him being him. How hard is it to be crazy?" Now I want to do something, you know, sane. I want to be in love or something so that people can see the diversity of what I can do.'

His last two film productions were aimed in that direction. In *Gang Related*, a courtroom drama by writer-director Jim Kouf, Tupac stars with James Belushi, Leila Rochon, and in small parts James Earl Jones and Dennis Quaid. Belushi and Tupac are partners, two corrupt homicide detectives, who get involved in shady stuff and chalk it up to gang-related activity – the usual formula. But *Gridlock'd*, Tupac's first independent film, is another story. Written and directed by the actor Vondie Curtis Hall, it is credibly based on Hall's real-life experience of trying to get help and find his way through the big-city bureaucracies of drug clinics and rehabs. As members of a spoken-word trio, Tupac (as Spoon), Tim Roth (as Stretch) and Thandie Newton (as Cookie) play Detroit junkies who make a desperate effort to go straight, all the while facing inevitable death with gallows humor. 'You ain't gonna die, it's just a flesh wound,' Tupac says to Roth after a shooting. The line has eerie echoes; it works as part of the story which doesn't trade on Tupac's real-life woes but paints a gritty portrait of urban reality, satirizing the simplistic political notion of dead-end society. In a bold move for a first-time black filmmaker, Hall breaks with Hollywood fantasy conventions, choosing a documentary style that manages to avoid all the pitfalls of TV-series realism.

Roth's appearance brings to mind *Meantime*, the signal Eighties BBC film about life on the dole that he made with English director Mike Leigh. Roth's impressive British technique meshes with Tupac's naturalism, making them a good team. He remembers their working relationship fondly: 'My mate-name for Tupac was "New Money," because he was the upstart, full of the *esprit* of being a big pop record star and he was certain to be a smashing film star. He used to call me "Free Shit" because of the extra perks he thought I got in my dressing room, trailer, what have you.' Together, they avoided the honey-quotient of actors getting high on playing druggies.

Gridlock'd deftly shifts dramatic tone from slapstick comic (a welfare office riot) to horrific comic (a hospital waiting-room nightmare). Hall, who starred in the memorable Eighties theater production *Williams & Walker* (about the moral crises felt by Twenties blackface performers Bert Williams and George Walker), lets the actors explore the complexities of good luck and bad breaks. Remembering Tupac, he said: 'When you think about George Walker and Bert Williams, they were completely different individuals off the stage and 'Pac was a lot more stuff than he seemed when outside the rap arena. The producer Preston Holmes got him the script and he said, "I want to do this movie." The brother showed up, he had the script down, had the character's arc. He could talk about the beats, he could make reference to all the shit. I thought, "This is not the cat the media is throwin' out there." He's smart, funny, well read.

'That's what saddened me about his death, you could see the compassion *and* silliness. In the media all you see is the picture with the hat skewed to the side, not even the pictures of what he was looking like when we were working. Just a straight up black man.

'I went to the memorial benefit his mother gave. Ex-Panther after ex-Panther spoke. When you talk to the folks 'Pac grew up around, you sensed why the brother was like that: sitting around with his mother's friends, having the revolutionary brothers have dialogue at table and sense his mother's spirit and brilliance. It was evident when he was on set. He could reference any shit – it was because he was around fuckin' intellectuals when he was born. [He had] a diverse taste in music. The guy pulls up the girl in the Cranberries. He knew every artist out there. All these films, all this music; he sort of absorbed all this stuff.

'One time when we were driving in L.A. in his Rolls-Royce Corniche, he had the Cranberries blaring. He was on Crenshaw Boulevard. Some brothers pulled up, said, "'Pac, what you listening to?" "Just the radio," he said. But it was the CD.'

Hall appreciated Tupac's eclectic qualities. He knew that actors, like rappers, when intuitively in sync, reveal their poignant secrets. *Gridlock'd* marked the first time since *Juice* that Tupac had had worthy collaborators who understood his pressures. Hall envisioned a trenchant hope: 'Tupac's movie career could have brought out more sides of his personality, so that people could know him better.'

Tupac had always wanted to act out rev-olution in real life. Years earlier, explaining the meaning of THUG LIFE, his motto and tattoo, he talked of a plan to start a camp for children on the order of L. L. Cool J's but with a different, militant purpose: to teach kids how to use firearms. Tupac had launched into an energetic proselytizing, full of race-war threats and mounting panics that only made sense as an expression of his own churning anxieties As he spoke, and his fears uncoiled, he exuded more and more unreachable certainty.

It was this ambition and mood that inspired the movie-parody concept of the 'California Love' video. Directed by Hype Williams, the hip hop video director specializing in Hollywood knock-offs, Tupac was cast as an apocalyptic scavenger, modeled on characters in *The Road Warrior*. 'California Love' exhibits his firebrand mania in images already accepted in pop culture. Though its source is trivial, Tupac embraced its form to validate his personal longing for apocalyptic action. Williams hypes it up with overlapping images and sped-up chases, disco fantasias, fight scenes that have nothing to do with the song's lyrics – all of which totally contradict, and perhaps parody, his second, conventional video of the song set at a party in contemporary L.A. These compacted hip hop visions convey how hard it has become for young folks to stabilize their passions, or choose sensible paths. They're overflowing with feelings – emotions that need to be sorted out, examined, balanced, corroborated.

Rap Sheet editor Darryl James, writing of meeting Tupac, observed, 'The Tupac who stood in front of me then was just a cool kid who was funny as hell and just wanted people to like him.' That's the Tupac immortalized in 'I Ain't Mad at Cha', a video he co-directed that imagines his death by gunfire and his ascension to heaven where he greets black pop stars from Billie Holiday, Redd Foxx to Jimi Hendrix and Sammy Davis, Jr. James remembers the hopeful young star who said, 'I never had shit growing up, so I had nothing to lose. Now I want to show what I've been through to other people who've been through the same thing to show how narrowly I escaped. I stand up for something: I want to take the bad and turn it into good.'

'I Ain't Mad at Cha' dramatizes Tupac's bonding with his homey (played by Bokeem Woodbine), shifting back and forth between heaven and earth so Tupac can keep an eye on his friend's reactions and see him being inspired by Tupac's death to keep on keeping on. It recalls another unexpected favorite film of his, Steven Spielberg's *Always*, in that love is so strong it keeps going beyond the grave. Tupac's theatrical instincts were shrewdly apparent in 'I Ain't Mad at Cha.' The caring expressed in the video and its link-up with the black showbiz tradition are true to the kinds of sincerity and fraternity that hip hop revived for a new generation of black pop fans.

Picking up on the song's message of forgiveness, Tupac's video dramatizes the particular confederacy between his spirit and those of legendary pop stars. Looking past the egotism of this mini-drama, it vividly depicts Tupac's desire to connect and identify with others who have left an 'immortal' mark on the world through their achievement in the performing arts. It's significant that his heaven is not filled with political dissidents and rebels; the stress of Death Row had taken him beyond those factional concerns.

'I Ain't Mad at Cha' tells all those who had offered him political solutions that he has seen his own world and time in a different light. He has defined his personal struggle in new terms. In addition to being a black American male – an endangered species – he is contending with the complications of being an entertainer, of standing with one foot in the system and one foot in the street, reaching for the very top. In the pursuit of artistic expression and a public career – in spite of compromises and obstacles – Tupac has found challenge and reward enough. The optimism of this video conveys Tupac's desire to transform his earthly struggle into a quest for enduring fame and lasting remembrance . . . for paradise and redemption.

Tupac rarely admitted this drive, preferring instead to speak through hip hop's usual bravado in which 'keeping it real' meant limiting himself to ghetto stereotypes – what video director Mark Romanek calls 'brick-wall videos' that present hip hop performances in typical, predictable slum settings. In 'I Ain't Mad at Cha,' Tupac goes one step beyond cliché, daring to resist the 'street' trend for a music video vision that brings him closer to an epiphany – and closer to examining the hereafter alluded to in so many of his raps. Partly inspired by Bone Thugs-N-Hamony's 'Tha Crossroads' video that spans the black church to the afterlife, Tupac represented hip hop sentiments in a setting that might even have charmed Reverend Daughtry. Keeping it 'real' in this case meant an unusual effort to keep hip hop spiritual.

Video-making fully utilized Tupac's rap and dramatic ambitions. Leila Steinberg testified to the hip hop faith he had shown in 1993 when Mac Mall, a struggling Bay area rapper, needed a video to promote his single, 'Ghetto Theme.' 'I played it for 'Pac,' Steinberg remembers, 'and he said, "I'm gonna be a director, so this is where I'm gonna start, with the video, I'm gonna direct, you gotta let me." Actually he didn't give us a choice.' The chance to make images that expressed his feelings for life in the hood inspired Tupac. 'I love the song,' he said. 'I feel it. This is my project.' Putting his seal on a ghetto anthem – even on someone else's – showed Tupac's awareness of the importance of confirming hip hop's complicated experience. 'Video's a signal,' he said. 'So you turn it up!'

'I Ain't Mad at Cha' envisions sorrow, remorse and forgiveness, as clear and concise as Tupac would ever manage. The video's wishfulness may seem naïve because of hokey directorial devices and low-budget scenery, but it suggests that, up to the time he adopted his *alter-ego* Makaveli, Tupac sharpened his ambitions while he outraced his dreams.

GRIDLOCK'D

review by Roger Ebert

It is possible to imagine *Gridlock'd* as a movie of despair and desperation, but that would involve imagining it without Tupac Shakur and Tim Roth, who illuminate it with a gritty, goofy comic spirit. This is grim material, but surprisingly entertaining, and it is more cause to mourn the recent death of Shakur, who gives his best performance as Spoon, a musician who wants to get off drugs.

Spoon and his friend Stretch (Roth) arrive at this decision after rushing Spoon's girlfriend Cookie (Thandie Newton) to an emergency room, comatose after a drug overdose. The three of them have a jazz trio. Ironically, she's the clean liver, always eating veggieburgers and preaching against smoking. While Cookie hovers in critical condition, Spoon and Stretch spend a very long day trying to find a rehab program for themselves.

> "If he'd played his cards right, he could have gone on to be a very established actor." — Tim Roth

The heart of the movie is their banter, the grungy dialogue that puts an ironic spin on their anger and fear. Tim Roth is a natural actor, relaxed in his roles, with a kind of quixotic bemusement at life's absurdities. Shakur, the hip hop star turned actor, matches that and adds an earnestness: In their friendship, Spoon is the leader and thinker, and Stretch is the sidekick who will go along with whatever's suggested.

It's Spoon who decides to kick, telling his friend (in a line that now has dark undertones), 'Lately I feel like my luck's been running out.' Writer-director Vondie Curtis Hall, making his directing debut after a TV acting career on *Chicago Hope* and other shows, combines the hard-edged, in-your-face realism of street life with a conventional story that depends on stock characters: evil drug dealers, modern Keystone Kops, colorful eccentrics. The movie isn't as powerful as it could have been, but it's probably more fun: This is basically a comedy, even if sometimes you ask yourself why you're laughing.

That's especially true in a scene that moviegoers will be quoting for years. Spoon, desperate to get into an emergency room and begin detox, persuades Stretch to stab him. As the two friends discuss how to do it (and try to remember which side of the body the liver is on), there are echoes of the overdose sequence in *Pulp Fiction*. What Tarantino demonstrated is that with the right dialogue and actors, you can make anything funny.

The daylong duel with the drug dealers and the encounters with suspicious cops work like comic punctuation. In between is the real life of the movie: the friendship of the two men and their quest to get into rehab. They circle endlessly through a series of Detroit social-welfare agencies that could have been designed by Kafka: They find they can't get medicards without being on welfare, can't get into detox without filling out forms and waiting ten days, can't get into a rehab center because it's for alkies only, can't get the right forms because an office has moved, can't turn in the forms because an office is about to close. If this movie reflects

Tupac quickly developed a rapport with his Gridlock'd *co-star, British actor Tim Roth.*

real life in Detroit, it's as if the city deliberately plots to keep addicts away from help.

In movies about stupid bureaucracies, the heroes inevitably blow up and start screaming at the functionaries behind the counters. Hall's script wickedly turns the tables: The clerks shout at Spoon and Stretch. Elizabeth Pena plays an ER nurse who maddeningly makes them fill out forms while Cookie seems to be dying. When Spoon screams at her, she screams back in a monologue that expresses all of her exhaustion and frustration. Later, at a welfare center, an overworked clerk shouts back: 'Yeah, we all been waiting for the day you come through that door and tell us you're ready not to be a drug fiend. After five, ten years, you decide this is the day, and the world stops for you?' This material is so good, I wish we'd had more of it. Maybe Hall, aiming for a wider audience, hedged his bets by putting in scenes where the heroes, the drug dealers and the cops chase one another on foot and in cars around downtown Detroit. Those scenes aren't plausible and

they're not about anything.

Much better are the moments when the two friends sit, exhausted, under a mural of the great outdoors and talk about how they simply lack the energy to keep on using drugs. Or when Spoon remembers his first taste of cocaine in high school: 'I didn't even know what it was. Everybody else was throwin' up. But for me it was like going to the moon.' Or when they watch daytime TV and do a running commentary. Or when they're almost nabbed for a murder they didn't commit.

Still, maybe Hall made the smart bet, by positioning this story halfway between real life and a crime comedy. The world of these streets and tenements and hospitals and alleys is strung out and despairing, and the human comedy redeems it. By the time a guy is trying to help his friend by stabbing him, we understand well enough what drugs will lead you to. For its premiere audience at the Sundance Film Festival, *Gridlock'd* played like a comedy, with big laughter. Too bad Tupac couldn't be there.

GANG RELATED

review by James Bernardinelli

Gang Related will forever be known as Tupac Shakur's last film. In fact, that's how it's being marketed. As final features go, this isn't a bad one (for the ultimate in ignominious send-offs, see Donald Pleasance's curtain call in *Halloween 6*), and Shakur is in top form. The movie is a generally well-written yarn about police corruption that gets out of hand. For 90 per cent of its 110 minute running length, *Gang Related* is taut, well-paced, and clever. It's too bad that the conclusion, despite retaining a sense of unpredictability, is a let-down. Characters act irrationally to facilitate a few more ironic twists of plot.

On the whole, however, *Gang Related* is an enjoyable, if extremely profane, example of movie-making. The script, from writer/director Jim Kauf (who previously penned the screenplay for both *Stakeout* movies, and last directed with 1989's *Disorganized Crime*) mixes action, tension, and low-key comedy. Our heroes (who are actually anti-heroes) are Davinci (James Belushi) and Rodriguez (Tupac Shakur), a pair of bent cops who have just been caught in the Murphy's Law corner of the Twilight Zone. What at first seems like a relatively straightforward caper turns into a nightmare as circumstances conspire to plunge them into a tangled web of bad breaks and worse luck.

Their plan is seemingly simple: sell cocaine taken from the police evidence room to a drug dealer, kill him using a gun also lifted from the evidence room, then replace the gun and coke before anyone is the wiser. The results: an apparent gang related slaying of human refuse, plus Davinci and Rodriguez get to pocket the profits of their illicit drug sale. With the help of Davinci's stripper girlfriend, Cynthia (*Waiting to Exhale*'s Lela Rochon), the pair have successfully pulled this con nine times. Ten isn't their lucky number. On this occasion, their victim is an undercover DEA agent, and they're put in the uncomfortable position of having to investigate a murder they committed. And that's before things start to go really wrong . . . .

While *Gang Related*'s script isn't a masterpiece, the situation it postulates is suitably delicious. The film probably contains enough action to qualify as a thriller, but it's really more of a black comedy. Kauf has fun toying with his characters and their situations, constantly one-upping himself in the 'whatever can go wrong, will go wrong' department. I won't give away any specifics beyond the initial setup, because that would spoil the primary entertainment value of the movie. Sadly, however, Kauf is at a loss when it comes to wrapping things up, and the anticlimactic, routine finale lacks the panache evident throughout most of the running time. The final scene is in keeping with the rest of the film, but the events leading up to it are dubious at best. But, because only a few minutes are so out of synch, min-

> 'Shakur's untimely death has robbed the motion picture community of a promising star.'
> — James Bernardinelli

'Did you hear the one about the two cops who wasted a Drug Enforcement Agent?' – 'Pac as Rodriguez in his final feature film, Gang Related *(1997).*

imal damage was done to my appreciation of the movie as a whole.

It's no surprise that Tupac Shakur is good in his role as a bad cop with a conscience. In films like *Poetic Justice* and, more recently, *Gridlock'd*, Shakur has shown himself to be a talented actor, and it goes without saying that his untimely death has robbed the motion picture community of a promising star. The actor who really surprised me here was James Belushi, who is very good as Davinci, the cynical mastermind behind the kill-the-drug-dealer-and-get-the-money scheme. I've never been terribly impressed by Belushi's range, but his performance here is relentlessly on-target. The supporting players are also good, with solid work turned in by Lela Rochon, James Earl Jones (as a high-priced lawyer), Wendy

Crewson (as the prosecutor who is unpleasantly surprised by disappearing witnesses and evidence), and Dennis Quaid (as a homeless man who plays a pivotal role in the proceedings).

Kauf, whose *Stakeout* was a lighter blend of the same kind of elements at work here, knows just how to play the material to keep it enjoyable. That's not an easy task, considering that the main characters are pretty reprehensible and the basic plotline is about covering up the accidental murder of a cop. Nevertheless, in part because of a series of good performances and in part because Kauf approaches things with confidence, the results are positive. *Gang Related* may not be *Pulp Fiction*, but it's not a bad foray into tangential territory.

100

PART FOUR

A THUG DEATH

THE LIVING END

by Frank Williams

'When I die, the consciousness I carry, I will to black people. May they pick me apart and take the useful parts, the sweet meat of my feelings.' – Amiri Baraka

Soulja's Story: 'Pac's Theme

He, who lived each day relentlessly throwing a finger at death. He, the poster boy for ghetto self-destruction. He, the sensitive poet and alcoholic. He, who was dying right before our eyes all along. He, who treated urban sickness with green sacks of weed. He, the thug and mama's boy. He, the eternal Gemini, communicating both b-boy love and agony. He, the nomad who combed the streets and studios looking for a home . . . has finally found one.

On Friday, September 13, 1996, at 4.03 p.m. Pacific Standard Time, Tupac Shakur went into cardiopulmonary arrest. The cause of death was respiratory failure. A heart attack. 'He coded,' said a hospital spokesman referring to code blue, the medical term for death. 'Doctors tried to revive him but he didn't come back.'

After the coroner's office examined Tupac's body, they determined that his heart attack was due to multiple gun wounds to the chest. This time, the one thing Tupac Shakur prided himself on, his will to live, had disappeared into the unforgiving hands of nature.

Death Around the Corner

'Don't shed a tear for me nigga. I ain't happy here / I hope they bury me and send me to my rest / headlines reading, "murdered to death" / my last breath.' – from Tupac's 'If I Die 2Nite'

As he predicted in nearly every rhyme since *2Pacalypse Now*, Tupac Amaru Shakur died in a flurry of gunfire, bullets piercing his tattooed, muscular, 150-pound body. After 25 years of sleeping with demons, Tupac is gone – murdered by the same black

on black madness that inspired him to share his imagination with the world. Just a few hours after the Mike Tyson/Bruce Seldon fight in Las Vegas on September 7, Tupac and Death Row Records' CEO Marion 'Suge' Knight were driving near the Las Vegas Strip. They were leading an estimated ten-car convoy with their bodyguards trailing right behind them on the way to Suge's Club 662, where Run-DMC and Craig Mack were scheduled to perform that night.

At approximately 11.15 p.m. that Saturday night with Suge behind the wheel, a white Cadillac pulled up alongside their black BMW 750 and opened fire. One witness to the shooting said one of the men jumped out and shot inside the car, filling it with thirteen shots. Not wearing a bullet proof vest at the time, Tupac was hit four times in the chest. Knight was only slightly wounded, grazed on the head by bullet fragments and glass.

Rushed to the University Medical Center, doctors in the Trauma Intensive Care Unit tried desperately to stop the extensive internal bleeding in Tupac's chest. Two of the four shots that struck near his 'Thug Life' tattoo caused the bleeding. While Suge was released at 11.00 a.m. the next morning, Tupac remained in critical condition, breathing only with the help of a life support machine.

In an effort to save him, surgeons performed at least three operations and removed his right lung. While a distraught hip hop nation hoped for his survival, Tupac teeter-tottered on the brink of death. Six days later, having never regained consciousness, Tupac was dead.

But even while he was holed up in the

first floor hospital room, rumors began to spread like wildfire. Initially, the shooting was believed to be the result of an altercation Tupac had earlier in the night at the MGM Hotel. But Sgt. Greg McCurdy of the Las Vegas Metropolitan Police Department said after officers reviewed a surveillance tape from the hotel they determined that, 'Investigators have no reasons, at this time, to believe that the altercation has any connection to the shooting.' According to a source (speaking only on the condition of anonymity) from the night's entourage, Knight allegedly corraled his employees, refusing to let them leave Las Vegas until an internal investigation of the incident was completed.

Quickly, like vultures descending on their prey, the mainstream media jumped in, labeling the shooting as the latest chapter in the heated East Coast/West Coast rivalry. Reports circulated that cops in New York were looking for Notorious B.I.G. (a.k.a. Chris Wallace) to question him about the shooting. Though Las Vegas detectives said they were looking into the much heralded rivalry, there was no evidence indicating that Biggie was held for questioning.

A police source (who also wished to remain nameless) indicated that the shooting came as the result of a long-standing gang rivalry between the Death Row camp and a Compton street gang. Sources in Los Angeles also cited the death of an alleged Crip gang member at a Death Row *Soul Train* Awards after-party as a possible flashpoint in the dispute. Kelly Jamerson, a 28-year-old roofer, was stomped to death at the party last February. An argument between the rival gang members at the party led to his death.

In the September 23 issue of *Newsweek* magazine, an unnamed police source said that the shooting of two Crips from Compton just four days after Tupac's death was a direct retaliation for the Las Vegas drive-by. Marcus Duron Childs and Timothy Flanagan, both 21, were working on a car in a Compton driveway when a man walked up to them with a handgun and opened fire. They both died as a result of their injuries.

Other sources in both the music industry and those familiar with the underground Los Angeles gang network said more shootings were expected. Death Row Records and Suge Knight himself refused to comment. The label only released a statement that read: 'Suge Knight and the entire Death Row Records family are saddened by the passing of our brother and rap recording star, Tupac Amaru Shakur. A true warrior, Tupac vigorously fought for his life until his heart failed this past afternoon.'

There were no arrests at the time of this writing in mid-September. Police hoped a tip hotline would elicit witnesses to help solve the case. Investigators in the Vegas homicide bureau interviewed Knight twice, but expressed frustration that the former UNLV football player gave them few leads.

Days after Tupac's death, Death Row Records held a memorial service for him in Los Angeles. In New York City, Nation of Islam minister Conrad Muhammad convened a host of hip hop celebrities at Harlem Mosque Number Seven in an effort to promote unity in the wake of the rapper's death. Tupac's body was cremated the day after he died. His family later held a private service at the Davis Funeral Home in Las Vegas.

Dear Mama

Hours after Tupac was shot, I hopped a flight to Las Vegas. On assignment from my newspaper day job, I was charged with the task of surveying the damage. This might be exciting to some, but piecing together the details of another drive-by shooting of a young black male isn't a career high point to me. Inside the waiting room, a bevy of b-boys, flygirls, groupies, and curious spectators anxiously circled the area waiting for the latest update.

Worried family members wiped red eyes and shuffled about the small room. Tupac's crew, the Outlaw Immortalz, looked tense and perplexed, perhaps wondering how a night of partying turned into a morning of nail biting. Quincy Jones' daughter and

Tupac's girlfriend at the time, Kidada Jones, sat nervously shifting in the waiting room.

Reverend Jesse Jackson, in town to watch the championship fight, hugged Tupac's mother, Afeni Shakur, and comforted the rapper's friends. On the curb outside the hospital, Jackson pointed fingers not at the shooters, but at society as a whole. 'Tupac has had many close calls,' Jackson told me. 'But this is about more than Tupac. It's about the culture of violence that we live in, this survival of the fittest mentality that too often calls out for revenge, for retaliation.'

Watching Tupac's mother, Afeni Shakur, walk alone towards the chaplain's office, I thought of the many other black mothers who'd been in this position: wringing their hands as wounded sons lay gutted by bullets in hospital beds. In spite of the hit records, the expensive jewelry and never-ending controversy, this was her son. Not a media caricature of 'gang life' or over-sexed coon played up by MTV. This was a boy's face she had wiped; dirty diapers cleaned in a righteous act of motherhood.

Shrugging off my media badge, I walked silently with her down a long hallway decorated with Ansel Adams photos. Instead of being insensitive and probing her for reaction, I hoped simply to provide a smile.

All the shoot 'em up videos with rappers boasting of bucking niggas down never show these stark details – the actual aftermath of bullets tearing flesh and the anguished look of a dreadlocked mother pacing a waiting room. 'In play life, the violence is not serious,' Jackson said, 'it's a game. Our youth have become so immunized to how final death really is.' I guess Dre from Outkast was right when he said: 'It took yo' mama nine months to make it, but it only took a nigga 30 minutes to take it.'

How Long Will They Mourn Me?

The day before Tupac died, Dat Nigga Daz (of Tha Dogg Pound) called into 92.3 The Beat radio station in Los Angeles and urged the entire city to pray for his label mate.

Obviously emotionally shaken, Daz told listeners to cherish life. More importantly, he said something maybe the bullshit and set tripping had finally taught him. 'More people should try to be my friend first and not my enemy,' Daz said. 'So at least I can decide if I want you to be my enemy.'

As shocked callers rang up with poems or detailed accounts of encounters with Tupac, popular DJ Theo reminisced on the rapper he met while both were paying dues in the Bay Area. 'Tupac,' Theo said, 'had a certain fire in his eyes that you don't see very often.'

Elsewhere in the rap community, news of Tupac's death was greeted with disbelief and a hint of hopelessness. Some thought it might finally be good riddance to gangsta rap. Others say it was simply the last stop for a young man headed for tragedy since birth.

'I don't think it will affect rap music,' rap pioneer and Def Jam Records founder Russell Simmons said about the possible ramifications of the rapper's death. 'Tupac wasn't headed for this anymore than say Sean Penn or Kurt Cobain. It was just that rebelliousness for the sake of it, that wild rock 'n' roll side of him that did this. The attitude in our world, especially in youth culture, promotes all of this.'

Fans began to hold vigils from Texas to Washington, D.C. to Las Vegas. In Los Angeles, mourners placed flowers at Tupac's Woodland Hills home. Effects of his death crossed racial and economic lines, with confused white parents in suburbia reporting sobbing teenagers, and even single mothers in the 'hood recounting how they were inspired by his heartfelt lyrics.

'It's a big loss,' Simmons said. 'He was one of the best poets of our time. He was very insightful and added a level of sophistication to rap that was unmatched. It doesn't matter what type of education he had. Tupac communicated such an honest and diverse range of feelings in his music.'

Definition of a Thug Nigga

'I heard a rumor I died / murdered in cold

blood, dramatized / pictures of me in my final state, you know I cried.' – from Tupac's 'Ain't Hard to Find'

It would be easy to cull the meaning of Tupac's short but turbulent life from his lyrics. If you listened hard enough, the sketchy outline of his soul revealed itself. His lyrics were a series of bloody, open sores, summing up the trials of black boys reared in crack-crazed neighborhoods everywhere. With his mix of tough guy charisma and true ghetto flavor, Tupac captivated a nation with songs that possessed a defiant spirit almost unrivaled in modern pop music.

On June 16, 1971, as black America was knee-deep in a black pride movement, Tupac Shakur was born in the Bronx, New York. His mother, Afeni, was heavily involved with the black Panther Party in New York. She was even thrown in jail while pregnant with Tupac and freed just two months before her only son was born. Tupac's father was unknown. A *New York Times* article reported that his mother said she had slept with two different men and was unsure which man was the father.

Showing talent early, friends say the shy boy was destined for fame. 'I knew Tupac as a ten-year-old boy,' said Charles Barron, a family friend from Tupac's childhood Brooklyn church. 'And he wrote some poetry to me then. He was sincere, very sincere.'

'Pac's first public performance was as a thirteen-year-old at an Apollo Theater production of Lorraine Hansberry's *Raisin in the Sun*. It was at this fund-raiser for Jesse Jackson's 1984 presidential bid that Jackson first met his mother.

Not long after, he moved with his mother and sister to the Baltimore area, where he enrolled in the High School for Performing Arts. When not talking shit or getting into trouble, he studied acting and ballet. Before long, his family was packing up again.

In 1988 they relocated to the Bay Area. There Tupac soon started forming the persona that would become the character sketch for 'Thug Life.' His initiation into 'the life'

began with peddling drugs in a Marin City housing project residents nicknamed 'the jungle.' Using the name MC New York, he cultivated his love for rap music, weaving his talent for poetry into rhymes that reflected the realities of hardcore street life.

Bay Area hip hop fans know Tupac from his early days when he rapped with Vallejo MC Ray Luv in a group called the One Nation MC's. But he first gained national exposure when he teamed with zany funk masters Digital Underground on 'Same Song.'

His performance on that 1990 song earned him a record deal with Interscope Records. Tupac's debut album, 1991's *2Pacaplyse Now*, injected a sensitivity to the gangsta rap genre that was rare at the time. On 'Brenda's Got a Baby,' Tupac tackled the realities of teenage motherhood and then spoke fondly of unconditional homeboy love on 'When My Homies Call.'

He received praise when he starred as the double-crossing teenage thug in the movie *Juice*, and later as the ambitious and charming Lucky in 1993's *Poetic Justice*. Between the jabs thrown at then Vice-President Dan Quayle on his second album, 1993's *Strictly 4 My N.I.G.G.A.Z.*, he continued his criticism of police harassment ('Point the Finga') and gained a new batch of fans, mostly females, with the inspirational 'Keep Ya Head Up.' On that song he emotionally rhymed: 'I wonder why we take from our women / why we rape our women / do we hate our women?'

On his most critically acclaimed album, *Me Against the World,* Tupac showed a more mature and introspective side, pondering his own celestial future: 'I wonder if heaven got a ghetto for thug niggas / a stress free life and a spot for drug dealers?' That 1995 LP yielded his most famous song, the Grammy Nominated 'Dear Mama,' a poignant tale of his undying love for his mother.

Yet for all his musical industriousness, Tupac could not shirk the nihilism and violence he so frequently rapped about. Along the way to superstardom, Tupac would be accused of inspiring a Texas teenager to kill

Tupac and Suge in full effect at the Tenth Annual Soul Train *Awards, March 1996.*

a state trooper, shooting at two off-duty Atlanta police officers in 1993, and then go on to serve a fifteen-day jail term for attacking director Allen Hughes. He would also lose more than one friend (former rap partners Kato, and then Stretch of the group Live Squad) to the same violence that finally killed him.

At a Marin City community festival in 1992, a stray bullet from his gun discharged in a fight, accidentally killing six-year-old Qa'id Walker Teal. Tupac said the boy's death, like the thought of never knowing who his father was, haunted him.

On November 30, 1994, in the midst of his trial for allegedly raping a woman in a Manhattan hotel the year before, Tupac was shot five times outside a recording studio in Times Square. While still in a wheelchair and recovering from his wounds, he was convicted of sexual abuse for the 1993 incident and sent to jail. He served nine months in the Clinton Correctional Facility in New York on the charge before being released on $1.4 million bail, pending the outcome of an appeal.

Tupac said in interviews that since Suge Knight was one of the few people who looked out for him while he was in jail, he promised to join the label when he was freed. After his release on October 12, 1995, Tupac immediately signed with Death Row Records, where he recorded his first album for the label.

The Dr. Dre-produced 'California Love' spearheaded the success of the double CD. This year's *All Eyez on Me*, with help from Snoop Doggy Dogg, Jodeci and nearly all of the Death Row camp, sold over 2.5 million copies and was certified five times platinum. It entered the pop charts at number one, and began selling out at record stores when news of 'Pac's death hit the streets.

Shortly before he was murdered, Tupac had finished two, as yet unreleased, movies. In the film *Gridlock'd* he plays a heroin addict fighting his addiction, and in *Gang Related*, he plays a detective. He also leaves the world with two new albums – *The Don Killumminati – The 7 Day Theory*, recorded under the name Makaveli, and *One Nation*, an album geared toward healing some of the East/West beef by featuring Tupac along with prominent East Coast MCs like Black Moon's Buckshot and others.

ALL EYES ON HIM

by R. J. Smith

It was early the morning of Friday the 13th, and in a Las Vegas intensive care unit the world's most famous rapper was drifting along in a 'medicinally induced coma.' Across town, a lounge singer grabs the mike. Between Jimmy Buffet and Bell Biv DeVoe covers, he stares hard through the smoke to the back of the small room. The singer points a rhinestone-festooned finger at a powerfully built young black man with a shaved head, standing before a row of video poker machines.

'Oh my God,' he says with a shocked voice. 'Ladies and gentlemen, a miracle has taken place. Tupac Shakur is with us tonight!'

Rimshot, please. The crowd hoots, the kid obliges an obscure smile, and the show band glides into 'California Love.' 2-3-4 . . . .

Hours later, the 25-year-old Shakur was pronounced dead of respiratory failure and cardiopulmonary arrest. He had come to Vegas for the September 7 Mike Tyson-Bruce Seldon fight. Afterwards, he and Death Row Records CEO Marion 'Suge' Knight were driving to Knight's Club 662 (named for the numbers you punch when spelling M-O-B on a Touch-Tone phone). Shakur was standing in a black BMW driven by Knight, his head poking through the sunroof. A white Cadillac pulled alongside him, about thirteen rounds were fired, and Shakur went down.

You could drive a flotilla of limousines through the gap separating the white lounge singer's mockery from the grief of the black fans who gathered outside the University Medical Center. That's how it was for Tupac Shakur – there may have never been a pop star who signified so differently for so many different people. The more his fame grew, the more the split widened.

Whites who knew little else about Shakur learned about that tattoo on his torso, the one that spelled THUG LIFE until the surgeons played their Scrabble.

Less known was what it said on his back: *Exodus 18:1 1*. The biblical passage goes like this: 'Now I know that the Lord is greater than all gods: for in the thing wherein they dealt proudly *he was* above them.' Somewhere in those words is a knowledge his black fans grasped better than anybody else. Here was a man giving his life over to a power greater than himself. A man caught up 'in the thing,' and unable to break free. He knew it, too, and he did not care.

For 28-year-old rapper E-40, a Bay Area native who has recorded with Shakur, Tupac's death is an unreadable act of God. 'This was fate. It was time,' he says. 'Anybody could get shot. You could be sitting there watching TV, and a stray bullet could go through your sheetrock wall and hit you in the head.

'You know what I think? Tupac is looking down on us, saying, "Y'all don't know what you're missing up here." We the ones in hell.'

For many whites who listen to hip hop, Shakur's death is not so much an occasion for sorting out one's feelings as *finding* them. But in the days after his death I heard more than one African-American with little use for Shakur as a rapper say they were surprised by their remorse.

'He's a person you recognize,' says 33-year-old poet and novelist Paul Beatty. 'He's the kind of person a lot of us know; talented, but in so much pain, and having problems dealing with it . . . .

'You see all that cognitive dissonance in his life – a lot of black people know that from all of that stuff is very hypocritical all the time, and he was the embodiment of all that.'

Swamp Dogg, the 54-year-old singer, songwriter, and producer, ran into Shakur at

108

an L.A. supermarket just days before he went to Vegas. 'I feel a hell of a loss, and I can't understand why,' says Swamp Dogg. 'Other rappers have died or gone to prison and I didn't feel anything. I'll never know, but I *thought* I heard a person who wasn't really bad, who was doing bad things to hang with the bad guys. There was a softness about this guy.'

That softness was the secret of Shakur's charisma. An interior dialogue away from the kind of stardom few taste, he was a fine actor, razor eyes complicating a matinee-idol face. His rapping technique was leaden, and hadn't grown much over four records, but there was a plain speak in his lyrics that could singe.

Shakur didn't care about such gifts. His life was bigger than his career, and everywhere he went his celebrity seemed like the last thing on his mind, as he hurled taunts and made promises which were easier for others to keep.

Especially when he was standing up in Knight's BMW, not wearing his bulletproof vest. In the wake of his killing, innuendo and superstition have rushed to fill the air. The rumors won't stop: It was a Bloods vs. Crips thing (Knight has ties to the Bloods); it was an East Coast vs. West Coast thing, inspired by the blood feud between Knight and Bad Boy's Sean 'Puffy' Combs (an ancillary rumor had Combs holed up in a Hollywood hotel, sweating out Shakur's final days); it was an inside job (how many carsful of how many bodyguards failed in their mission?); Shakur was actually dead for days before it was announced; Shakur isn't dead at all.

That last one goes like this: Just days after Shakur's death, Death Row Records head Suge Knight announced he'll be releasing a posthumous Tupac record. (Don't mutter *2Pac Unplugged* so Knight can hear you.) The rumor currently sweeping the East Coast is that this next record will feature a cover photo of Tupac's bullet-riddled body hanging from a cross. Here's the kicker: The record will be titled *Makaveli*, after

Machiavelli, the Florentine politician who advocated faking one's own death in order to sneak up on his enemies and kill them by surprise.

Hey, even the unconvinced white kids would go for *that*.

Even if that rumor doesn't pan out, the lounge singer's right: Shakur is with us, now and forever. He changed the direction of hip hop – hijacked it, some would say – and ceremonialized its status as the art politicians love to hate. Dan Quayle bashed him, and so have Bob Dole, C. DeLores Tucker, and Bill Bennett. He helped turn hip hop into circle-the-wagons music. Now that he's gone, will the circle be unbroken?

You have to give Tupac Shakur credit for going out like a champ. Months ago he filmed the video for 'I Ain't Mad at Cha;' just days after he died, a completed version was rushed to MTV.

The song, from his most recent album, the quintuple-platinum *All Eyez on Me*, is about a gangster forgiving an old pal who's left the life. The tune has its cake and eats it, too – Shakur makes such a magnanimous show of his forgiveness you'd think he was buying his friend a new car or something. But when he chuckles he ain't mad at the striver, he protests too much – there's a patronizing smile on his face, and his kindness is meant as a withering dismissal.

You wonder why it could possibly be a sin to want to make something of your life. The video, depicting Shakur's death in a flurry of bullets, followed by his return to earth as an angel, pushes beyond whatever extremes are found on the record. I don't know what's more shocking: that Shakur wears his halo so well, or that his hip hop heaven features Redd Foxx, Miles Davis, and Sammy Davis, Jr. (paradise has gone nondenominational). It may steal its idea from a better Bone Thugs-N-Harmony video, but 'I Ain't Mad at Cha' steals its soul from Vegas. The homeboy he should be chilling with up there is Liberace. Leave it to Shakur to turn his wake into a floor show.

'I'm a general and I'm a smart general and I'm not gonna attack at no blind soldier. I'm gonna attack those who attack me.' – Tupac Shakur

'Mad at Cha' is sentimental kitsch, a lavish display of phony feelings. But this should come as no surprise. Shakur's most famous song, the 1995 Grammy-nominated 'Dear Mama,' celebrated motherhood with the pathos of a convict's hand pressed up against the glass. His songs of violence were always followed by songs of regret. Lurking just behind the gangsta was a sentimentalist who knew no bounds.

Then again, when did Shakur ever respect limits? When had he ever learned them? As likely as it is that he'd have been better off – i.e. *alive* – if he'd stayed in jail (he'd been bailed out by Knight last October, pending the appeal of a sexual-assault conviction), Shakur might have been better off actually having been raised in a gang.

As it was, he matriculated in a milieu of scientific socialism, a pan-African nationalism more glamorous from afar than up close. His mom was a member of the Black Panther group the New York 21, charged – and then acquitted – of conspiring to blow up department stores and police stations.

His stepfather, Mutulu Shakur, was a nationalist, and his godfather, Geronimo Pratt, is currently serving out a life sentence.

'He didn't look at those people in a romantic way,' says 26-year-old hip hop writer dream hampton. 'There was nothing romantic about his step-dad being in lockdown 23 hours a day, nothing romantic about his mother going underground. There was nothing stable about it.'

Tupac Shakur was born on 16 June 1971. A move in 1988 from the East Coast to Marin City, California, and his mother's crack addiction, stunted whatever sense of structure he had nurtured. 'Tupac was never part of a gang,' says Hampton. 'In Oakland he was dissed. Drug dealers were selling his mom crack, so they would kind of dog him. Look at him in early Digital Underground footage. He was always this skinny guy.'

A humiliated agnostic, a gangster without the discipline a home team provides, Shakur always seemed ready to jump out of his skin. His willingness to fight Knight's battles with the East Coast powers – here's a man who couldn't see the ridiculousness of throwing West Side up at the Grammys while standing beside Kiss – just underlined his own rootlessness. Shakur was raised on the East Coast, began rapping in California as MC New York, went to jail back East, and came out a Cali shogun. He wasn't just a man of many parts. Parts is all he was.

'Me and Tupac was joined at the hip,' Suge Knight told reporters a few days after Shakur's death. Which is how they were the one time I saw Shakur up close, the rapper almost comically concealed in the shadow of Knight.

It was Thanksgiving, and the gangstas were giving out turkeys in the ghetto. A line snaked down the steps, round the side, and along the block of a South Central Los Angeles community center. The free food, paid for by Death Row, was supposed to be doled out at eleven in the morning. The annual event gave Knight a chance to show off Shakur as his latest signing – Knight had just posted Shakur's $1.4 million bail – but the pair had yet to show. So the old folks and the moms with babies in their arms waited patiently, staring through the windows at the stacks of frozen turkeys locked inside. Everyone was unbearably polite. 'Free Tupac!' people began chanting. Only slowly did another replace it: 'Fuck Tupac! Free the turkeys!'

A couple of hours later the Death Row car arrived, and whatever anxiety had been rising in the hundreds of poor folks was dispelled by the appearance of Shakur. Wiped out by the Smile. He turned on the beacon, slowly ascended the center's steps, and charmed his way to heaven. Of all his skills, the Smile was perhaps his finest.

But quick as a shot, the trademark disappeared. The other thing I most remember about that day is how, having soothed the hungry, Shakur disappeared into the shadow. He might have been the star, but Knight controlled the vibe, and Shakur did nothing to undermine it. He kept changing by the moment – first snarling at a Dutch TV crew, then mildly looking over to listen to Knight, then donning the posture of a visiting dignitary. He was all reaction, a charged particle orbiting his boss.

Knight put the money out for his freedom, but if Shakur did the dance, it was because he wanted to. When he was in the slammer, Shakur told reporters he was a changed man. But then he got out and realized contrition was out of the question. He played the thug ranker than ever. He pretended that this was fate; maybe he believed it. His best performance was as a man who made a deal he couldn't undo.

THE DAY AFTER TUPAC SHAKUR DIED

by Amy Linden

The day after Tupac Shakur died, I was hanging on my street. There was a group of youngish black guys lounging around a car, which was blasting Tupac's 'California Love.' 'A tribute?,' I wondered, and the guys nodded. We started talking in that way that total strangers in NYC often do. Tupac's death was a damn shame; we all agreed: 'Fucked up. Some fucked up gangsta shit gone crazy.' (This, by the way, from guys who, neighborhood lore has it, are low-level dealers.) Tupac was 'hanging with some fucked-up people.'

'It's sad,' I offered.

'Yeah,' one of the guys said, 'I mean nobody wanted him dead. They just wanted Tupac to shut the fuck up.'

Wanting Tupac to 'shut the fuck up' was the prevalent sentiment here in NYC. Tupac's turmoils, both internal and outward, were viewed as annoying and time-consuming. It was like watching a toddler throw a tantrum. I recall a conversation, weeks before Tupac's murder, with a friend who used to be a rap publicist. The theme? Our boredom with the endless cliché of alt-rockers OD-ing and rappers shooting someone. Somebody, we decided, should flip the script. Tupac, we laughed, could use some smack. Not enough to kill him, just to calm his ass down.

I suppose here I should confess that I was never a fan of Tupac, although I thought he was terrific in the movies. OK, I liked a few tracks, 'Brenda's Got a Baby,' 'Dear Mama,' and 'California Love,' but I had no love for Tupac's brand of flashy, gold-encrusted machismo. And it wasn't because I live in Brooklyn and Tupac represented L.A.; I can think of a bunch of West Coast rappers I like.

Tupac didn't say things I was interested in hearing, and, most importantly, he didn't say them in a way that broke any ground or expanded hip hop's possibilities. As far as I'm concerned, Tupac brought nothing remarkable to the game. And in fact, Tupac's career, and in particular the Death Row era, represented the qualities that I see as hip hop's worst. The blatant consumerism. The by-the-numbers playerism. All that Big Willie shit. The pointless sexism, done without the humor of a Sir Mix-a-Lot. Tupac's continuing love affair with aggression seemed played out in a year that brought De La Soul's stinging attack on gangsterism. Tupac's trumped-up feud with Biggie and Puffy rang hollow in a year that the architect of the West Coast sound, Dr. Dre (himself no angel), said enough's enough. And in a year that brought the blistering reflection of Nas, the wise wordplay of A Tribe Called Quest, the seething attack of Jeru the Damaja, the sloppy Southern swagger of Outkast, or the moody sexiness of Method Man, Tupac clutching a bottle of Moët and ogling bitches in bikinis looked old-fashioned.

All that doesn't matter now because Tupac Shakur is already in the process of being anointed. That's what happens when you die young and you die stupidly. And the hip hop nation is once again being asked to atone for something we didn't do. We didn't make Tupac obsessed with his own death. We didn't tell him to sign up with a man who knows nothing about flavor but everything about fear. Like the star he is now being compared to, Kurt Cobain, my gut tells me that Tupac would have died prematurely no matter what he did for a living. The shame is that Tupac, like a lot of kids, black and white, bought into the lie that money gets you happiness, that violence is the way to solve problems, and that you have to live the life you're being paid to put on record. The best way to honor the memory of Tupac is not to make him more than he was but to convince the hip hop nation that keeping it real ain't half as important as staying alive.

EASY TARGET: Why Tupac Should Be Heard Before He's Buried

by Mikal Gilmore

I don't know whether to mourn Tupac Shakur or to rail against all the terrible forces – including the artist's own self-destructive temperament – that have resulted in such a wasteful, unjustifiable end. I do know this, though: Whatever its causes, the murder of Shakur, at age 25, has robbed us of one of the most talented and compelling voices of recent years. He embodied just as much for his audience as Kurt Cobain did for his. That is, Tupac Shakur spoke to, and for, many who had grown up within hard realities that mainstream culture and media are loath to understand or respect. His death has left his fans feeling a doubly sharp pain: the loss of a much-esteemed signifier and the loss of a future volume of work that, no doubt, would have proved both brilliant and provocative.

Certainly, Shakur was among the most ingenious and lyrical of the present generation of rappers, often pitting his dark-toned, staccato cadences against lulling and clever musical backdrops, achieving an effect as memorable for its melodic contours as for its rhythmic verve. In addition, his four albums – *2Pacalypse Now*, *Strictly 4 My N.I.G.G.A.Z.*, *Me Against the World*, and *All Eyez on Me* – ran the full range of rap's thematic and emotional breadth. In the first two albums alone, you could find moments of uncommon tenderness and compassion (the feminine-sympathetic portrayals in 'Brenda's Got a Baby' and 'Keep Ya Head Up'), astute political and social observation ('Trapped,' 'Soulja's Story' and 'I Don't Give a Fuck'), and also declarations of fierce black-against-black anger and brutality (the thug-life anthems 'Last Wordz' and '5 Deadly Venomz'). What made this disconcerting mix especially notable was how credible it all seemed. Shakur could sing in respectful praise and defense of women, then turn around and deliver a harangue about 'bitches' and 'ho's' – or could boast of his gangster prowess one moment, then condemn the same doomed mentality in another track – and you never doubted that he felt and meant every word he declaimed. Does that make him sound like a confused man? Yes – to say the least. But Shakur was also a man willing to own up to and examine his many contradictory inclinations, and I suspect that quality, more than any other, is what made him such a vital and empathetic voice for so many of his fans.

Shakur was also a clearly gifted actor (his first performance, as an adolescent, was in a stage production of *A Raisin in the Sun*) – though he wasn't especially well-served by mediocre young-blacks-coming-of-age films such as *Poetic Justice* and *Above the Rim*. The 1992 film *Juice* (his first) wasn't much better, though it contains Shakur's best performance to date (two other films, *Gang Related* and *Gridlock'd*, are set for release in 1997). In *Juice*, Shakur played Bishop – a young man anxious to break out of the dead-end confinements of his community who settles on an armed robbery as the means of proving his stature, his 'juice.' Once Bishop has a gun in his hand, everything about his character, his life, his fate, changes. He shoots anything that obstructs him – including some lifelong friends. He kills simply to kill as if by doing so he will eventually shoot through the one thing that hurts him the most: his own troubled heart. 'I am crazy,' he tells a character at one point. 'But you know what else? I don't give a fuck.' Shakur speaks the final line with such sure and frightening coldness, it is impossible to know whether he informed his delivery with his own experience or whether he was simply uncovering a disturbing but liberating personal ethos.

Tupac's last trip – the car into which Tupac's assassin fired thirteen shots, stands in desolate isolation behind a Las Vegas Police Department cordon.

But it was with his two final recordings – *Me Against the World* and *All Eyez on Me* – that Shakur achieved what is probably his best-realized and most enduring work. The two albums are major statements about violence, social realism, self-willed fate and unappeasable pain, though it's as if they were made by two different, almost opposing sensibilities. Or they could be read as the combined, sequential statements of one man's growth – except in Shakur's case, it appears that the growth moved from hard-earned enlightenment to hard-bitten virulence. *Me Against the World* (released after he was shot in a 1994 robbery and during his imprisonment for sexually abusing a woman) was the eloquent moment when Shakur paused to examine all the trouble and violence in his life and measured not only his own complicity in that trouble but how such actions spilled into, and poisoned, the world around him.

On *All Eyez on Me*, released a year later on Death Row Records, Shakur gave way to almost all the darkness he had ever known – and did so brilliantly. Indeed, *Eyez* is one of the most melodically and texturally inventive albums that rap has ever produced – and also one of the most furious. Tracks like 'California Love' and 'Can't C Me' are rife with sheer beauty and exuberance, and even some of the more dangerous or brooding songs ('Heartz of Men,' '2 of Amerikaz Most Wanted,' 'Life Goes On,' 'Only God Can Judge Me,' 'Got My Mind Made Up') boast gorgeous surfaces over their pure hearts of stone. On both albums, in song after song Shakur came up against the same terrible realization: He could see his death bearing down on top of him, but he didn't know how to step out of its unrelenting way. So he stood there waiting and while he waited, he made one of rap's few full-length masterpieces, *Eyez*.

The hardest-hitting, most eventful song of the *Eyez* project – and possibly of Shakur's career – appears as the B side on the 'California Love' single: a track called 'Hit 'Em Up.' According to many in the rap community, the song is an attack aimed (mainly) at Sean 'Puffy' Combs' Bad Boy label, (specifically) at recording artist Biggie

114

Smalls, who records for the label. In the last couple of years, these figures had become arch-rivals of Marion 'Suge' Knight, owner and co-founder of Death Row Records, and Shakur indicated that he suspected they were involved in his 1994 shooting. As a result, 'Hit 'Em Up' was much more than just a song – it was Shakur's salvo of revenge and warning. 'I fucked your bitch you fat motherfucker,' he says, addressing Biggie Smalls as the track opens, referring to a rumour about B.I.G.'s wife and Shakur. But that boast is trite compared with what follows: 'Who shot me?' he barks, and then answers, 'But you punks didn't finish. Now you're about to feel the wrath of a menace, nigga.' A minute later, Shakur steps up his rage a couple notches. 'You want to fuck with us, you little young-ass motherfuckers?' he rails. 'You better back the fuck up, or you get smacked the fuck up . . . We ain't singin', we bringin' drama . . . We gonna kill all you motherfuckers . . . Fuck Biggie; fuck Bad Boy . . . And if you want to be down with Bad Boy, then fuck you, too . . . Die slow, motherfucker . . . . You think you mob, nigga? We the motherfucking mob . . . You niggas mad because our staff got guns in their motherfucking belts . . . We Bad-Boy killers / We kill 'em.'

I have never heard anything remotely like Tupac Shakur's breathless performance on this track in all my years of listening to pop music. It contains a truly remarkable amount of rage and aggression – enough to make anything in punk seem flaccid by comparison. Indeed, 'Hit 'Em Up' crosses the line from art and metaphor to real-life jeopardy. On one level you might think Shakur was telling his enemies: We will kill you competitively, commercially. But listen to the stunning last 30 seconds of the track. It's as if Shakur were saying: 'Here I am – your enemy and your target. Come and get me, or watch me get you first.'

So: a man sings about death and killing, and then the man is killed. There is a great temp-

tation for many to view one event as the result of the other. And in Tupac Shakur's case, there are some grounds for this assessment: He did more than sing about violence; he also participated in a fair amount of it. As Shakur himself once said, in words that *Time* magazine appropriated for its headline covering his murder: WHAT GOES 'ROUND COMES 'ROUND. Still, I think it would be a great disservice to dismiss Shakur's work and life with any quick and glib headline summations. It's like burying the man without hearing him.

I suspect also that Shakur's death will be cited as justification for yet another campaign against hardcore rap and troublesome lyrics. It has become one of the perennial causes of the last decade. In 1989, the FBI got into the act by contacting Priority Records to note the bureau's official distaste for the ground-breaking group NWA's unyielding, in-your-face song 'Fuck tha Police.' In 1990, *Newsweek* ran a cover story titled 'Rap Rage, Yo!' calling rap a 'streetwise music,' rife with 'ugly macho boasting,' and three years later the magazine reiterated its disdain with a Snoop Doggy Dogg cover that posed the question: WHEN IS RAP 2 VIOLENT? In 1992, conservative interest groups and riled police associations pressured Warner Bros. Records to delete 'Cop Killer' from Ice-T's *Body Count* album (subsequently, Warner's separated itself from Ice-T). And in 1995, moralist activists William Bennett and C. DeLores Tucker succeeded in pressuring Warner's to break the label's ties with Interscope Records, due to Interscope's support of a handful of hardcore rap artists – including Tupac Shakur. You can almost hear Bennett and Tucker preparing their next line of argument: 'Look what has come from the depraved world of rap: real-life murder on the streets! Isn't it time to stop the madness?' It isn't altogether unlikely that such a campaign might have some effect – at least on wary major labels. Already, according to reports in the *Los Angeles Times*, some record executives are

115

Tupac Amaru Shakur (16 June, 1971 - 13 September, 1996).

questioning whether any further associations with rap and its bad image will be worth the heat that labels will have to face.

It is true, of course, that certain figures in the rap community have taken their inflammatory rhetoric and violent posturing to an insane, genuinely deadly level. It is also saddening and horrible to witness such lethal rivalry among so many young men with such innovative talents – especially when these artists and producers share the sort of common social perspective that should bring them together. Death Row and Bad Boy could have a true and positive impact on black America's political life – but that can't happen if the companies seek merely to increase their own standing by tearing away at perceived-enemy black opponents. From such actions, no meaningful or valuable victories are to be had.

At the same time, there's nothing meaningful or valuable to be gained by censoring hardcore rap – or at least that course would offer no real solutions to the very real problems that much of the best (and worst) rap signifies. For that matter, such a course would only undermine much of rap's con-

siderable contribution to popular culture. Rap began as a means of black self-expression in the late Seventies, and as it matured into the wide-ranging art form of hip hop, it also became a vital means of black achievement and invention. In the process, rap began to report on and reveal many social realities and attitudes that most other arts and media consistently ignored – that is, rap gave voice and presence to truths that almost no other form of art or reportage was willing to accommodate. Works like NWA's 'Fuck tha Police' and *Niggaz4Life* may have seemed shocking to some observers, but NWA didn't invent the resentment and abuse that they sang about. Nor did Ice-T, Ice Cube, or the Geto Boys invent the ghetto-rooted gang warfare and drive-by shootings that they sometimes rapped about. These conditions and dispositions existed long before rap won popular appeal (also long before the explosive L.A. riots of 1992), and if hardcore rap were to disappear tomorrow, these conditions would still exist.

What disturbed so many about rap – what it is actually deemed guilty for – is how vividly it represented the circumstances that the music's lyrics and voices illuminated. It wasn't pleasant to hear about murderous rage and sexist debasement – to many, in fact, rap came across as an actual threat. As one journalist and author friend told me when I recommended that he listen to Snoop Doggy Dogg's *Doggystyle*, 'I don't buy records by people who want to kill me.' Interestingly, such music fans didn't seem to brandish the same scrupulous distaste when rock groups like the Rolling Stones, the Sex Pistols, The Clash and several others also sang about murder, violence, rage and cultural ruin.

Tupac Shakur, like many other rappers, intoned about a world that he either lived in or witnessed – in Shakur's case, in fact, there was a good deal less distance between lyrics and life than is the case with most pop-music figures. Sometimes, Shakur saw clearly the causes for his pain and anger, and aspired to rise above being doomed by that delimitation; sometime he succumbed to his worst predilections. And far too often he participated in actions that only spread the ruin: He was involved in at least two shootings, numerous vicious physical confrontations, and several rancid verbal assaults; he was also convicted and served time for sexual abuse. Moreover, he probably made a certain element of the rap world genuinely dangerous by embodying the ideal that 'real' rappers had to live the lethal lives they sang about. In the end, perhaps Shakur's worst failing was to see too many black men and women with backgrounds similar to his as his real and mortal enemies.

But listen to Tupac Shakur before you put his life away. You will hear the story of a man who grew up feeling as if he didn't fit into any of the worlds around him – feeling that he had been pushed out from not only the white world but also the black neighborhoods in which he grew up. You will also hear the man's clear intelligence and genius: his gifts for sharp, smart, funny perceptions, and for lyrical and musical proficiency and elegance. And, of course, you will hear some downright ugly stuff – threats, rants, curses and admitted memories that would be too much for many hearts to bear. Mainly, though, you will hear the tortured soul-searching of a man who grew up with and endured so much pain, rancor and loss that he could never truly overcome it all, could never turn his troubled heart right-side up despite all his gifts and all the acceptance he eventually received.

In case anybody wants to dismiss this man's reality too readily, consider this: We are experiencing a time when many of our leaders are telling us that we are vulnerable to people who live in another America – an America made up of those who are fearsome, irresponsible, lazy or just plain bad; an America that needs to be taught hard lessons. And so we have elected to teach these others their hard lessons. In the years immediately ahead, as a result of recent political actions, something like one million kids will be pushed into conditions of poverty and all that will come with it – including some of the horrible recourses left to the hopeless. Imagine how many Tupac Shakurs will emerge from this adventure – all those smart kids who, despite whatever talents they will possess, will not be able to overcome the awfulness of their youth and who will end up with blood on their hands or chest, or both.

Indeed, what goes 'round comes 'round. The America we are making for others is ultimately the America we will make for ourselves. It will not be on the other side of town. It will be right outside our front doors.

RAP WARS
by Dana Kennedy
Did The Violence Claim Another Life?

'It's cool to do hardcore shit and be that way, but . . . death is a whole different thing, man. Especially if it didn't have to happen, you know?'
— Dr. Dre, minutes after hearing of the death of Tupac Shakur

Death is not normally a whole different thing for Sergeant Kevin Manning, a homicide investigator for the Las Vegas Metropolitan Police Department. But the fatal shooting of 25-year-old gangsta-rap star Tupac Shakur, gunned down in front of about 45 people on a Saturday night in the heart of Las Vegas, is harder to solve than most of the 121 other homicides that have occurred in the city so far this year. The question is simple: Who did it and why? Theories abound – it was gang related, it was drug related, it was bad blood between East Coast and West Coast rappers – but there are no definite answers . . . yet. 'It's unbelievably frustrating,' says Manning, in his office in the shabby northern end of the city. 'It's like trying to drive through a stone wall.'

That wall went up on 7 September, just seconds after Shakur, sitting in the passenger seat of a car driven by Death Row CEO Marion 'Suge' Knight on Flamingo Road, was shot four times by one of four men in a white Cadillac. (He died from his wounds on 13 September.) Knight's black BMW was followed by a convoy of about ten cars; there were dozens of people milling about the street. 'But nobody saw anything,' says Manning grimly. 'Strange, huh?'

Not really, in the pugnacious, vicious, often lethal world of gangsta rap. But then, Manning and the two detectives working on the case probably never parsed the lyrics of Tupac Amaru Shakur, especially songs like 1995's 'If I Die 2Nite': 'I ain't happy here / I hope they bury me and send me to my rest / Headlines reading Murdered to Death, my last breath.' His music vividly describes the violence and sense of surrealism that hold sway when ghetto kids turn into millionaire rappers who live – and sometimes die – by Godfather-esque rules. 'No one expects Sly Stallone to be Rambo, but they expect Tupac or Ice-T to be who their persona is,' says African-American scholar and playwright David Trotman. 'To have street credibility, you have to be real. And I guess this is the ultimate street credibility, to give your life for it.'

When it comes to ultimate street cred, however, the prize still goes to Suge Knight, 31, the widely feared head of Death Row. A former gang member from the crime-ridden L.A. suburb of Compton who built Death Row into a $100 million-plus business in just four years, Knight and his operations are now embroiled in the investigation into Shakur's death. A shrewd businessman who signed Shakur to his label last year just before springing the young rapper from prison and whose artists include Snoop Doggy Dogg and Tha Dogg Pound, Knight is also involved in the feud between L.A.-based Death Row and New York-based Bad Boy Entertainment – a feud that has often divided the $800 million rap industry. Earlier this month, the two camps brawled at the MTV Awards in New York. It's because of Knight, who is 6'4" and weighs about 315 pounds, and his strong-arm tactics, many say, that no one dares to talk about the Shakur case.

Mention Knight's name, and Las Vegas police sergeant Walter Quering rolls his eyes. Knight owns a gated mansion near Mike Tyson and Wayne Newton on the south-eastern edge of Vegas. Last fall the

LAPD notified the Las Vegas police that Knight had opened a nightclub just off the Strip. (Knight denies ownership.) The bar is called Club 662. 'Look at the dial pad,' says Quering, pointing at his phone. 'The numbers 6-6-2 correspond to M.O.B. – Member of Bloods.'

Knight has been a proud member of the Bloods street gang since growing up in Compton. The interior of Club 662 is blood red, the gang's colors; so is the recently repainted exterior of his childhood home. Rap insiders, who are almost unanimously afraid to allow their names to be used, say Knight rules Death Row absolutely. 'Death Row is run mainly by loyalty, the way things should be with a family,' says a rap-industry exec. 'I respect [Suge's] smarts and what he's been able to create. But it was their way or no way. It's like they learned from gangster movies how to behave.'

By all accounts, Knight conducts himself like a Hollywood version of an old-style don. Knight has been convicted of robbery and assault (1994), has pleaded guilty to a federal weapons charge, and was sued in 1991 by Eazy-E for threatening the now-deceased rapper with baseball bats and pipes during a contract dispute. Knight reportedly boasted of making a record-company president get on his hands and knees and 'walk around like a dog.'

Knight's artists followed his violent lead. Not only did Dogg and Shakur have run-ins with the police – Shakur was convicted of sexually assaulting a twenty-year-old fan; Dogg beat an accessory-to-murder rap this year – but they goaded East Coast rappers as well. Their feud with Bad Boy Entertainment president Sean 'Puffy' Combs, 25, and one of his artists, the Notorious B.I.G., had been simmering at the time of Shakur's death. Shakur, who was shot five times and robbed in a much-talked-about 1994 incident, publicly accused Combs and B.I.G. of setting him up, which they denied. Recently, Shakur bragged on 'Hit 'Em Up' that he slept with B.I.G.'s wife: 'I fucked your bitch, you fat

motherfucker.' Last year, after a Death Row staffer was fatally shot in Atlanta, Knight reportedly blamed the murder on Combs, who promptly hired full-time bodyguards. Combs reportedly denied any connection to the shooting.

At first, many rap stars and execs figured Shakur's shooting was the result of that East Coast/West Coast beef. But within days, speculation turned in other directions. There is talk that the shots were actually aimed at Knight because of his questionable ties. Some wondered whether the shooting was retaliation for a skirmish that Shakur had gotten into with another man during the Tyson heavyweight fight at the MGM Grand earlier that night. 'That was a professional hit,' says a rap industry source. 'That wasn't something that happened that night. That was planned.'

But by whom? The most chilling – and perhaps far-fetched – theory is that Knight himself could be involved. Rumors had been flying that Shakur was eager to leave Death Row, but a label spokesman declined to comment. Sergeant McCurdy wonders aloud why Death Row hasn't offered a reward for the person who brings in Shakur's killer. (Knight could not be reached for comment for this story.) 'They were friends and [Shakur] was Death Row's top-selling artist,' says a source close to Shakur. 'But the only thing I could ask myself: "Is Tupac worth more alive or dead? Was he at his pinnacle?" There's a lot of [his] music in the can and the best stuff has not come out [yet].'

When it comes to unraveling the mystery of Shakur's death, there is plenty to come out yet, too. Maybe it never will. (The 1995 Atlanta murder of Knight's aide Jake Robles has never been solved, nor did police ever arrest a suspect in connection with the 1994 shooting of Shakur.) And in interviews with friends and associates, a complex portrait of the slain rapper emerges. Though Shakur had the words thug life tattooed on his torso, he had studied at Baltimore's prestigious High School of the Performing Arts

119

and never truly lived the hardcore life he glorified. 'If you knew Tupac, you knew he was a true artist,' says former assistant Kendrick Wells.

But throughout his career, Shakur seemed to court danger. 'Tupac always searched for the next level of the game,' says a former associate. 'Where we come from, the negative is just how people live. He had graduated each level. He'd gone from Marin [Marin City, California] to Oakland, to L.A., where it was imagined – and realistically so – to be more dangerous. Then he went to the East Coast, where he kicked it with big-time drug dealers and killers, and the next natural progression was Death Row.'

Shakur was born in 1971, just after his mother, former Black Panther Afeni Shakur, was released from a Bronx prison where she was being held on a bombing charge (she was later acquitted). The rapper never knew who his father was. For a time, Afeni, who kept a vigil at Shakur's deathbed, was addicted to crack. Her son wrote about this in his 1995 Grammy-nominated 'Dear Mama': 'And even as a crack fiend mama / You always was a black queen mama.'

Many believe Shakur badly needed a father figure and was especially vulnerable when Knight ponied up the $1.4 million bond last year to free him from prison pending the appeal of his 1995 sexual-assault conviction. Shakur signed with Death Row, and his first album for the label, *All Eyez on Me*, debuted at Number One on the charts last spring and has sold some five million copies. On the latest *Billboard* album charts, *Eyez* jumped from Number 69 to Number Eighteen. Shakur's already exaggerated B-boy machismo became even more accentuated while at Death Row. 'He got swallowed up by it,' says a longtime friend. 'He was too young to see who was taking advantage of him and who wasn't.'

Sources close to Death Row suggest that

Dr. Dre, the wizard-like rap producer and former gangsta rapper who had founded Death Row with Knight in 1992, was smarter. Dre abruptly left Death Row in March 1996 to form his own label after what had reportedly been months of tension between him and Knight. An ex-Death Row employee hints that Knight often roughed up his own staff when he felt they weren't working up to capacity.' I got away from it just in time, but Tupac unfortunately didn't,' the ex-employee says. 'If he'd lived, he would have made it out. Just like Dre. And you would've seen who he was.'

Enough people apparently saw who he was anyway – even some East Coast rappers. 'I always had love for Tupac,' says Buckshot Da B.D. Eye, a New York-based rap artist and CEO of Duck Down Records, who was invited in July to go to L.A. to work on Shakur's upcoming album, *One Nation*, along with a host of other East Coast rappers. 'This project was Tupac's way of saying there was no real war with the East Coast,' says B.D. Eye.

That was the real Tupac, agrees L.A.-based rapper E-40. 'People say he was a troublemaker; that wasn't true, but trouble had no problem finding him,' says E-40. 'In his life, Tupac uplifted a lot of spirits, and I'm sure he's chilling in heaven right now looking down on us.'

Back on earth, however, the Las Vegas police are not nearly so sanguine. 'We think we know why no one's talking,' says Sergeant McCurdy. 'They all want to take care of it themselves.' Perhaps they will – and maybe then someone else will die. In the end, Dr. Dre sums it up as bluntly as if he were reciting a freshly written lyric. 'Who knows when it's your time?' he says. 'When God says it's your time, you have to go. That's it.'

(Additional reporting by Heidi Siegmund Cuda, Michael Gonzales, and Matt Diehl)

THE NEW TUPAC FANS

by Ruby Bailey

In the parking lot of a west side Detroit school, there's one corner where, residents say, drug deals go down daily.

At the opposite end of the lot, so-called gang bangers have been said to gather, flashing the telltale finger signs of the Bloods and the Crips.

The center of the lot is where the cheerleaders sometimes hold impromptu rehearsals and the Girl Scouts wait to board buses for field trips.

The contradictory uses for this parking lot make it an all-the-more appropriate place to serve as a memorial for Tupac Shakur, the rapper who promoted thug life yet condemned violence, who insulted women but said he loved his mother.

It is here that a group of young African-American men stand about twenty deep, ranging in age from 15 to 47. Shakur's 'If I Die Tonight' pounds from the speakers. They play it over. And over. And over again.

'I'll live eternal / Who shall I fear? / Don't shed a tear for me nigga / I ain't happy here. I hope they bury me and send me to my rest / Headlines readin' murdered to death.'

Meet Shakur's newest fans. They are among those across the country who, while hearing of Shakur's antics in life, never discovered his music until his death a little more than a month ago. These men are now drawn to Shakur's music, they say, because he prophesied so often about his own demise. And with good reason. Shakur, who at 25 had several skirmishes with the law and a prison term for sexual assault under his belt, barely survived a 1994 attempt on his life.

So as the lyrics bounce off the walls of the school building, the words come back to haunt this group of black men, who know others who 'went out the same way' as Shakur, says Maurice Lipscomb, who owns the boom box but not the compact disc that's playing in it. 'The same way: In a hail of gun fire,' says Lipscomb, 29. 'And for no good reason.'

And it's that similarly violent way Shakur died – less than a week after he was ambushed in Las Vegas while riding with Marion 'Suge' Knight of Death Row Records – that has drawn this group and other new converts to the rapper's music.

It is a morbid curiosity, but it is nonetheless fuelling business. Sales of Shakur's most recent album, *All Eyez on Me*, tripled within a week of his shooting. Within two weeks, the album jumped from Number 69 to Number 6 on the *Billboard* pop chart. Album sales peaked the week of September 22 at 76,000. The week ending October 6, the album sold 62,000 copies, according to Soundscan, the Hartsdale, NY firm that monitors music sales.

Shakur's death is also expected to propel his November 5 posthumous release, *Makaveli – The Don Killuminati – The 7 Day Theory*, to debut at Number One on the charts. Shakur also filmed two movies, *Gang Related* and *Gridlock'd*, before his death. They are scheduled to be released in January.

Increased record sales after the death of a singer are nothing new in the industry, but there are those who are willing to bet Shakur's afterlife success will be long lasting, due in part to those who are not fans.

'They're going to gravitate to it,' says Dr. Dre, disc jockey on New York's HOT 97-FM and former host of *Yo! MTV Raps*. Dr. Dre (not to be confused with Dr. Dre, former head of Death Row Records) attended the Nation of Islam's recent Rap Day of Atonement in New York, a memorial of sorts for Shakur and the violent urban culture in which he lived and died.

Requests for Shakur's music have 'laid back a little bit' at the station, says Dr. Dre.

'But it's always going to be more popular. He was Tupac. And more people are coming to know just who Tupac really, really was.'

Local record stores report that it's those who never purchased and seldom heard the rapper's music who caused the sell-out stampede after his death. Now the stores are restocked, and the albums are selling briskly, again to those just discovering Shakur's rap renditions of thug life.

'I just can't explain it, but I've just had a need to buy his music,' says Sharron Clark, a 32-year-old accountant, as she prepared to purchase the album in a downtown record store. 'I've never supported that kind of music, but there was something so tragic about the way he died, something so weird about the way he always said he would die, just like that, that made me buy it. It's almost like I'm looking for answers.'

Chico 'the Quiet Storm' Hicks, a local nightclub disc jockey, agrees. 'The way he was struck down will pretty much guarantee sales for a long time to come. People liked him, but they didn't talk about him as much as they do now. He didn't seem to affect people with the drive he does now.'

The sure-to-come hype for the new album release, the movies and any yet-to-be-released videos Death Row Records has on hand will ensure Shakur – or at least his label – sales for what could be years to come, says Mike Bernacchi, professor of marketing at the University of Detroit-Mercy.

> **'His death was a lot like his life; controversial, attention getting. The song lives beyond the singer.'
> — Mike Bernacchi**

'His death was a lot like his life: controversial, attention-getting,' says Bernacchi. 'The song lives beyond the singer. He may make more money in the hereafter.'

For some, the question isn't how long he will be remembered, but which side of the multifaceted rapper people will remember.

Just days after his death, Death Row released his single and video, 'I Ain't Mad at Cha,' which showed the rapper dying in a drive-by shooting. Once in heaven, Shakur sings to a friend who abandoned thug life, supporting his decision.

Had Death Row allowed 'I Ain't Mad at Cha' to be his final release, 'the last Tupac would have been the angelic Tupac,' says Kevin Taylor, music researcher for Black Entertainment Television (BET).

'Unfortunately that's not where the label is going to leave it,' says Taylor, '"I Ain't Mad at Cha" won't be the last image. He's going to come back with this gangsta knucklehead stuff.'

Taylor describes the upcoming album as 'gruff' and says it revisits the East Coast-West Coast rap division and insults rappers Sean 'Puffy' Combs and Dr. Dre, the former head of Death Row.

'Five years from now, he will be a reference point,' says Taylor. 'The question, and perhaps the problem is, what will he refer to, the glamor of thug life or the nonsense of it?'

DEADLY BUSINESS
by Dana Kennedy

Although more than a dozen people, including two women, have confessed to the September 7 shooting of rapper Tupac Shakur in Las Vegas, his murder remains unsolved. Las Vegas police – and even homicide detectives in Compton, California, who have been investigating the case – say those claims are from bogus publicity seekers and admit they have no real leads. 'We've heard every theory, but we don't know anything,' says Lieutenant Danny Sneed, seated in the bunker-like headquarters of the Compton police. After twelve shootings in Compton, some in direct retaliation for the attack on Shakur, the police arrested 23 local gang members in a predawn sweep – but there are still no official suspects. 'It's a mystery,' says Sneed.

It's no mystery, counter current and former Compton Crips, only one of whom will give his name, who say they know the shooter and claim police could crack the case if they wanted. The story on the street in Compton – admittedly just one of the theories that abound in the Shakur case – is that the shooting was done by a Crip in connection with the fight involving Shakur and Death Row Records president Marion 'Suge' Knight (long associated with the Crips' rivals, the Bloods) in Las Vegas after the Mike Tyson-Bruce Seldon fight at the MGM Grand.

'The cops don't want to find out who did it – they think whoever did it did them a favor,' says aspiring rapper Jerome 'Butter' Wilson, nineteen, who says he has been a Crip on the deceptively placid-looking streets of Compton since age nine and served time in the California Youth Authority. 'Tupac shot a cop, after all. [In 1993, he was charged with, but not convicted of, shooting two Atlanta police officers.] They're just happy someone took Tupac out for them.'

Far from being a mystery, the identity of the killer is well-known to some, claims Wilson. While his story could be street hyperbole, Wilson spouts specific details about the case – including the type of gun with which Shakur was shot – that police have not released publicly, and at least one California police source grudgingly concedes he may be telling the truth. According to Wilson, who's with the In-Hood Crips (another subgroup of the same gang), the killer belongs to the Southside Compton Crips – and it isn't Orlando Anderson, a Southside Crip who was questioned on 2 October in connection with Shakur's shooting, but later released.

Wilson claims that two people he knows were with the gunman in the white Cadillac with California plates when it pulled up alongside Knight's black BMW 750 sedan following the clash at the MGM Grand. In Wilson's version, Knight, 31, and Shakur, 25, encountered half a dozen members of the Crips with whom they had scuffled ringside before the Tyson bout. 'They were out to get Suge and Tupac got in the way,' says Wilson. 'Tupac beat one guy up, then the guy went and told his homeboys. They got strapped and got in the Cadillac and ended up killing a million-dollar man. Tupac wasn't really a gang-banger, but you can't go up against the hood like that.'

Whether or not Wilson's tale is true, he is right on one account. When it comes to the nearly $1 billion-a-year rap industry, it doesn't matter if you're a superstar like Shakur, a ruthless, behind-the-scenes kingpin like Knight, or just a local gang member with a demo tape like Wilson – it's risky to go up against the hood. Shakur's 13 September death exposed just how deadly – if phenomenally profitable – the business of rap can be. (Shakur's posthumous album,

123

Tupac's visual legacy lives on in this striking piece of New York street art.

The Don Killuminati: The 7 Day Theory, a coarsely produced, cobbled-together effort, debuted on the *Billboard* charts at Number One and has sold more than a million copies since its release November 5.)

But most chilling, Shakur's murder, while it may be spurring a move toward more positive, less violent rap, also highlights how even success and fame cannot always insulate rap's biggest powers from the violent culture that spawned and, in many cases, still surrounds them. 'This incident not only has people in the industry thinking, it has black kids thinking, it has mothers thinking,' says New York rapper Chuck D of Public Enemy. 'I've never seen a situation like this in the black community over a cultural person. [Tupac's] almost like Elvis.' (And there are even fervent fans who believe Tupac lives. Chuck D, echoing postings on the Internet, calls Shakur's death an 'unclear incident. But until Tupac shows up, we'll just have to assume he's dead.')

If Tupac is like Elvis, then Suge Knight, of course, was his Colonel Parker. But Knight too is struggling with the ghosts of his not-so-distant past. His Corleone-esque control

of the thriving Death Row Records began to unravel with the acrimonious departure of the label's co-founder and creative force, Dr. Dre, in March and the murder of Shakur, the label's biggest star. To make matters worse, the FBI reportedly is investigating the label for alleged gang connections and racketeering. At press time, Knight, who could not be reached for comment for this story, remains in L.A. County Jail awaiting a ruling on four possible parole violations (stemming from a 1992 assault on two aspiring rappers at a Hollywood recording studio) and Death Row's future is in doubt.

While most people in the rap industry say much of the so-called feuding between East Coast and West Coast rappers is no more than hype to sell records, the thug life mythologized by Shakur and other gangsta rappers is still very real. 'You haven't seen the last of this violence,' warns a former Compton Crip who did not want to be identified. 'Suge's a Blood. They bring no money back into the hood. He's become an untouchable nigger. Tupac was the intended hit. The idea is to kill everything around Suge. They want him to die slowly. Tupac was his boy. Everyone who is making Suge money is in danger.'

The sleek corporate offices of Death Row Records look out over Wilshire Boulevard in Beverly Hills, less than twenty miles from Compton but worlds apart. Since Knight founded the label in 1992, he claims it has sold more than 26 million records and grossed in excess of $170 million. But gang members like Jerome Wilson can still remember Knight when he hung out with the Bloods in Compton and was an usher at the neighborhood Cineplex. 'I've known that fool since back when he had no money,' says Wilson. But now that Knight does have money, and more than most can imagine, many of his former friends in the hood resent him. 'A lot of motherfuckers are mad because guys like him aren't real anymore,' says Wilson. 'Us rappers out here rap about the struggle we're going through. That's why the first album you make is always the best, because it's real.'

That may be so, but Death Row plans to make plenty of money off its late star. (Not to mention how his murder boosted sales of Shakur's previous releases – for example, his previous album *All Eyez on Me* re-entered *Billboard*'s Top Ten.) Besides *Killuminati*, Shakur had recorded enough material before his death for at least three more albums. 'With Tupac dead, they stand to make more money than they ever dreamed possible from him,' says one rap industry source who feared giving his name. 'Did you see the speed with which they got Tupac's video off to MTV? Three days after he died? The future of Death Row has never looked brighter.'

Maybe. Maybe not. Knight, the brains – and, at six foot four and 330 pounds, the brawn – behind Death Row, is behind bars for the time being. Gangsta godfather Dr. Dre, whose breakthrough hit with NWA was 'Fuck tha Police,' has severed all ties with Death Row and, with songs like the new 'Been There, Done That' on his just-released *Dr. Dre Presents . . . The Aftermath*, is pro-

claiming that he has renounced his violent gangsta past. As a result, Death Row Records, like the rap industry itself, is at a crossroads. The label's only real remaining stars are Snoop Doggy Dogg, who just released *Tha Doggfather*, which debuted at Number One and has sold more than half a million copies, and Tha Dogg Pound. Death Row has signed such unlikely future stars as has-been pop-rapper turned wannabe gangsta MC Hammer, and eighteen-year-old Gina Longo. Longo, the only white performer signed to the label, is the daughter of Lawrence Longo, the deputy DA of L.A. County who, perhaps not so coincidentally, recommended a plea bargain for Knight last year in the assault case. (Longo has since been under investigation by the DA's office for conflict of interest.) 'When Dre left Death Row, that was the end, everybody knew it,' says an industry source who does not want to be identified because he fears Knight. 'No Dre, no Death Row. The fact that they had Snoop and Tupac kept them in the game . . . but it was all about the masterful influence of Dre and his creative skills.'

Even if Death Row, which, after all, is now calling itself the 'new and untouchable Death Row,' manages to stay in the game, it may never regain the kind of prominence and Godfather-like swagger of the Tupac era. It may be replaced, if not by a kinder and gentler rap culture, then by a savvier, more sophisticated one. 'It was sad what happened with Tupac, because he had something going,' says Yo Yo, a popular and respected L.A.-based female rap artist whose fourth solo album, *Total Control*, was just released on EastWest Records. 'He could have moved on. But it was his choice to stay in that game. Like Dr. Dre is [moving on], and people need to see that. Here's this guy who was once considered to be the hardest gangsta rapper from the group NWA, and now he's like: "You got guns, I got straps. It's time to move on. You can't keep dwelling on the same shit."'

Dr. Dre's shedding of his gangsta skins

may be one of the first signs that West Coast rap is slowly evolving from its hardcore origins. 'It's too early to tell which direction the music will take because [Tupac's] death just happened in September,' says Big Jon, creative director at EMI Music Publishing. 'But from the inside, I can say people are more aware now, more conscious. I think you'll see people like Snoop coming out with straight party jams. People will see how you can't take nothing for granted.'

But it is on the East Coast where some of the smoothest entrepreneurs in rap are laying claim to the next generation. And none are cannier than 26-year-old Sean 'Puffy' Combs, the head of Bad Boy Entertainment in New York City. Combs has long played a kind of politic Jay Leno to his longtime rival Suge Knight's cranky David Letterman. 'I'm not a gangster,' insists Combs, even though he and Bad Boy's Notorious B.I.G. (who declined to comment) have long and loudly feuded with Shakur and Knight. 'I never professed to be that. We never made any negative statements toward Tupac or Death Row. We never made negative records, we never did anything. We just try to make positive moves and make music.'

Combs admits that the culture of the rap industry, no matter how powerful the participants, often still mirrors rough street life. In 1995, at a birthday party in Atlanta, Jake Robles, a friend of Knight's, was shot and killed. Knight blamed Combs and his entourage, though Combs denied any involvement. And at last month's hip hop conference in Miami, shots were fired at a party given by Heavy D's Uptown Records. 'I've been in a lot of parties where shots rang out, so it wasn't like nothing I was new to,' says Combs. 'A lot of time in parties, urban parties, shots ring out. It's a sad thing, but it has nothing to do with the music. It's the environment.'

That environment, Combs says (perhaps a bit disingenuously, considering all the money he's made off of gangsta rap), is what he hopes to change with his booming Bad Boy Entertainment – and a reported $75 million deal with Arista may provide ample incentive to toe the line. The word hood isn't used as much in New York, but Combs claims to be funnelling some of his company's profits back into the inner city. He is only too happy to provide a list of the projects he plans, casting himself as something approaching the Mother Teresa of rap. He says he's buying a building in Harlem to house his year-old outreach organization for inner-city kids, called Daddy's House Social Program. (Combs boasts that he is donating more than twenty percent of his gross to Daddy's House.) 'My company right now is 100 percent black,' says Combs. 'And it's 100 percent people who didn't have any prior experience. People that just needed a chance, just like me when I got my foot in the door.'

Monica Lynch, longtime president of New York-based Tommy Boy Records, says rap needs that kind of fresh blood. 'I think that musically and creatively rap has reached an impasse and things sound a little bit stale right now,' says Lynch. 'There are a lot of people out there bored with rap, and there need to be musical innovations, new types of musical hybrids in rap.'

Back in Compton, and eating heartily from a cafeteria tray laden with macaroni and cheese, chicken wings, apple pie, and grape soda while his beeper goes off every few minutes, Jerome Wilson wonders who will help him get his foot in the door. He has a demo tape but is not sure how to shop it around. Plus he's ambivalent about what he sees as selling out. 'Don't kid yourself; a lot of these rappers aren't really gangsters,' says Wilson, who claims he's 'been shot three times, stabbed. These guys talk like they're living the life, but all they're doing is getting rich off people in the ghetto.'

Living the life for many high-profile rappers actually means wearing the best Versace and Moschino, downing Cristal, checking their Skypagers, and dialing up their tiny $1,000 StarTAC cell phones. But as

Tupac, Hammer and Snoop at the 23rd Annual American Music Awards, January 1996.

in the case of Shakur, or even less promi- nent rappers like his backup singer Yafeu Fula, nineteen, (a witness to Tupac's shoot- ing whose own November 10 murder remains unsolved), their money won't always protect them. Said Reverend Jesse Jackson after Shakur's death, 'Sometimes the lure of violent culture is so magnetic that even when one overcomes it with material success, it continues to call.'

In the meantime, the trail leading to the identity of Shakur's killer and his motivation for gunning down the star seems to be growing cold. Wilson says he doubts the killer will be caught anytime soon – if ever. 'Right now he's lying as low as a leprechaun with his legs cut off,' says Wilson. 'He's not talking and nobody else is talking either.'

Shakur's fellow West Coast rapper Ice Cube rejects the notion that the young star was killed because of the kind of music he performed. It all comes back to the dangers of going up against the hood, even when you're a big star. 'Gangsta rap didn't kill Tupac,' Ice Cube says. 'His music didn't come out of the speaker and kill him. Anybody can get murdered. Anyone can die.'

(Additional reporting by Heidi Siegmund Cuda, Beth Johnson, Billy Johnson Jr., Tiarra Mukherjee, Tom Sinclair, and Frank Swertlow)

THE TUPAC SHAKUR MURDER INVESTIGATION
One Year Later Still No Arrests
by Bryan Robinson

No leads, no suspects, no arrests. One year after rap artist Tupac Shakur died from gunshot wounds suffered during a drive-by shooting in Las Vegas, his murder remains unsolved.

'The latest developments [in this case] are that there are no developments,' said Sergeant Kevin Manning, who is leading the investigation for the Las Vegas Metro Police. 'There is nothing going on with this case. No suspects. Nothing.'

Since his death, there have been many rumors about why Shakur was murdered. One of the most prevalent was that Shakur was a victim of an ongoing war between two Los Angeles-based gangs, the Bloods and the Crips. Shakur associated with several members of the Bloods, and his boss and mentor at Death Row Records, Marion 'Suge' Knight, also had ties to the Bloods. Another theory was that Shakur died as a result of a professional rivalry between the West Coast's most prominent rap label, Death Row Records, and the East Coast's most successful hip hop label, Bad Boy Entertainment. However, Las Vegas investigators say these theories have led nowhere.

'There have been a lack of witnesses and a lack of evidence,' said Sergeant Manning. 'Without those two things, it makes it [the investigation] kind of difficult.'

But some of Shakur's friends and relatives say that the Las Vegas police department has purposely dragged its feet. 'It was clear to me from day one that the Las Vegas police never had any intention of solving the case of my son's murder,' Shakur's mother, Afeni, told the May 1997 issue of Vibe magazine. These critics allege that the police were not fans of Tupac, who had been arrested eight times between 1991 and 1996 and whose lyrics sometimes promoted violence against police. Shakur had served eight months in a New York jail for sexual abuse in 1995 and had been arrested in 1993 for allegedly shooting two off-duty police officers in Atlanta. (These charges were later dropped because of lack of evidence.)

Because of his criminal record and association with gang members, critics say, Las Vegas police may see Tupac Shakur as nothing more than a famous gangster who died living the 'Thug Life' he had tattooed on his stomach.

'I've been told by the police that who he [Shakur] was has nothing to do with the investigation,' said Cathy Scott, author of the recently published book, *The Killing of Tupac Shakur* and a reporter for *The Las Vegas Sun*. 'One officer told me that "Just because Tupac was famous does not mean we're going to assign more detectives than usual. Tupac was a young black man in America, and young black men get murdered."'

However, Scott compared Shakur's case to another young black man who also was murdered, Ennis Cosby, the son of Bill Cosby. 'There was a whole police blitz on that case,' Scott said. 'There were at least twenty cops and detectives searching for Ennis Cosby's killer, and they got their man. [Mikhail Markashev, the man accused of killing Ennis Cosby, is scheduled to go on trial in the spring of 1998.] In Tupac's case, there has been two detectives, one sergeant, and one criminologist assigned to the case.'

Ennis Cosby, an aspiring teacher, had a wholesome image and was the son of a beloved comedian who was once considered 'America's Dad' by fans of *The Cosby Show*. Shakur was a gangsta rapping renegade whose mother was a member of the Black Panthers. Both Cosby and Shakur were young black men killed in the prime of their lives. However, as suggested by Scott and other critics, the progress in these two murder investigations has differed because of Tupac Shakur's reputation. Police may see Shakur's murder as less tragic, less senseless, than Ennis Cosby's murder.

The Las Vegas investigators say that nothing indicates that Shakur's murder was gang-related. However, many critics say that the murder indeed was a gang shooting. (According to the Las Vegas police's 1996 annual report on gangs in Clark County, 122 out of the 484 gang-related cases the police investigated were sent to the district attorney's office for prosecution. This is a success rate of slightly better than 25 percent among gang-related cases for the Las Vegas Metro Police. Shakur's murder may have been among the 75 percent of the gang-related cases that never made it to prosecution. But the Las Vegas police have been successful in solving general homicides. According to the most recent department statistics, Las Vegas police have solved 62 out of the 106 reported homicides in Clark County in 1997. This is a success rate of approximately 58 percent among general homicides.)

Tupac Shakur was shot four times in the chest as he rode in a car driven by Suge Knight on September 7, 1996. He and Knight had attended a boxing match between Mike Tyson and Bruce Seldon at Las Vegas's MGM Grand Hotel and were on their way to a party at Knight's Las Vegas

> **'I believe that everything you do bad comes back to you. So everything that I do that's bad, I'm going to suffer for it. But in my heart, I believe what I'm doing is right.'**
> **— Tupac**

club when the shooting occurred. Just before they left the MGM Grand, Shakur, Knight, and their entourage from Death Row Records were involved in a fist-fight with Orlando Anderson, a reputed member of Knight's alleged rivals, the Crips. No one really knows how the altercation started, but it was captured on hotel security cameras. Shakur and Knight left after hotel security guards stopped the melee.

An entourage of about ten vehicles with Death Row Record employees was following Knight's car at the time of the shooting. Police say that despite all these witnesses, no one has admitted seeing the shooting or triggerman. Shakur died on 13 September 1996. And Knight, who was only grazed by the bullets, told ABC's *Primetime Live* during an interview this year that he did not know who shot Shakur, and that even if he knew, he would not tell the police. Knight is currently serving a nine-year sentence for violating probation for his involvement in the altercation just before the shooting. (At the time of the incident, Knight was on probation for a variety of weapons and assault charges.)

Despite his ties to the Crips and his fight with Shakur, Orlando Anderson is not considered a suspect in Shakur's murder by Las Vegas investigators. They claim that Anderson could not have shot Shakur because he was still being questioned at the MGM Grand about his melee with Shakur at the time of the shooting.

However, Los Angeles police familiar with Anderson's alleged gang history reportedly consider him a suspect in Shakur's murder. According to Cathy Scott, some officials within the Los Angeles Police Department feel that the Las Vegas police have blown the Tupac Shakur case and that Anderson is 'their man.' Afeni Shakur also holds Anderson responsible for her son's murder; she has filed a wrongful death suit against him. Anderson himself filed a suit on 8 September against Shakur's estate, seeking damages for assault and battery from the melee.

'I'm not a cop, and I'm not pretending to solve this murder, but it seems that some very unusual things have happened with this investigation,' said Scott. 'For example, the crime scene was not secured for the first twenty minutes after the shooting. There were no helicopters to look after the area. Two witnesses who were riding in cars behind Tupac's car, Frank Alexander and Rob Stein [who were associates of Shakur], have said that they have not even been called by the police. Meanwhile, the police have said that no one is coming forward with any information. It seems that both sides are waiting for the other to make the first move.'

Nonetheless, some people are not surprised by the lack of progress in Tupac Shakur's murder investigation. 'I don't think any of his [Tupac's] people at Death Row seem very motivated [to talk to the police about the murder],' said James Bernard, executive editor of *XXL*, a new magazine on hip hop. 'After all, a lot of them are under federal investigation. Unfortunately, and this is not an excuse, but what happened to people like Tupac and Biggie Smalls [also known as Christopher Wallace, Tupac's reported professional rival who also died during a drive-by shooting in March 1997] happens to black men all the time every day. The mindset is that you don't go to the cops.'

In his life and death, Tupac Shakur has been a victim of both his reputation and this gangsta code of silence by his associates. Police say his entourage refuses to cooperate, showing more loyalty to a street code than to a slain friend. Critics of the investigation say the police see Shakur as a dead criminal, a thug with a long arrest record who gained notoriety by rapping anti-police lyrics and glamorizing the gangsta lifestyle. The police, critics allege, feel absolutely no pressure to solve Tupac Shakur's case.

Close friends of Tupac Shakur have said that during his short life, Shakur always emphasized that he wanted to stay true to the people he represented in his music. However, based on his music, Shakur was an enigma. He was rap's Dr. Jekyll and Mr. Hyde, who seemed to simultaneously represent the opposite ends of a spectrum. Sometimes, Shakur promoted compassion towards single black mothers and male responsibility towards the family in songs such as 'Brenda's Got a Baby' and 'Keep Ya Head Up.' However, at other times, he would call black women 'bitches' and brag about the gangsta lifestyle in songs such as '2 of America's Most Wanted' and 'I Get Around.'

Sadly, it seems that in death, the Mr. Hyde part of Tupac Shakur has won. The mystery surrounding his murder appears to have the elements of a true gangsta death. A shower of bullets. A dead body. And a combination of an indifferent police department and uncooperative witnesses. No suspects. No arrests. Only the gangsta code of silence.

DEAD POETS SOCIETY

by Cathy Scott

Just before 3 p.m. on a spring afternoon last May, a car drove up to a crowded car wash on a street corner in Compton, California. An argument broke out between two groups of men and a minute later the sound of gunfire erupted. When the smoke cleared, four men were sprawled out, bleeding, on the ground. Two were already dead. And a third died early the next morning.

The US is a nation long hardened to the idea of black-on-black murder. Although a shooting in a white rural school is cause for a national outcry, a gun battle in an African-American ghetto barely raises an eyebrow.

The slaughter at the car wash would have been quickly forgotten but for the notoriety of one of the dead – 23-year-old Orlando 'Little Lando' Anderson. A member of a Los Angeles gang known as the Southside Crips, Anderson was the man widely suspected in the murder of rapper Tupac Shakur.

The killing of Anderson is but the latest in a string of murders that have blighted the reputation of rap culture and the image of young African-American men. Among the most famous victims are two of the biggest names in rap music: Tupac Shakur and Biggie Smalls.

Eighteen months after Smalls's murder, and two years after Shakur's, there have been no arrests. The slayings raise many questions but provide few answers. Does the police's failure to clear up the murders simply reflect the apparent randomness of the violence, or is it the result of a troubling reluctance to solve murders in which the victims are black? Or have the investigators failed because some facts are being concealed. Some people in the African-American community believe that a dark pattern links the murders. And many see a conspiracy to cover up the real facts of the cases.

It's perhaps no big surprise that conspiracy theories are alive and well in the African-American community. Such theories are the refuge of the disaffected and the disenfranchized. Those who already perceive themselves to be disempowered find it easy to believe in obscure forces. The assassinations of Malcolm X and Martin Luther King, Jr., continue to be questioned. The theory that the CIA helped flood crack cocaine into the black neighborhoods of Los Angeles has been debated from the streets of South Central all the way to Capitol Hill. There were howls of horror when Spike Lee announced in a magazine advertisement that 'AIDS is a government engineered disease,' but the fact is that many believe that theory to be true. A 1990 poll of New York City's African-American community showed that 29 percent believed that AIDS may have been 'deliberately created in a laboratory in order to infect black people,' and 60 percent thought the government could have 'deliberately' made drugs available to poor people.

It's common, of course, for rumors of conspiracy and cover-up to accrete around icons like Shakur and Smalls, especially when there is a wall of silence surrounding their deaths. Out of the dozens of people contacted and interviewed for this story, few would comment on the record. And those who would were, more often than not, attorneys speaking on their clients' behalf. 'This is a non-story. No one is interested anymore,' explains Kenny Meiselas, the attorney for Sean 'Puffy' Combs, who is the CEO of Smalls' record label, Bad Boy Entertainment. It seems this is a crime few want to solve. But not solving the murders of Shakur and Smalls might just be the biggest crime of all.

Shakur and Smalls were modern-day American storytellers. Their mix of rhythms and rhymes were a raw and vivid chronicle of the life of young African-American men in the US.

Shakur came of age in a housing project on the outskirts of San Francisco. Brilliantly talented, he started writing poetry, eventually turning his poems into songs. Arrested eight times between 1991 and 1996, he definitely had a thug image. But his rough-and-tumble lyrics made him a huge star. Shakur went on to record one gold and four platinum albums before his death and gave young black America a new voice. Shakur was also a rising film star, having appeared in such movies as *Poetic Justice*, with Janet Jackson; *Gridlock'd*, with Tim Roth; and *Gang Related* with Jim Belushi. *Poetic Justice* director John Singleton praised Shakur's acting at the time, saying, 'He's what they call a natural. You know, he's a real actor.' It seemed Shakur had it all. Lots of money, fancy cars, and the company of beautiful women. He had escaped from a life in the ghetto, but he couldn't seem to get the ghetto out of his blood.

Biggie Smalls grew up dealing crack on the streets of Bed-Stuy, Brooklyn. Then he discovered his natural talent for rap. He quickly rose to prominence by rapping about what he knew best: sex, drugs, and violence. He was a street poet who fashioned himself after a Chicago mobster and shared Shakur's love of the gangsta lifestyle.

'I spoke to Tupac on the phone a lot, but I never met him,' says Voletta Wallace, Smalls' mother. These days Wallace sits in the black-and-green-furnished condo in Teaneck, New Jersey, she inherited from her son. 'It's designed as if it were made for *Lifestyles of the Rich and Famous*,' she says. Though his fans knew him as Biggie or the Notorious B.I.G. – thanks to his six-foot-three, 300-plus-pound frame – she still calls her only child Christopher. 'When Christopher started his music, Tupac was his friend,' she says in a steady, confident voice. 'They would go to clubs, and they would hang out together. They were very, very close.'

Even though Smalls and Shakur started as friends, as their reputations grew, the friendship cooled. And for those who see connections between their deaths, the narrative begins on November 30, 1994. That was the first time someone tried to kill Tupac Shakur.

Just after midnight, Shakur was on his way to a recording session at Quad Studios. As he entered the lobby he was ambushed by three men. After a scuffle, Shakur was shot five times, taking a bullet to the head, and left for dead. The gunmen fled as Shakur stumbled into the elevator. He went up to the eighth floor, where Smalls was recording with his producer, Combs.

Accounts of what may or may not have happened start here. To the horror of much of the industry, an angry Shakur publicly accused Smalls of knowing that he was going to be set up. Smalls denied any involvement in the shooting, saying that Shakur had simply been the victim of a botched robbery. But Shakur refused to back down on his accusations.

The day after the Quad Studios shooting, Shakur, heavily bandaged, was found guilty on one count of sexual abuse for having molested a female fan in November 1993. Soon after, he was sentenced to a prison term of one and a half to four and a half years. While Shakur maintained his innocence, his financial resources were being stretched to the limit by the legal action, and he couldn't make bail.

While his lawyers worked on his appeal, Shakur was locked up in a New York prison.

It was during this time that Smalls exploded on the rap scene. He was the 1995 *Billboard* rap artist of the year and became Bad Boy's biggest talent when his debut album, *Ready to Die*, went platinum. By October 1995, Shakur had served eight months in prison and was desperate to get out. He signed a record contract with Marion 'Suge' Knight, CEO of Death Row Records. Knight, a six-foot-three, 315-pound former bodyguard with a violent criminal record, was one of the most powerful and feared men in the music business. He had built Death Row into the most successful rap label in history, with $100 million in sales. But he was also said to be connected to the Bloods, a Compton gang and rival of the Southside Crips. In return for Shakur's signing with Death Row, Knight posted his $1.4 million bond.

Shakur and Smalls, the two biggest gangsta rappers in America, were now on the two biggest hip hop labels. Shakur wasn't going to let old rivalries die. Knight and Shakur repeatedly ridiculed Smalls and Combs in public and in the press. And the head between the two rappers escalated after Shakur boasted in a song that he had an affair with Smalls' wife. That was the start of what became known as the East Coast-West Coast war. Smalls and Shakur would soon find themselves overtaken by the violence they rapped about.

On September 7, 1996, Shakur attended the Mike Tyson-Bruce Seldon heavyweight fight in Las Vegas and was on his way to a party. Knight was at the wheel of his black BMW 750 sedan; Shakur was riding shotgun. At a stoplight at the busy intersection of Flamingo Road and Koval Lane, a late model white Cadillac with four men inside pulled up next to Knight's car. Suddenly, a gunman sitting in the backseat started shooting at the passenger side of the BMW. Knight's head was grazed by a bullet, but Shakur wasn't as lucky. He frantically tried to climb into the backseat to avoid the gunfire but was struck by four bullets. The gunfire ended as quickly as it began. Shakur was executed in cold blood. The Cadillac fled the scene. Shakur never regained consciousness and died six days later, on Friday the 13th. He was just 25.

In the search for answers for Shakur's murder, speculation again focused on Smalls. 'My son had nothing to do with Tupac's murder,' Voletta Wallace says. 'He was shocked and upset.' Wallace says her son laughed at comments made by Shakur accusing Smalls of being involved in the Quad Studios shooting. After Shakur was killed, Smalls' mother says, he quit laughing.

By October 1996, the Las Vegas Metropolitan Police Department had a possible suspect in the murder, Orlando Anderson, but was unable to link him directly to the killing. If Shakur was murdered by Anderson, a Southside Crip, the reason seemed relatively simple: Shakur's association with Suge Knight and the Bloods, the Crips' rivals, was well known. Shakur had even appeared in photographs wearing a red scarf – the gang color of the Bloods. Anderson had another, more immediate motive for the killing: Security video at the MGM Grand Hotel showed that just three hours before the shooting, Shakur and his entourage, including Knight, had beaten and stomped Anderson in the hotel lobby. Could the killing have been revenge for the assault? Shakur's mother, Afeni, thinks so. In fact, she filed a wrongful-death lawsuit against Anderson. Her lawyer announced that two crimes were committed against Shakur: one by Anderson and the other by an incompetent police investigation. The case was scheduled to go to trial this past September. Now that Anderson is also dead, it never will.

Following Shakur's murder, Knight was incarcerated. The courts decided that the assault he and Shakur had carried out on Anderson at the MGM Grand was a violation of Knight's probation from a prior assault conviction. He has been sentenced to nine years in prison at the California Men's Colony, in San Luis Obispo, but many in the industry claim they still fear him. Knight refused to be interviewed for this story. (While writing the article, I was warned off by entertainment writers and attorneys. Their biggest fear, they claimed, was Knight and his reputation of strong-arm tactics.)

At the time of Shakur's murder, the police blamed witnesses for not providing them with enough information to make any arrests. But there was one witness, Yafeu Fula, who said he could possibly identify Shakur's killer. Fula was a rapper in Shakur's backup group and was riding in the car behind Knight's on the evening Shakur was mortally wounded. But the police let him go home to New Jersey without interviewing

Biggie Smalls' coffin leaves the Frank E. Campbell Chapel, Brooklyn, March 14, 1997.

him about possible suspects.

On November 10, two months after Shakur died, Fula was visiting his girlfriend at a housing project in Orange, New Jersey. In the middle of the night, gunfire erupted inside a dark hallway. When the police arrived, they found the nineteen-year-old Fula slumped against a wall near a stairwell. The bulletproof vest he was wearing didn't save him: He died hours later, having been shot in the face at point-blank range. 'Execution style,' was how Orange police described it.

Orange and Las Vegas police insist that Fula's death was unrelated to the Shakur investigation and that it was not the result of trying to silence a witness. The day after Fula's murder, Sergeant Kevin Manning of the LVMPD said that Fula was simply one more young black man to be gunned down. 'The odds were against him,' because of his race, not because he was a witness to Shakur's murder.

In the months following Shakur's murder, more rappers began taking precautions, hiring bodyguards and wearing bulletproof vests. Even with the apparent danger, though, Smalls took a break from New York and travelled to Shakur's home turf, Los Angeles. 'Yes, Christopher was comfortable,' Wallace says. 'Maybe he was too comfortable.'

On March 9, 1997, two weeks before the release of his second album, *Life After Death*, Smalls, 24, was celebrating at a party at the Petersen Automotive Museum in Los Angeles. About midnight, the L.A. fire marshal broke up the party because the crowd of 2,000 exceeded the building's fire-code capacity. Combs and Smalls headed to another party. Smalls was sitting in the passenger seat of a GMC Suburban. Combs sat in a car in front of him, and security guards followed in a Chevy Blazer. The streets were packed with people as the caravan waited at a stoplight on Wilshire Boulevard and Fairfax Avenue. Suddenly, a dark-colored car pulled up alongside Smalls's vehicle, and an unidentified black male wearing a suit and bow tie opened fire on the passenger side with a 9mm pistol. Smalls was hit seven times in the chest and was dead on arrival at the Cedars-Sinai Medical Center.

The immediate assumption on the streets was that Smalls' killing was a reprisal of Shakur's death. 'Nonsense,' Kenny Meiselas says. 'The incidents were not connected. I think everyone who has investigated the cases or has had direct information about them knows they were not.'

The most plausible explanation for Smalls' death was that he owed money to someone, possibly to a street gang he had employed as security while in Los Angeles. The *Los Angeles Times* backed up this theory when it reported, using unnamed police sources, that Smalls' shooting was suspected to be over a financial beef the rapper had with a Crips gang member whom some say Smalls hired to protect him on his trip to L.A. Bad Boy, though, denies ever hiring gang members for security.

The murders led to an explosion of theories about the deaths of the two biggest performers in rap. Some say that the killings were the result of an effort to rub out black gangsta rappers. Still others think that they were deliberate hits by rival rap camps with gang affiliations. Some conspiracy theorists go so far as to say that the federal government was involved and that the police have conspired not to solve the crimes. 'The other thing I heard,' Wallace says, 'was that the shot was not meant for my son. The shot was meant for Puffy.' That Combs, and not Smalls, may have been the intended victim has not been ruled out by the LAPD. 'It's pending,' detective Fred Miller said recently.

But, stranger still, many believe that Shakur is not dead, that he faked his own death, perhaps to avoid returning to jail. Some subscribe to what has become known as the Seven-Day Theory; Shakur was shot on the seventh, the numbers of his age, 25, add up to seven, and his posthumous album, for which Shakur adopted the name Makaveli, was entitled *The Don Killuminati: The 7 Day Theory*. Chuck D, an elder statesman of rap and now a reporter for Fox News, responded to the death with a list of eighteen reasons that led him to believe Shakur was still alive. They included number six: 'The name of Tupac's next album is Makaveli. [Machiavelli] was an Italian war strategist who faked his own death to fool his enemies. Perhaps Tupac is doing the same thing!'

The theories are often outlandish, but what's perhaps equally bizarre is how widely they are believed. (After Shakur's death, I wrote a book called *The Killing of Tupac Shakur*. In an effort to quell the rumors, I included a photo of a very dead Shakur on the autopsy table. But every day, I get e-mails, letters, and phone calls from fans who refuse to accept that the rapper is gone.)

Critics of both the L.A. and Las Vegas police investigations have claimed that if Shakur and Smalls had been white men, the cases would have received more attention. The police, of course, see it differently. They feel they have been continually frustrated by hundreds of witnesses and friends who refuse to talk. Among some sections of the younger African-American community, a code of *omerta* is observed. Their distrust of the police is so ingrained, and so powerful, that they refuse to cooperate, even when a close friend has been killed or when their own lives are in danger.

In the Quad Studios shooting, the police contend that Shakur, the victim, refused to cooperate, so the investigation was simply closed. 'His lawyer never called back. No one called back,' explains detective George Nagy of the New York Police Department. 'They more or less handled it their own way.'

But Nagy – clearly frustrated – then goes on to outline the police's attitude in an extraordinarily bold admission of the way things really are: 'Why would a guy go out of his way to investigate a case when the guy who was shot didn't even care?' he asks. 'Why are you going to try hard when you have a million other cases?'

When Shakur was killed in Las Vegas, Nagy says, Las Vegas police didn't contact the NYPD to see if the murder might be related to the Quad Studios shooting. But Las Vegas police have a different story. They say they did contact New York detectives but were unable to learn who was handling the case.

The US Justice Department, meanwhile, is reportedly looking into another conspiracy. The FBI is investigating Death Row's possible links to drug trafficking and money laundering by L.A. street gangs and the New York Mafia. David Chesnoff, Knight's attorney, confirms that a grand jury was convened to look into Death Row and Knight about two years ago, shortly after Knight was jailed. The grand jury has not yet made its findings public. 'Unlike the President Clinton grand jury investigations, we don't get to read about what they're doing in the newspapers,' Chesnoff says.

Knight has repeatedly denied that any money from illegal activities financed Death Row. He has suggested that the federal probe is racially motivated. 'Suge is an exceptionally smart and talented person who got tainted with a bad image that's really undeserved,' Chesnoff says. 'He's one of the few entrepreneurs who has made significant contributions to the community from which he came. I predict that, like a phoenix, he is going to rise from the ashes.'

And then, out of the conspiracy box, came rumors that Smalls, too, was under investigation. The *Los Angeles Times* reported that federal agents were monitoring him in the week before his death as part of an investigation of criminals allegedly connected to Bad Boy.

If Smalls was under surveillance, were the agents watching when he was murdered? 'I was told that ten minutes before he was shot, Christopher was under surveillance by the FBI,' Wallace says. 'Then when he is shot, all of a sudden they're not there. Maybe the FBI knows who shot him. Maybe the FBI is the one who shot him.' The feds, meantime, aren't talking.

Bad Boy, though, is unaware of any federal surveillance of Smalls on the night of his death, and according to Kenny Meiselas, no one at Bad Boy has ever been contacted about an investigation by the FBI. Meanwhile, Combs no longer answers reporters' questions about the shootings. 'Puffy's thinking is that talking to reporters has not necessarily changed what they print,' Meiselas says. 'It's been frustrating for him.'

But Wallace wonders if Combs may know more about her son's death than he is telling the police. 'Does Puffy know something about my son's death? Maybe he's afraid to talk. Maybe he's intimidated,' she

says. 'But at least do something. Give a hint. Don't just sit back and act as if he was my son's best friend and confidant . . . . There are a lot of people out there who know something about my son's death. But they're afraid to come forward.'

Meiselas disagrees. 'Puffy loved Biggie like a brother,' he says. 'He has done everything possible to assist police in finding the person who took his friend and creative partner away.'

During the Puff Daddy and the Family World Tour earlier this year, Combs repeatedly implored the crowds to remember Smalls. This could have been a sincere gesture or, of course, the memorial could simply be cynical showbiz. 'Believe me,' Wallace says, 'it's not the buddy-buddy thing that the media says their relationship was. They had a beautiful relationship. But it was a business relationship . . . Puffy was not Christopher's best friend.' When Wallace hears Combs talking about how he is looking after her financially, she bristles. 'Puffy's not taking care of Biggie's mother,' she says. 'Biggie is taking care of Biggie's mother. Puffy doesn't buy my food, pay my mortgage. Everything was in Christopher's name. He died a very rich man and a very smart man,' she says proudly.

LAPD detectives say the Smalls case is still alive. The investigation began with twenty detectives, however; today, four homicide detectives are assigned to the case. Meanwhile, the Las Vegas Metropolitan Police Department says that the Shakur investigation, which from the start was handled by two detectives and one sergeant, is also continuing. Two years later, its investigation, though open, has stalled.

The real story behind the deaths of Shakur and Smalls may never emerge. It says a lot about the communities the victims came from and the society that surrounded them that both murders have become so encrusted with conspiracy theories and myths. Smalls' and Shakur's deaths have absorbed the rage, the sorrow, the confusion, and the pain in communities in which most people have lost friends and relatives to violence.

WHO KILLED TUPAC SHAKUR?

by Chuck Philips

The city's neon lights vibrated in the polished hood of the black BMW as it cruised up Las Vegas Boulevard.

The man in the passenger seat was instantly recognizable. Fans lined the streets, waving, snapping photos, begging Tupac Shakur for his autograph. Cops were everywhere, smiling.

The BMW 750 sedan, with rap magnate Marion 'Suge' Knight at the wheel, was leading a procession of luxury vehicles past the MGM Grand Hotel and Caesars Palace, on their way to a hot new nightclub. It was after eleven on a Saturday night – September 7, 1996. The caravan paused at a crowded intersection a block from the Strip.

Shakur flirted with a carful of women – unaware that a white Cadillac had quietly pulled up beside him. A hand emerged from the Cadillac. In it was a semiautomatic pistol, aimed straight at Shakur.

Many of the rapper's lyrics seemed to foretell this moment.

'The fast life ain't everything they told ya,' he sang in an early hit, 'Soulja's Story.'

'Never get much older, following the tracks of a soulja.'

Six years later, the killing of the world's most famous rap star remains officially unsolved. Las Vegas police have never made an arrest. Speculation and wild theories continue to flourish in the music media and among Shakur's followers. One is that Knight, owner of Shakur's record label, arranged the killing so he could exploit the rapper's martyrdom commercially. Another persistent legend is that Shakur faked his own death to escape the pressures of stardom.

A year-long investigation by *The Los Angeles Times* reconstructed the crime and the events leading up to it. Evidence gathered by the paper indicates:

The shooting was carried out by a Compton gang called the Southside Crips to avenge the beating of one of its members by Shakur a few hours earlier.

Orlando Anderson, the Crip whom Shakur had attacked, fired the fatal shots. Las Vegas police discounted Anderson as a suspect and interviewed him only once, briefly. He was later killed in an unrelated gang shooting.

The murder weapon was supplied by New York rapper Notorious B.I.G., who agreed to pay the Crips $1 million for killing Shakur. Notorious B.I.G. and Shakur had been feuding for more than a year, exchanging insults on recordings and at award shows and concerts. B.I.G. was gunned down six months later in Los Angeles. That killing also remains unsolved.

Before they died, Notorious B.I.G. and Anderson denied any role in Shakur's death. This account of what they and others did that night is based on police affidavits and court documents as well as interviews with investigators, witnesses to the crime and members of the Southside Crips who had never before discussed the killing outside the gang.

Fearing retribution, they agreed to be interviewed only if their names were not revealed.

The slaying silenced one of modern music's most eloquent voices – a ghetto poet whose tales of urban alienation captivated young people of all races and backgrounds. The 25-year-old Shakur had helped elevate rap from a crude street fad to a complex art form, setting the stage for the current global hip hop phenomenon.

Tupac Amaru Shakur was born in 1971 into a family of black revolutionaries and named after a martyred Incan warrior. Radical politics shaped his upbringing and the rebellious tone of much of his music.

His godfather, Black Panther leader Elmer 'Geronimo' Pratt, spent 27 years in prison for a robbery-murder in Santa Monica that he insisted he did not commit. Pratt was freed after a judge ruled in 1997 that prosecutors concealed evidence favorable to the defendant.

Shakur's stepfather, Black Panther leader Mutulu Shakur, was on the FBI's Ten Most Wanted list until the early 1980s, when he was imprisoned for robbery and murder. His mother, Afeni Shakur, also a Black Panther, was charged with conspiring to blow up a block of New York department stores – and acquitted a month before the rapper was born.

Shakur grew up in tough neighborhoods and homeless shelters in the Bronx, Harlem and Baltimore. He exhibited creative talent as a child and was admitted to the Baltimore School for the Arts, where he studied ballet, poetry, theater and literature.

In 1988, his mother sent him to live with a family friend in the Bay Area to escape gang violence in Baltimore. Living in a tough neighborhood north of Oakland, he joined the rap group Digital Underground and signed a solo record deal in 1991.

Shakur's debut album, *2Pacalypse Now*, sparked a political firestorm. The lyrics were filled with vivid imagery of violence by and against police. A car thief who murdered a Texas state trooper said the lyrics incited him to kill. Law enforcement groups and politicians denounced Shakur. Then-Vice President Dan Quayle said the rapper's music 'has no place in our society.'

Shakur's recordings explored gang violence, drug dealing, police brutality, teenage pregnancy, single motherhood and racism. As his stature as a rapper grew, he pursued an acting career, drawing admiring reviews for his performances in *Juice* and other films.

But he never put what he called the 'thug life' behind him.

During a 1993 concert in Michigan, he attacked a local rapper with a baseball bat and was sentenced to ten days in jail. In Los

Angeles, he was convicted of assaulting a music video producer. In New York, a nineteen-year-old fan accused Shakur and three of his friends of sexually assaulting her.

While on trial in that case, the rapper was ambushed in a Manhattan recording studio, shot five times and robbed of his gold jewelry. Shakur later said Notorious B.I.G. and his associates were behind the attack.

Shakur, convicted of sexual abuse, was serving a four-and-a-half-year prison term when he was visited by Suge Knight, founder of Death Row Records in Los Angeles. Knight offered to finance an appeal of his conviction if Shakur would sign a recording contract with Death Row.

Shakur accepted the offer and was released from prison in 1995 on a $1.4-million appellate bond posted by Knight. Hours later, Shakur entered a Los Angeles studio to record *All Eyez on Me*. The double CD sold more than five million copies, transforming Shakur into a pop superstar whose releases outsold Madonna's and the Rolling Stones'.

On September 7, 1996, Shakur, still out on bond, traveled to Las Vegas to attend a championship boxing match between Mike Tyson and Bruce Seldon at the MGM Grand Hotel.

The sold-out arena was jammed with high rollers: Wall Street tycoons, Hollywood celebrities, entertainment moguls. The fight also attracted an assortment of underworld figures: mobsters from Chicago, drug dealers from New York, street gangs from Los Angeles.

Shakur arrived around 8:30 p.m. accompanied by armed bodyguards from the Mob Piru Bloods, a Compton street gang whose members worked for Knight's Death Row Records. Shakur and Knight sat in the front row, smoking cigars, signing autographs and waving to fans.

'Knock You Out,' a song Shakur had written in honor of Tyson, blasted over the loudspeakers as the boxer entered the ring. Tyson flattened his opponent so quickly that many patrons never made it to their seats.

After congratulating Tyson, Shakur, Knight and a handful of bodyguards in silk suits headed for the exit. In the MGM Grand lobby, one of Shakur's Bloods bodyguards noticed a member of the rival Southside Crips lingering near a bank of elevators.

The Bloods and Crips have a 30-year history of turf wars: beatings, drug heists, drive-by shootings. The Crips dress in blue, the Bloods in red. When the two gangs aren't pushing dope or terrorizing citizens, they take pride in retaliating against each other.

The hoodlum standing in the lobby was Orlando 'Baby Lane' Anderson, 21, a Crip who had recently helped his gang beat and rob one of Shakur's bodyguards at a mall in Lakewood. Anderson had a string of arrests for robbery, assault and other offences. Compton police suspected him in at least one gang killing.

After the beating of Shakur's bodyguard, Anderson had dared to rip a rare Death Row medallion from the man's neck – an affront to Knight's honour and a slight to the Bloods.

The Bloods had been fuming for weeks, waiting to exact their revenge. Now, unexpectedly, there was Anderson, standing before them.

Shakur charged the Crip. 'You from the South?' he asked.

Before Anderson could answer, Shakur punched him. His bodyguards jumped in, pounding and kicking Anderson to the ground. Knight joined in too – just before security guards broke up the 30-second melee, which was captured by a security camera.

Shakur and his entourage stomped triumphantly across the casino floor on their way out of the hotel. They walked half a block down the Strip to the Luxor hotel, where Death Row Records had booked more than a dozen rooms. After dropping off Shakur and the bodyguards, Knight drove about fifteen minutes to a mansion he owned in a gated community in the city's south-eastern valley.

The plan was to regroup later at a benefit concert for a youth boxing program featuring Shakur and other Death Row acts. The midnight concert was to be held at Club 662, a nightspot just opened by Death Row. The club's name was an emblem of how gangs had infiltrated the rap business. On a telephone keypad, 662 spells 'mob.'

A bruised and shaken Anderson gathered himself off the floor in front of dozens of startled onlookers. MGM security guards and Las Vegas police tried to persuade him to file a complaint against his assailants, but he declined.

Anderson headed out to the Strip and crossed over a pedestrian bridge to the Excalibur Hotel, where he had checked in with his girlfriend. News of the beating swept through the gang underground. Before he reached his room, Anderson's pager was beeping with calls from his Crips cohorts, according to what he later told associates.

Anderson phoned his comrades and set up a meeting at the Treasure Island hotel. He changed his clothes and hopped into a taxi, heading for the hotel with the huge neon skull and crossbones out front.

Treasure Island had served as a Crips headquarters during boxing matches for years. The gang would rent a fleet of luxury vehicles, ride across the desert in a caravan, hand their keys to the valets and head to a block of rooms booked under fake names. Drug trafficking paid for all this.

The ritual had little to do with boxing. Many gang members never attended the fights. They came to party and bask in the post-fight revelry: the drinking, the gambling, the drugs, the prostitutes. Other street gangs followed suit, flying in from Harlem and Atlanta, taking over establishments up and down the Strip.

By the time Anderson's taxi reached Treasure Island, more than a dozen gangsters were holed up in a Crips-reserved room. Marijuana smoke clouded the hallway.

Many of those close to Tupac believed that the Las Vegas Police did not treat the identification of his murderer as a priority.

Alcohol was flowing as Anderson opened the door. The gang was furious. The topic of discussion: Who gets to pull the trigger?

According to people who were present, the Crips decided to shoot Shakur after his performance at Club 662. The plan was to station two vehicles of armed Crips outside the nightspot and lie in wait.

The gang put in a call to a Crips hideout in Las Vegas, a rented house used to stash drugs and firearms and shelter gang members on the run from crimes committed in Los Angeles. They told a man there to bring some backup weapons over to the hotel. Soon.

For the Crips, the beating of Anderson was an egregious affront warranting swift and fatal retaliation. Still, the Crips thought, why not make a little money while they were at it? They decided to ask Shakur's biggest enemy to pay for the hit.

The gang arranged a rendezvous with Notorious B.I.G. The Brooklyn rapper, whose real name was Christopher Wallace, hated Shakur and had been feuding with him for more than a year.

Once tight friends, the two entertainers now ridiculed each other at events, in interviews and on recordings. In one song called 'Hit 'Em Up,' Shakur bragged about having sex with Wallace's wife and vowed to kill him. The threats between the rappers and their labels, Death Row and Bad Boy Entertainment, escalated into a series of assaults and shootings – one of which resulted in the killing of a Death Row bodyguard in Atlanta in 1995.

Fearing for his safety, a friend of Wallace's arranged for the Crips to supply bodyguards for the rapper whenever he traveled west. Over the years, the gang was paid to provide security for Wallace at casinos in Las Vegas, clubs in Hollywood and award shows in Los Angeles. Besides cash, Wallace gave the gang access to stars, groupies and the inner sanctums of the music business.

Wallace began flashing Crips gang signs and calling out to the homies at concerts, sometimes even inviting gang members on stage. Privately, he prodded the gang to kill Shakur – and promised to pay handsomely for the hit.

On September 7, 1996, the Crips decided to take him up on the offer.

They sent an emissary to a penthouse suite at the MGM, where Wallace was booked under a false name. In Vegas to party, he didn't attend the Tyson-Seldon fight but had quickly learned about Shakur's scuffle with Anderson. Wallace gathered a handful of thugs and East Coast rap associates to hear what the Crips had to say.

According to people who were present, the Crips envoy explained that the gang was prepared to kill Shakur but expected to collect $1 million for its efforts. Wallace agreed, on one condition, a witness said. He pulled out a loaded .40-calibre Glock pistol and placed it on the table in front of him.

He didn't just want Shakur dead. He wanted the satisfaction of knowing the fatal bullet came from his gun.

It was a gangsta rap parade. Fans waved. Women flirted and asked for autographs. Photographers snapped pictures.

Knight was leading a caravan of at least five Death Row cars heading toward Club 662. Shakur and Knight turned heads as the convoy proceeded slowly north on Las Vegas Boulevard.

Around 11 p.m., police stopped Knight for cranking the black BMW's stereo too loud and not properly displaying its license plates. Shakur and Knight joked with the officers and talked them out of issuing a ticket. Then the BMW turned right on Flamingo Road and headed east toward the club.

Moments earlier, Anderson and three other Crips took an elevator down to the Treasure Island lobby. They walked out into the valet parking area.

Hovering under the hotel's skull-and-crossbones logo, the four Crips waited silently as the valet brought out a 1996 white Cadillac and opened the doors. They piled in and eased the sleek new sedan into traffic. A fifth Crip in an old yellow Cadillac met them at the curb and followed close behind. He rode solo, with an AK-47 assault rifle lying across the front seat.

The traffic in front of Treasure Island was bumper to bumper. Cars honked. Billboards flashed. Neon-lighted fountains trickled nearby.

The driver of the white Cadillac lighted a cigarette. Behind him sat Anderson. The Crip in the front passenger seat handed Anderson the loaded Glock from Notorious B.I.G. The four men discussed staking out the club where Shakur would perform.

After waiting at a stoplight between Caesar's Palace and the Barbary Coast hotel, the Cadillacs turned onto Flamingo and headed east toward Club 662.

As they passed the Bally's hotel on the right, the driver saw a caravan of luxury cars ahead on the left. The vehicles, packed with Mob Piru Bloods and Death Row employees, were stopped at a red light across from the Maxim Hotel. The crosswalk was filled with tourists.

Leading the convoy was Knight's black BMW. Shakur was in the passenger seat. They were alone in the car, unarmed.

The Crips couldn't believe their luck. They decided to chuck their plan and strike immediately.

The Cadillac raced up on the convoy and pulled up beside the BMW. Shakur didn't notice. He was flirting with a carful of women in a lane to his left.

'I saw four black men roll by in a white Cadillac,' said Atlanta rapper E.D.I. Mean, who was in the vehicle directly behind Shakur's. 'I saw a gun come from the back seat out through the driver's front window.'

Bullets flew, shattering the windows of the BMW. Shakur tried to duck into the rear of the car for cover, but four rounds hit him, shredding his chest. Blood was everywhere.

'We heard shots and looked to the right of us,' Knight said. 'Tupac was trying to get in the back seat, and I grabbed him and pulled him down. The gunshots kept coming. One hit my head.'

In the chaos, neither Knight nor Mean could make out who had fired. The driver of the yellow Cadillac just behind the assailants never got a chance to fire his AK-47.

'It all happened so quick. It took three or four seconds at most,' Mean said.

Then the white Cadillac screeched around the corner. A bodyguard near the back of the Death Row caravan fired at the fleeing sedan. In a ruse designed to confuse Shakur's entourage, the Crip in the yellow Cadillac chased the white Cadillac around the corner, as if in hostile pursuit.

Knight made a U-turn, his bullet-riddled BMW squealing around the concrete median. The Death Row convoy followed him back to the Strip, where he rammed his car onto a curb.

Las Vegas police were soon on the scene. After summoning an ambulance for Shakur, they ordered everyone else in the Death Row convoy out of their cars at gunpoint. The police forced Knight, who was bleeding from a head wound, to lie face down on the pavement.

By the time the detectives figured out that Knight and his caravan were victims, not suspects, the Crips had returned to their hotel rooms and gathered their belongings.

Staggering their departures to avoid attracting attention, Anderson and his fellow gang members hit the highway, each in a different car. Two younger gang members drove the white Cadillac back across the desert.

Interstate 15 moves fast at night.

It was still dark when the Crips disappeared over the California border.

Surgeons at University Medical Center in Las Vegas removed Shakur's right lung in an attempt to stop the internal bleeding. When his condition deteriorated, they put him on a ventilator. He died six days after the shooting, with his mother at his side.

Wallace returned to New York, where he recorded a CD called *Life After Death*, which has veiled references to the shooting in several songs. According to the Crips, Wallace paid the gang $50,000 of the promised $1 million through an intermediary a week after Shakur died.

In March 1997, Wallace discussed his feud with Shakur during an interview with a San Francisco radio station. Asked whether he had a role in the rapper's death, Wallace said he 'wasn't that powerful yet.'

Three days later, Wallace was in Los Angeles for the *Soul Train* Music Awards and an after-party at the Petersen Automotive Museum. He was gunned down as he sat in his Chevrolet Blazer at a traffic light on Wilshire Boulevard. No one has ever been charged in the killing.

Two days after Shakur was shot, gang warfare erupted in Compton as the Bloods sought revenge on the Crips. A rash of drive-by shootings left three people dead and twelve injured, including a ten-year-old girl. Informants told police that Anderson had been seen brandishing a Glock pistol.

Las Vegas police interviewed Anderson once. They said they could not build a case against him as Shakur's killer because witnesses in the rapper's entourage refused to cooperate with them.

Anderson said he had nothing to do with Shakur's death. 'If they have all this evidence against me, then why haven't they arrested me?' he said a year after the shooting. 'It's obvious that I'm innocent.'

Anderson was shot dead May 29, 1998, at a Compton carwash in a dispute police say was unrelated to Shakur's slaying.

The three other Crips who were in the white Cadillac that night in Las Vegas still live in Compton. None of them has ever been questioned by police about the crime.

Despite the public setting and the victim's notoriety, no one has ever been arrested for the killing. Shakur's family, many of his followers and some black entertainers cite the case as evidence of a double standard in the justice system. Had a white celebrity been gunned down in the open, they contend, police would have found those responsible without delay.

Las Vegas police say their investigation stalled not for lack of effort, but because witnesses in Shakur's entourage refused to cooperate.

That, however, is only part of the explanation. A *Times* review found that police committed a string of costly missteps:

They discounted an incident, hours before the shooting, in which Shakur took part in the beating of a gang member in a Las Vegas hotel lobby.

They failed to follow up with a member of Shakur's entourage who witnessed the shooting and told police he might be able to identify one or more of the assailants.

The witness was killed several weeks later in an unrelated shooting.

They did not pursue a lead about a sighting of a rented white Cadillac similar to the car from which the fatal shots were fired at

Shakur and in which the assailants escaped.

Las Vegas homicide Sergeant Kevin Manning, who oversaw the investigation, defended his department's work. He said detectives fielded thousands of phone tips, interviewed hundreds of witnesses and chased numerous leads during a year when the homicide unit was besieged with a record 168 murders.

'Tupac got the same treatment as any other homicide here,' said Manning. 'But you know what? We can't do it alone. We rely on cooperative citizens to step forward and help us solve crimes. And in Tupac's case, we got no cooperation whatsoever.'

The *Times* reported Friday that court documents as well as interviews with investigators and gang members, including witnesses to the crime, indicate that Shakur was attacked by the Southside Crips, a Compton gang, to avenge the earlier beating of one of their members. The *Times* also reported that the man who had been beaten fired the fatal shots.

The following account of how the Las Vegas police investigation went aground is based on the same sources and on interviews with Nevada police, six Los Angeles-area investigators involved in the probe and three independent gang experts.

Gang killings are extremely difficult to solve because there is usually little evidence and few witnesses are willing to talk. Shakur's associates were particularly unlikely to volunteer information. Like the rapper himself, many had criminal records and a deep-seated hostility toward police. To some extent, the feeling was mutual: Shakur first gained notoriety with lyrics depicting violence against police.

There was a deeper problem: Las Vegas

'Part of being a thug is to stand up for your responsibilities.' — *Tupac*

police were slow to grasp that the roots of the killing lay in a feud between rival gangs in Compton, and were slow to act once they did realize it. To identify those responsible, police would have to take their investigation to Compton and develop informants within the gangs.

The Vegas cops were ill-suited to do that. They had little experience with gang investigations or gang culture. The Compton Police Department did have entree to the gang underworld. Its investigators had known many gang members since they were babies. They took their first mug shots. They testified at their trials. They visited them in jail. In return, they often got valuable information.

But Las Vegas police worried that the Compton investigators were too close to the gangs and their rap-industry patrons and might leak information. The Vegas detectives kept their distance from the gang squad, and their investigation quickly hit a dead end.

'How is a cop from Vegas supposed to go out to Compton and get a powerful street gang to cooperate in a murder probe?' asked Jared Lewis, a Modesto police detective who is director of Know Gangs, a group that presents seminars on gang homicides for police agencies nationwide.

'Gang homicide investigations are very complex,' he said. 'This was no easy case to solve, by any stretch of the imagination. I can understand why it ended up the way it has.'

Las Vegas police had heard about the beating in the MGM Grand lobby and reviewed a security videotape of it. But they did not know who Anderson was or why the incident mattered. Manning, the homicide commander, issued a statement at the time saying, 'Investigators have no reason . . . to believe that the altercation has any connection to the shooting.'

A week after the shooting, Compton gang investigators reviewed the videotape at the request of Las Vegas police. They identified the beating victim as Anderson,

explained his gang affiliation and said the bodyguards seen flailing at him were Bloods.

'We told Vegas right then we thought the Southside Crips were responsible for the murder and that Orlando was the shooter,' said Bobby Ladd, then a homicide investigator with the Compton gang unit and now a Garden Grove police officer.

Las Vegas police stuck to their position that the beating was irrelevant. Manning told an interviewer, 'It appears to be just an individual who was walking through the MGM and got into an argument with Tupac . . . . He probably didn't even know it was Tupac Shakur.'

Having ruled Anderson out as a suspect, Las Vegas police did not try to track him down for questioning or show his photograph to members of Shakur's entourage, a dozen of whom remained in Las Vegas for a week after the shooting while the rapper fought for his life in a local hospital.

Police also failed to retrieve additional security video that might have captured Anderson's movements after he was beaten. Security cameras are pervasive in Las Vegas, sweeping hotel lobbies, hallways, parking areas and other public places around the clock.

Crips gang members say Anderson and his accomplices passed in front of video cameras as they gathered at the Treasure Island and MGM Grand hotels to plot the killing and, later that night, when they picked up the white Cadillac in the valet parking circle outside Treasure Island.

Because casinos routinely tape over surveillance footage every seven days, the potential evidence was lost.

'Overlooking the gang fight at the MGM was a mistake,' said Wes McBride, president of the California Gang Investigators Association. A retired gang intelligence sergeant for the Los Angeles County Sheriff's Department's Operation Safe Streets division, McBride runs a gang training program for police academies.

'In gang culture, that fight was a killing

offense,' he said. 'If you embarrass a gang member in public, they will retaliate with a vengeance.'

Lou Savelli, a New York gang-unit sergeant and vice president of the East Coast Gang Investigators Association, concurred. 'If a drive-by shooting happened in New York and we found out that there was a gang beating three hours earlier involving the murder victim, I guarantee that would be my Number One lead,' he said.

Manning now says Las Vegas police may have misjudged the significance of the fight in the MGM lobby. In a recent interview, he said police discounted Anderson as a suspect based on information that he had been detained by hotel security long enough that he would not have had time to arm himself and organise the Crips' ambush of Shakur several hours later.

Manning said that information had proved incorrect. He declined to elaborate.

Investigators say it takes special effort to develop a rapport with gang members. Because gang culture places a premium on respect, gang detectives will treat thugs and their families with great courtesy, even deference. In return, they sometimes provide confidential information that helps solve crimes.

That did not happen in the Shakur case.

From their first moments on the scene, Las Vegas police unintentionally alienated the witnesses most likely to be able to identify the rapper's assailants.

After summoning an ambulance for Shakur, police ordered Knight, bleeding from a head wound, and other members of Shakur's entourage out of their cars at gunpoint.

'The police shoved guns in our faces and threatened us,' said rapper E.D.I. Mean, who was in the car directly behind Shakur's. 'They made us lie face down in the middle of the street. Even after they realised we were telling the truth, they never apologized.'

Las Vegas police say they had no way of knowing at first whether Knight and the others were victims or suspects. After establish-

ing that they were the former, patrol officers had them sit along a curb until homicide detectives arrived. That took nearly two hours.

Then Manning and his men ushered the witnesses one by one into squad cars and took their statements.

They were, Manning said, 'extremely uncooperative.' Knight, founder of Death Row Records in Los Angeles, summed up relations between the witnesses and the police during an interview with ABC-TV's *PrimeTime Live* two months later. Knight said that even if he knew who killed Shakur, he would not tell Las Vegas authorities.

'It's not my job,' he said. 'I don't get paid to solve homicides. I don't get paid to tell on people.'

Las Vegas detectives were disgusted. 'It's the typical gang mentality,' Manning said. 'Their best friend got shot and nobody saw nothing. The way I see it, if somebody tells me they don't want to talk, what's the point of calling them back over and over again? In this country, citizens have rights.'

There was, however, one witness willing to help: a nineteen-year-old rapper named Yafeu 'Kadafi' Fula. He had spent part of his childhood in the same households as Shakur and was particularly close to him. Fula, who was with Mean in the car behind Shakur's that night, told police he might be able to identify one or more of the assailants.

Fula was among the dozen or so members of Shakur's circle who remained in Las Vegas after the shooting, keeping vigil at University Medical Center, where Shakur was on life support. During that week, detectives made no attempt to follow up with Fula.

His only contact with police was confrontational. On September 9, two nights after the shooting, patrol officers stopped a motorist outside the hospital. Fula and some other Shakur associates who knew the man protested and got into a scuffle with police. Fula was handcuffed and searched but not charged.

After Shakur's death on September 13,

145

Fula left Las Vegas, traveling to Atlanta and Los Angeles and then New Jersey, where his relatives lived.

Compton investigators, meanwhile, had assembled mug shots of a handful of gang members, including Anderson. They hand-delivered the photos to Las Vegas.

Manning said detectives called Fula's lawyer to set up a meeting with the teenage rapper so they could show him the pictures. Manning said the calls were not returned.

Police did not try to locate Fula on their own. By November 10, it was too late. Fula was gunned down in a housing project in Irvington, NJ.

Early on the morning of October 2, 1996, Compton police, FBI agents and members of the Los Angeles County Sheriff's Department swept through Compton, arresting nearly two dozen gang members and seizing weapons and ammunition. Their aim was to stifle a gang war that had erupted after the shooting of Shakur.

Orlando Anderson was among those sitting in the Compton police lockup. He had been picked up on a warrant stemming from a gang killing six months earlier. The other gang members were being held on drug, weapon and other charges. Compton police believed that some of them were involved in Shakur's slaying or knew something about it.

Two Las Vegas detectives took part in the roundup at the invitation of Compton police. One of them questioned Anderson for about twenty minutes.

The visiting detectives brushed aside a suggestion that they question the other gang members. This stunned the Compton cops and sheriff's deputies, who thought the obvious thing to do was to use the threat of prosecution to try to extract information about Shakur's killing.

'We had a bunch of gang members in custody who knew exactly what happened with Shakur – some who we believed were in the Cadillac,' said Ladd, the former Compton investigator. 'Las Vegas expressed no interest whatsoever in talking to any of them. They barely even interviewed Orlando.'

Anderson was released two days later; prosecutors had declined to file charges against him for the gang killing. Las Vegas investigators never spoke to him again. He was killed May 29, 1998, in a drug-related shooting at a Compton carwash.

Savelli, the New York gang investigator, said the arrests in Compton were a missed opportunity.

'The success rate on these kinds of homicides hinges completely on having informants inside of the gang,' he said. 'You lean on gang members with rap sheets for information about the crime. If you don't get the information the first time, you go back. You get in their face. Two. Three. Four times. Eventually they talk. But relentless follow-up is essential.'

Manning said his detectives, operating outside their home state, lacked authority to interrogate the Compton gang members – that morning or later. Los Angeles authorities took issue with that assertion. They said that once local police invited the detectives to question the suspects, there was no legal reason for them not to do so.

Manning also said his detectives asked Los Angeles County sheriff's officers to question gang members on their behalf. Sheriff's investigators said they were not asked to interrogate the suspects about Shakur's killing. Rather, they said, the Las Vegas detectives asked them to pass on anything they learned about the case while questioning the gang members on the local charges.

Manning said he had no regrets about how his officers handled the situation.

'You can't just go in and push everybody aside and say, "OK, we're taking over,"' he said. 'Even if we did, do you think these guys are going to talk to us simply because we walk up and ask them to? Do you think we scared them so bad they would just puke their guts out and admit to everything?'

Two days after the shooting of Shakur, two

Crips were seen in Compton driving a white 1996 Cadillac bearing a rental sticker. An informant told the local gang unit that the Crips had visited a car stereo shop whose owner also did bodywork. In Las Vegas, one of Shakur's bodyguards had gotten off a shot at the white Cadillac as it fled. The word on the street in Compton was that the Crips brought the car to the stereo shop to have the damage repaired.

Compton police relayed this information to Las Vegas investigators, who added it to their file.

The Compton gang investigators then canvassed every rental agency in the area to determine whether any had rented a white Cadillac that had been driven to Las Vegas around the time Shakur was shot. They found that a Carson agency had rented such a car to a man with possible ties to the gang underground. They took a photograph of the car and detailed their findings in a report.

Compton investigators say they gave this additional information to Las Vegas police. Manning said his detectives never received it.

'We thought there was a possibility that we had located the Cadillac used in the crime,' said retired Compton Sergeant Robert Baker. 'It was a solid lead that should have been pursued.'

Investigators say it was understandable that Las Vegas police would have concerns about cooperating closely with their Compton counterparts. Compton had a history of political corruption, and some Police Department figures had been alleged to have gang ties.

In 2000, after years of feuding with the police brass, Compton Mayor Omar Bradley and City Council members disbanded the department and contracted with Los Angeles County to provide police services. But at the time of Shakur's shooting, the gang squad was regarded as one of the finest in Southern California.

People familiar with the investigation say Las Vegas police were concerned that city officials were too cosy with Suge Knight, who grew up in Compton, contributed money to Bradley's political campaigns and knew members of the police force. Knight's security chief, Reginald Wright, Jr., is a former Compton police officer whose father ran the gang unit.

Knight's name had figured in some of the speculation about Shakur's death. One theory was that Knight arranged the rapper's killing so he could exploit his martyrdom commercially. Las Vegas detectives worried that Wright's father and other officers might protect Knight or pass information to him. Knight's refusal to cooperate with them sharpened the Nevada detectives' suspicions.

To ease those concerns, Hourie Taylor, then Compton chief of police, removed the elder Wright from the Shakur investigation and replaced him with Baker. Nevertheless, Las Vegas investigators continued to keep their distance.

'The investigators with the best inside information about the Southside Crips worked in the Compton gang unit,' said McBride, the former Sheriff's Department gang investigator.

'They were good investigators. But even if Las Vegas didn't trust them, what did it hurt to listen? It's not like Vegas had to give up anything. In my mind, if you aren't even close to solving the case, what do you have to lose?'

Though the investigation into Shakur's slaying has been dormant for years, some former Compton officers refuse to give up hope of catching some of those involved.

'I believe Tupac's murder could have been solved – and it still could be,' said Tim Brennan, a Compton gang investigator now with the Sheriff's Department. 'All the clues are right there. What the investigation lacked was input from detectives who understood the gangs involved and how they operate and who all the players are. I believe justice could still be served.'

147

WHO KILLED TUPAC SHAKUR?

Epilogue

by Chuck Philips

The family of the late rap star Notorious B.I.G. denied Friday that he played a role in the murder of rival Tupac Shakur.

The family issued the statement in response to a *Los Angeles Times* story that reconstructed the killing of Shakur in Las Vegas in September 1996. The article reported that Shakur was attacked by members of a Compton gang called the Southside Crips, and that Notorious B.I.G. provided the gun and agreed to pay the gang $1 million.

Notorious B.I.G., whose real name was Christopher Wallace, was shot dead six months later in Los Angeles. His killing remains unsolved.

In the statement, Wallace's family described the *Times* story as 'irresponsible journalism.'

'Christopher Wallace was at his home in New Jersey on the night of Tupac Shakur's murder, with friends who will continue to testify for his whereabouts since he is unable to defend himself,' the statement said.

An attorney for Wallace's estate, Londell McMillan, also criticised the article. 'The story is patently false,' McMillan said. 'There have been numerous witnesses who have surfaced that clearly put Christopher in New York and New Jersey on September 7, 1996,' the night Shakur was shot.

One of Wallace's friends, rapper Lil' Cease, asserted Friday that he and Wallace were at Wallace's home in Teaneck, NJ, that night.

The *Times* account was based on court documents and interviews with police investigators and gang members, including witnesses to the crime. It said Wallace was in Las Vegas on the weekend of the shooting, registered at a hotel under a false name.

Shakur, other rap-industry figures and Los Angeles gang members also were in town, to attend a heavyweight boxing match.

Wallace was closely tied to the Southside Crips, whose members often provided security for him.

Wallace and Shakur, once close friends, had become bitter rivals who exchanged insults and threats on recordings, in concerts and at music-industry awards shows.

Before publishing its story, *The Times* sought comment from Wallace's mother, Voletta. Through a lawyer, she declined to comment.

> 'America is the biggest gang in the world. Look at how they didn't agree with Cuba, so ... (they) just cut them off.'
> *– Tupac*

148

DEAD MEN TELL NO TALES

by J. H. 'Tommy' Tompkins and Johnny Ray Huston

On September 6, 2002, nearly six years after Tupac Shakur was murdered, the *Los Angeles Times* published the first story in a two-part series on the rap superstar's murder. The articles were the work of *Times* staff writer Chuck Philips, a Pulitzer Prize winner, who, after what he called a 'year-long investigation,' claims to have discovered evidence that another rap superstar, Christopher 'Notorious B.I.G.' Wallace – once New York based and now, like Shakur, the victim of a drive-by assassination – was behind the shooting.

Philips's belief that Orlando Anderson fired the bullets that ended Shakur's life wasn't the explosive aspect of the story – Anderson had been cited as the prime suspect in various newspapers, in Randall Sullivan's book *LAbyrinth: A Detective Investigates the Murder of Tupac Shakur and Notorious B.I.G., the Implication of Death Row Records' Suge Knight and the Origins of the Los Angeles Police Scandal,* and on *Behind the Music.* Philips's bombshell was a claim that the hit had been paid for by Wallace. His article alleges Wallace was in Las Vegas the weekend of Shakur's fatal shooting, staying at the MGM Grand Hotel under an assumed name. According to Philips, Wallace didn't just offer the Southside Crips $1 million to kill Shakur – he supplied the murder weapon as well.

The story runs counter to Nick Broomfield's film, *Biggie and Tupac,* which uses many of the same sources as Sullivan, who investigated the murders for *Rolling Stone,* then wrote on them at greater length in *LAbyrinth.* Sullivan, who took pains to detail his sources, came up with very different conclusions. Relying heavily on the story of former Los Angeles police detective Russell Poole, he linked the murders of Shakur and Wallace to Marion 'Suge' Knight and his label (then called Death Row Records), the Mob Piru Bloods, and members of the LAPD, some of whom were implicated in the infamous Rampart police corruption scandal.

Philips, whose business coverage of Knight's peculiar approach to running a company has been notoriously soft, refuses to name his sources. The account, he wrote, 'is based on police affidavits and court documents as well as interviews with investigators, witnesses to the crime and members of the Southside Crips who had never before discussed the killing outside the gang.' Yet, 'fearing retribution, they agreed to be interviewed only if their names were not revealed.'

Speculation about the killers' identities and motives has generated conspiracy theories as elegant and complicated as anything spawned by the Kennedy assassinations. But Philips's story has weaknesses that are difficult to ignore. How – in a chain of events riddled with individuals and organizations whose self-interests give them reason to distort the facts – can his Wallace murder allegation be verified? What information came from police sources, and what came from gang members? This is important – not because the gang members are potentially unreliable but because the city of Los Angeles and the LAPD (reeling from the Rampart scandal and facing a civil suit filed by Wallace's estate) have a vested interest in Philips's conclusions. And why would Wallace – a successful entertainer who was anything but stupid – announce to a roomful of gang members, as Philips reports, his intention to have Shakur killed? Philips did not return calls seeking comment.

Philips's story requires one to believe that a 300-plus-pound celebrity was able to arrive in Vegas and check into the MGM Grand – the hotel hosting the Tyson fight – under an assumed name without being recognized by anyone (other than the anonymous

Tupac was described by MTV as 'the unlikely martyr of gangsta rap, and a tragic symbol of the toll its lifestyle exacted on urban black America.'

Southside Crips who've made the inflammatory claims); it also asserts that the spontaneously Wallace-led plot to kill Shakur took place within a two-hour time frame.

Dismissing Philips's assertions as 'falsehoods,' 'all lies,' and 'character assassination,' Voletta Wallace has already threatened to file a lawsuit. Christopher Wallace's widow, Faith Evans, told MTV that a tearful, fearful Wallace called her on hearing of Shakur's death, and his friend James Lloyd Jr. [rapper Lil' Cease] gave a number of interviews stating that Wallace was in New Jersey the night of Shakur's murder, first at a recording studio and then at home watching the Tyson fight on closed-circuit TV. (Paper and audio documents of the recording date have since been produced by the Wallace estate.) While hip hop public figures ranging from New York's Ed Lover to the Bay Area's Davey D have tried to slow down the rumor mills, Sullivan and Broomfield have also weighed in with criticisms.

'I think there is a real concern within LAPD to move on,' Broomfield told us. 'I think Bernard Parks has done everything in his power to make as little headway into the murder investigation [of Wallace] as possible.'

At the same time, Broomfield has his own complications and conflicts. Not only does he rely heavily on one source, Poole, for critical information, but also several other important sources, including Wallace's bodyguard, Eugene Deal, appeared on film only because Voletta Wallace asked them to.

Today, East Coast-versus-West Coast has come to signify a media battle between journalists (Sullivan is New York based) and police forces: It's interesting that Philips has focused on the ineptitude of Las Vegas police rather than the LAPD's inability to solve the murder of Wallace, which took place in Philips's own city.

But as the past week has shown, uncovering the truth about these murders may be an impossibly complicated task.

INTERVIEW WITH SUGE KNIGHT

by P. Frank Williams

Straighten up your spine, suckas. Think about this knockin' on your front door: A 6' 4", 330-pound (all muscle), gang-affiliated multimillionaire with nothin' to lose. His skin clean, focus right and his once-untouchable company paralysed but not folded, Suge Knight has found a strange peace while stuck behind prison walls for the last three years. And he's made millions of dollars while doin' time, scoring on projects like *2Pac's Greatest Hits* and the Outlawz. ('I can only spend $140 a month in here. Think of how much I saved! I'm saving, like, $10,000 a day.') Even the controversial Death Row Records-released *Suge Knight Represents: Chronic 2000* double album – which sparked drama between Suge and ex-friend Dr. Dre about the Chronic trademark – went gold. And though there's no doubt that bad blood still swirls between Suge and Snoop and Dre, at least Suge recognized quality music. ('I think Dre's new record is good.')

After being sentenced to a nine-year bid on a probation violation for helping Tupac beat down Orlando Anderson on that fateful September day in Las Vegas, Suge has been almost invisible. Parole officials at his current home, California's Mule Creek State Prison, list 33-year-old Marion H. Knight's release date as May 10, 2001. However, Suge insists that with good time served, he'll be out sooner – like this summer.

> **'My music is spiritual, if you listen to it. It's all about emotion; it's all about life . . . I would tell my innermost secrets.'**
> **– *Tupac***

'I got a release date and I'm coming home. I know a lot of niggas are scared, but time went so fast. When I come home, I want all those people who was talking shit about me to be able to look me in my eye and say the same things. People afraid for Suge to his bright. They been callin' up here, asking when I am gonna get out? When I hit bricks, it all belongs to me.'

And he don't wanna play checkers or sip tea when he steps into freedom. The 'former' CEO of Death Row Records begins his day at 7 a.m. with a meal in his two-man cell. ('I cook my own breakfast on my hot plate.') Then he fires up one of his trademark cigars, works out, showers, reads for a while and calls home. That leaves plenty time to sort out the future. ('In prison, you get the chance to see who really loves you. That little buck gives you a lot of time to think.')

If Suge is indeed the vicious Compton Piru mastermind known for gangsta tactics (like forcing cats to drink piss and angling Vanilla Ice over a fifteen-story balcony), then Simon (Suge's biblical alias) is a charming devil. Asked about a prison basketball game that left his foot in a cast, he responds, 'You know Suge Knight be playing above the time. I went up in the air like Vince Carter but came down like Kelly Price.

'I'm in prison. But my heart and mind is

151

Suge Knight was the subject of an investigation into alleged links between Death Row Records and organized crime.

free. Gangsta haters on the streets are doing more time than me. They need 30 police escorts with them every time they walk down the street.'

Sitting about five feet across from me in Mule Creek's bustling visiting room (kids, moms and girlfriends everywhere), Suge's eerily cheerful as he snacks on hot dogs, popcorn, ice cream and other items from a nearby vending machine. We chat for over four hours, and since no tape recorders or notebooks are allowed, I use napkins and paper towels to take various notes from the always-wild, occasionally venomous and consistently provocative mouth of Suge Knight:

'Before 'Pac got shot, Interscope didn't want to fuck with him. But by him being ghetto, I had to reach out to him, one black muthafucka to another. He was just pissed off that everybody just left him in there. Really, it was his girl Keisha who keep me up on him. It was her who really should have got the credit.'

'A lot of these muthafuckas let these white executives pump them up. But when Dre gets into a fight or beat down, Jimmy Iovine is not gonna get outta bed and go fight for Dre, is he? I would like to educate thug niggas on some million-dollar game: When Steve Stoute wants to get one dollar, he has to ask Jimmy for it. I bet you that when they was thinking about putting Puffy in jail, Clive Davis called up and said , "Let's try to work something out because this nigga has to pay me back all my money."'

'I think Jay-Z benefited from that fact that 'Pac and Biggie are dead. When they were around, he wasn't on that level. What I do

152

like about DMX – even though people say he bit 'Pac's style – is that he has a great work ethic. I like them Ruff Ryder niggas. They real ghetto niggas, rappin'. I like Lil' Kim because she's grimy and a ghetto bitch. She shows pussy 'cause she's really like that.'

'Hayy-O is a snitch. He has no credibility. He got on the stand and lied. There wasn't no truth in anything he said. He's a con man. If a nigga's a snitch, he will do anything to get free. And really, how could you be from the ghetto and be a rat? I think he sent the wrong message to kids. He reminds me of Sammy "the Bull."'

'I remember at the MTV awards. Snoop went to a New York radio station and said it was 'Pac with the East Coast-West Coast bullshit, not him. Snoop said he would do a song with Puffy, Biggie or anybody. 'Pac went crazy when he heard it on the radio. He was like, "I'm covering this muthafucka's back when he was out there doing that video for 'New York, New York.' Muthafuckas shot up the trailer. They was cryin'. I went and smashed for them. I'm doing all this good, and here he is speakin' about hookin' up with my enemies? Me and him gotta get down." This is what 'Pac told me. 'Pac went back and wrote a whole "Hit 'Em Up" version of his dissin' Snoop, from beginning to end. But I ain't never put it out because of the simple fact that I thought 'Pac was angry then and might have just been talkin' because he was pissed off. I have no intention of puttin' it out, but it's there.'

'We don't like that "'bout it, 'bout it" shit. We too gangsta for radio.'

'I seen Prince [the Artist] up in the clubs a few times and I hollered at him. Then the muthafucka was walkin' around with "slave" written on his face. He was sayin' that he didn't want to fuck with people at record labels. He should have stayed ghetto instead of runnin' back to Arista with his head between his legs.'

'Everybody's always like, "'Pac got a bad deal. 'Pac is dead because of us." But 'Pac always praised Death Row. Nobody ever

leaves here alive. I lost a lot of loved ones like him. If you around me, then I have your back. I never make no fake-ass records talking about 'Pac like Puffy did "Missing You." He did that to benefit himself. That was my nigga and I will never do no record like that. People talk all that shit, but can't nobody say me and 'Pac didn't have fun.'

'People act like it ain't no East-West shit. Like Jay-Z came out here thinkin' it was all good to kick it. He did songs with Dre thinking Dre was a real street nigga. But Dre ain't got love on the street like that.'

'People be so quick to judge me as a ghetto muthafucka. They won't let their kids spend the night at my house because I'm supposed to be such a ghetto, violent muthafucka, but my kids get everything they want and are raised well.'

'We [blacks] have so much hatred inside. It's a crab mentality. That's why we feed into that black-on-black feuding so much. Too many black people have that crab mentality which stops us from makin' money. We thinkin' white people's ice is colder than ours.'

P. Frank Williams: *Have you heard about the song Snoop put out about Death Row – dissin' you?*

Suge Knight: [Laughing] I ain't trippin'. As far as him and anybody else in the rap game ever tryin' to assassinate my character, that's impossible. You talkin' about a man who has always walked the walk and talked the talk. Ain't nobody ever whip my ass or slapped me all up. That's reality for them – not for me. When those muthafuckas get loaded, they're liable to say anything. I don't even trip off anything that Snoop says because there is always a lie behind it. He was tellin' everybody that, at the time his girl was pregnant, he was gonna name [the baby] 'Pac. Then all that shit happened in Vegas, so the naming never happened. But I'm not no paper soldier, so I'm not here to assassinate nobody's character. Say what you mean and keep it that way. If you wanna cross somebody, then do that. Don't act like it wasn't you.

P. Frank Williams: *So when you hit the street, you want people who've said whatever about you to say it in person?*

Suge Knight: When I come home, I want all those people who was talkin' shit about me to be able to look me in my eye and say the same things. People afraid for Suge to hit bricks. They been callin' up here, asking when I am gonna get out? When I hit bricks, it all belongs to me.

P. Frank Williams: *What's up with the Biggie murder? Were you involved with it?*

Suge Knight: I like Biggie. Like 'Pac, he was one of the best rappers in the business. Why would I try to do something to him? Who knows? Maybe one day he could have been signed to Death Row. I don't know why muthafuckas tryin' to pin that on me. I don't even know the muthafucka they tried to connect me with. Anybody with any kind of sense know I wasn't involved. Anytime you have somebody doing positive stuff and just doing their time and minding their own business, people will sit up there and lie. I never seen no shootin'. I only know what I heard and what I read. I had no involvement.

P. Frank Williams: *That was some wild stuff you said about Dre when we talked last weekend. Do you still feel the same way?*

Suge Knight: I have nothing negative to say about Dre. Like I said, I wish him the best. I ain't the one that called him a bisexual and faggot or none of that, like other people. That was done from Eazy-E and everybody else was before.

P. Frank Williams: *I heard you spoke to Dre. So what did you talk about? Was it a positive conversation?*

Suge Knight: [Laughing] Well, you know, with me it's always positive. We just talked about a few things.

P. Frank Williams: *I also heard you supposedly put money on both Crips and Blood books in here to make sure you don't have any problems.*

Suge Knight: If I stay in here until I am a hundred years old, I will still be a man. I could strip down naked in here and show all my tat and never have no problems. People know who I am and who I am down with. One thing about bein' a savage, it's that you stay that way. Why would I get in jail and become a pussy? It's a lot of these rap niggas that's been slapped and drank piss. But you can't find anybody who ever said they slapped Suge Knight in or out of jail. If you always been my enemy, it's still that way. That's funny to me. When I went to jail, it was because I was involved in something. It's not like I was standin' by and not doing nothin'.

P. Frank Williams: *You've had a lot of time to think in here. Any regrets? Has being away from the street and all the people given you a chance to reassess your life?*

Suge Knight: You mean as far as regrets?

P. Frank Williams: *I mean, have any of your opinions changed since you been in?*

Suge Knight: One of the things that prison does is make you a better judge of character. Like, if you take an artist or so-called friend or whoever, if they don't a have a good heart or they're not really your friend, you don't have to waste your time bullshittin' with 'em. You pick up on people much faster. In less than five minutes, you can have a conversation with somebody and tell if the person is a snake or he full of shit. There is a difference between me and most, which is that I am fresh off the block. I don't look for no special privileges. I'm a man who paid my dues. No person ever gave me nothing but God. Like I said before, a lot of these black guys go into these record labels tap dancin' and shakin' they ass to get in the door. One thing nobody can ever take from me is that I never been on no records, poppin' around in no videos or shakin' my ass. I don't be no cheer-leader. I come in like a businessman and I do business. I make sure that the people around me have the success that I have. And that's not that Hollywood success. I don't care about how many times somebody recog-nizes my face. My thing was to be the man who makes his little 30 or 40 million a year and still get a cheeseburger and fries and don't worry about an autograph.

P. Frank Williams: *So, why don't we have more black-owned businesses like Death Row Records? It was such a successful label with so many platinum artists. What hap-pened? Why couldn't it keep going? Why did it end with 'Pac dead, you in jail and Dre gone?*

Suge Knight: It's the oldest game in the world: divide and conquer. The sad thing about it is that you take artists like Snoop – they are not educated and at the top of their game – then they have people in their ears tellin' 'em if they only make $12 million, they should have made $100 million. But there's no way possible they should make that much. That makes them think, 'Death Row is fuckin' with me. I should go over here.' Then they go somewhere else and find that they're not treated as well. It's about black-owned and being empowered. If you take LaFace Records when TLC and Toni Braxton went bankrupt, people didn't say nothing negative about Arista. Now, of all the artists on Death Row, none of them went bankrupt. They was having chips and cars and all that. Now, if they fuck theirs off, then that's on them. There's a difference in running a business. Nothing negative about Dre, but when he first started with Aftermath, it was seven months and he was outta business. Even with Eve, she had to leave because of finan-

cial reasons and everything fell through. People don't know how hard it is to have your own business, even with Snoop's new label, a lot of them have been reachin' out to me, saying they aren't making enough money. Basically, people are never happy enough because they want more money. And they all have such bad deals.

P. Frank Williams: *Do you think police want to keep you in jail? Is there a con-spiracy?*

Suge Knight: I wouldn't say it's a conspiracy; you got good and bad people everywhere, like you got good and bad cops. At the same time, you have a lot of those people who don't know where my head is at. They will say shit, do punk-ass interviews and make punk-ass records about me. But most of them are snitches and informants, anyway. So they thinkin', 'When Suge come home, he's prob-ably pissed off.' But I am not trippin'. When people say the word 'revenge,' to me, the best revenge in the world is success.

P. Frank Williams: *How do you wake up every day and feel happy? Do you have that much faith in God? Is it your family that's supportive?*

Suge Knight: I'm passionate about every-thing, like my family and friends. I am a good judge of character and I only fuck around with my real homies, my real mutha-fuckas. Anybody that I am talkin' to is gonna be bonafide real. That means that your con-versations are better. There is no substitu-tion for happiness. Period.

P. Frank Williams: *So, Suge, you're talkin' about positivity, but are you still gonna put out this Snoop* Dead Man Walkin' *album?*

Suge Knight: I am in the penitentiary. The only thing that I do is my time. I'm quite sure that Death Row will be puttin' it out.

155

BIGGIE & TUPAC (REMIX)
Nick Broomfield Imitates Life Imitating Art
by Ernest Hardy

'You can be the shit, flash the fattest five . . .
Have the biggest dick, but when your shell get hit
You ain't worth spit, just a memory.'
– Biggie Smalls, 'You're Nobody ('Til Somebody Kills You)'

There are two formidable presences in Nick Broomfield's deceptively rambling, shrewdly ragtag documentary *Biggie & Tupac*, and they aren't those of either of the friend-turned-foe hip hop martyrs whose brief lives, mysterious deaths and complicated legacies (but mainly their deaths) the film is about. The first is controversial Death Row Records honcho Suge Knight – or, more accurately, his perceived, almost mythical power, which casts a dark (and at times darkly hilarious) pall over the entire film. The other is Voletta Wallace, mom of Christopher Wallace, a.k.a. rapper Biggie Smalls. Miss Wallace, whose round face glows when she talks about her son, gives the film not just its moral anchor – and outrage – but its heart as well. When Broomfield lets her know that he's having a hard time getting any of Biggie's acquaintances to speak on-camera, the film immediately cuts to a shot of Miss Wallace picking up her phone and dialing. A short while later, Lil' Cease, one of Biggie's protégés and closest friends, is sitting reluctantly before the camera as Miss Wallace looks on.

The timing of *Biggie & Tupac*'s long-delayed release looks now like a fortuitous stroke of luck. The hip hop community is still reeling from Chuck Philips' September 6 and 7 exposé in the *Los Angeles Times*, in which he traces the deaths of the two rappers to a 1996 altercation between Tupac's bodyguard, who had ties to the Bloods, and the late Orlando Anderson, who was a Crip. According to Philips, that event set the stage for the spiraling violence that would eventually claim the lives of the two rappers, both of whose prophetic obsessions with their own deaths permeated their music. The article's main controversy lies in its claim that it was Biggie who had Tupac killed, agreeing to pay the Crips $1 million for the deed, and even personally supplied the murder weapon in Las Vegas on the night that 'Pac was murdered. Philips never does explain how the world-famous, aptly named Biggie – whom he alleges was in Vegas on the night of a highly publicized Mike Tyson fight, when the city was crawling with both paparazzi and Negroes who'd instantly recognize the rapper – was able to slip in and out of the city with no one, save unnamed informants, seeing him or even knowing about his being there until Philips broke the story six years later. (Biggie's camp has angrily denied the claim, stating that the rapper was in New Jersey at the time of 'Pac's death.)

Three years in the making, *Biggie & Tupac* provides a riveting, almost point-by-point refutation of the *Times* article, although that was obviously not its intention. The film's greatest triumph is in the way it demystifies and dismantles the very thug/gangsta mystique that Philips' two-part article ended up reinforcing. The mountains of interviews, case files and evidence that Broomfield sifts through finger Suge Knight and the much-scandalized LAPD (whose corruption apparently has no bounds) as the true culprits, with Miss Wallace tracing the deadly feud, along with the whole con-

156

Director Nick Broomfield's Biggie & Tupac *told the story behind the murder of rap's biggest superstars and was one of the most talked about films at the Sundance Film Festival, 2002.*

trived East Coast-West Coast rivalry, to a beef between Suge Knight and Biggie's friend/producer/label boss Puff Daddy. Sitting in her home office, flanked by portraits of her boy and speaking in a soft Jamaican lilt, Miss Wallace stares straight into the camera and says, 'All it was is a Puffy and Suge Knight war. Suge Knight, for some reason, had a friend or a cousin or a nephew [who] got shot in Atlanta. He blamed Puffy and all hell breaks loose. So, if that's the case, Puffy and Suge Knight, solve your damn problem! C'mon, now! You're messing with lives here. Two lives were lost as a result of what? Stupidity.'

Broomfield is energized by Voletta Wallace's maternal fury, her fearlessness, and because of that, his film crackles. In his best-known documentaries, *Aileen Wuornos: The Selling of a Serial Killer* [1992], *Heidi Fleiss – Hollywood Madam* [1995] and *Kurt & Courtney* [1998], he wallowed in the tawdry, shamelessly bringing tabloid aesthetics and ethics to his 'investigative'

reporting. Maybe the difference this time lies in the fact that, in *Biggie & Tupac*, Broomfield is dealing with subjects who have already been so incredibly caricatured and misrepresented that the director was driven to new and higher levels of integrity just for the sake of developing a fresh angle on his characters.

It could also be that in turning over the stones of the two rappers' media personas, he discovered that who these young men were in private – often in stark contrast to their public images – was among the most shocking revelations he could bring. Biggie, contrary to his rapped tales of living in a one-room shack and going hungry, actually went to private school and had a cushy childhood; an old neighborhood friend scoffs at his tales of slinging crack and snatching purses and chains. 'No,' he laughs, 'not Christopher. He was a sweetheart.' Tupac, who perfectly embodied the equation that gangsta rap was born of real-life single black moms and reel-life Italian gangsters, was a voracious reader and a natural charmer who studied ballet, drama and literature as a child, despite the turmoil of having a Black Panther-turned-crack-addict mother and a string of addresses that were only temporarily called home. His biological father (whom the rapper didn't meet until late in his life) offers that, 'He wasn't the favorite son that everybody's pretending that he is now. [When Tupac became a star is when] he became the favored son.'

Armed with previously unseen home movies and rarely seen behind-the-scenes footage, and crisscrossing the country from Baltimore to Oakland, Brooklyn to Los Angeles, Broomfield fleshes out interviews with childhood friends, family members (Tupac's mom, Afeni Shakur, who controls his estate along with Death Row Records, is conspicuously absent) and former members of the rappers' inner circles. Former LAPD Detective Russell Poole – who, next to Miss Wallace, emerges as a true hero of the film – and former LAPD Officer Kevin Hackie guide the viewer through a Byzantine timeline and collection of data, and this is where Broomfield's shtick as the relentlessly probing, curious but slightly daft white Brit most effectively pays off.

With his deadpan delivery of questions and asides, and with the camera and boom mic jutting clumsily into the frame, Broomfield creates a proxy observer for the audience, particularly for mainstream viewers who may know little or nothing of the rappers or the worlds they rapped about.

But the film's platinum moment, when Broomfield finally interviews Suge Knight at Mule Creek Correctional Facilities, is powerful precisely for being such a letdown. Knight's weight has floated throughout the film. His threatening presence looms in interviews with Tupac's stepbrother, Mopreme, who tries to sidestep questions of Suge's influence on the rapper. It's felt in the almost visible trembling of a former bodyguard of 'Pac's who, though massively built, has retired to a private ranch and turned his life over to Jesus Christ – and just in case Jesus gets distracted, the man owns a snarling pack of rottweilers. When we finally meet Knight, who's hobbling on a cane, he bobs and weaves on questions about 'Pac, preferring to offer words of encouragement 'to the children.' With his eyes darting and his speech rambling, he's hardly the Faustian figure we've been prepped for; even the director's disappointment is palpable.

The 'showdown' with Knight, along with sundry incriminating revelations turned up throughout the film, has led to Broomfield being cited for bravery. And to some degree, he deserves it. (Even as he chides his cinematographer for having the jitters in the Mule Creek recreation yard, his own sense of fear and dislocation is palpable.) Still, if the truth be known, Broomfield's whiteness is his bulletproof vest.

A few years ago, when it was all the rage for disgruntled Negro rappers to assault critics and journalists, it wasn't Caucasian writers who were affected, and it wasn't the offices of *Spin*, *Rolling Stone* or *Details* that got trashed. For all their swagger, menace and bravado, hip hop's gangstas and thugs are a thoroughly domesticated breed. They know who to fuck with and who to leave alone. And – as the corpses of Biggie and Tupac verify – they know which lives are disposable.

PART FIVE

TUPAC RESURRECTED

JACKIN' BEATS

by Veronica Lodge

'We don't know where the masters are because we can't get an accounting from Death Row Records.' – Afeni Shakur on ABC's *Prime Time Live*, February 5, 1997

'I'm not mad, but I'm disappointed at Tupac's mother.' – Suge Knight in court commenting on Afeni Shakur wanting Tupac's recordings, while making his speech upon being sentenced to prison for probation violations, February 28, 1997

Tupac Shakur. A virtual wellspring of creativity and talent who spent endless hours in studios recording tracks, writing poems, songs and film scripts for movies he would like to see on-screen, like the story of Nat Turner or the illuminati. But the sanctity of his private work has been violated. Much of Tupac's unreleased material has now surfaced, resulting in more controversy as new issues arise regarding never-before-heard music. Within just a few days, this *Rap Pages* reporter was able to quite easily obtain thirteen Tupac bootleg CDs and cassette tapes without even having to make a phone call to do so. There were others that were available that I chose not to purchase, although I did make note of them. Afeni Shakur, Tupac's mother, can't control the release of her late son's music. How could this be? What's the history behind this?

The subject of Tupac's unreleased music was brought forth when Afeni Shakur filed a lawsuit against Death Row Records for $17 million last year in response to the claim made by Death Row CEO Suge Knight that Tupac owed Death Row $7 million.

Among the many complaints in that litigation was the failure of Death Row Records to pay royalties that were owed to her son. The legal briefs describe Tupac, who had been mysteriously gunned down in Las Vegas, as having died with no property, nor any substantial money of his own. At the time the suit was filed, it was pointed out by Rick Fischbein, an attorney for Tupac's estate, that Tupac had made Death Row

Records more than $100 million.

As part of her lawsuit, the former Black Panther presented an extensive list of expenses that Death Row Records had billed to Tupac and charged against his earnings. The suit described various expenses that were made to Tupac as being 'so pervasive, so blatant and so obvious, as to portray a pattern of fraud and deception involving millions of dollars.' The suit alleged that Death Row's claim that Tupac owed Suge money was fraudulently contrived, with Death Row citing figures calculated by deducting the fictitious expenses from monies owed to Tupac. The litigation cited specific expenses that Death Row had billed to Tupac, expenses that the suit called 'false and fraudulent.' The lawsuit contained detailed documentation along with corresponding check numbers.

Charges that were made to Tupac by Death Row included $23,857 for car repairs to a Porsche automobile. The suit made note of the fact that while Tupac didn't own a Porsche, Knight did. Other expenses the lawsuit questioned included a check for repairs for Death Row artist Michel'le Toussant's Range Rover, for which Tupac was charged $1,453.51. Among many other expenses, the lawsuit contended that Knight's Death Row Records' bill against Tupac's earnings were $57,600 for rent at an apartment that was occupied by other artists on the record label and not by Tupac, as well as $2,700 for child support paid on behalf of Nate Dogg, with check number 15404.

While the lawsuit brought into question many of the charges made by Death Row Records against Tupac's earnings, other issues were brought forth in the suit. Among them were issues that concerned the legacy of Tupac's music. A segment of the legal brief stated, 'Prior to his death, Tupac was the owner of some 152 musical works recorded by him which never had been released. Prior to his death, Tupac was entitled to the immediate possession of the unreleased recordings.' Subsequent to Tupac's death, plaintiffs, as representatives of Tupac's estate, became entitled to the immediate possession of the unreleased recordings.

The defendants [Death Row Records] are in possession of some or all of the unreleased recordings and they continue to wrongfully detain the same from the plaintiffs. The plaintiffs have demanded that the defendants return the unreleased recordings, but the defendants have refused and continue to refuse to deliver the same to plaintiffs. The value of the unreleased recordings is in excess of $100 million.

Donald David, an attorney for Tupac's estate, confirmed that Afeni Shakur has only received two DAT tapes from Death Row Records, and that the label is still holding onto the masters. David told *Rap Pages*: 'In order to mix a track properly for CD quality music, it's necessary that you have the underlying tracks from each of the instruments, voices, musicians, etc., to properly mix, amplify, eliminate and change whatever it is that comes to be the final composition.'

David contended that not only had Suge Knight still not given Afeni the master recordings, but also that he still has not delivered to her all of Tupac's unreleased songs. 'There are 151 tracks, but all we've received is 62.' When asked why Knight has not given these to Afeni, David's response was, 'I haven't been given a reason. Mr. Suge Knight is inaccessible right now,' referring to his present incarceration.

Rap Pages asked David if the songs appearing on bootlegs were also the tracks Knight had given to Afeni on DATs, or if they're part of other unreleased tracks that Knight is still holding on to. 'I can tell you, the one bootleg I saw, *Makaveli 2*, every one of them is on the DAT [given to Afeni],' he responded. 'This one was purchased in Harlem.' It was just before Suge Knight gave Afeni the DATs of these songs that the bootleg recordings of them began appearing on the streets.

As of present, issues in the lawsuit have still not been resolved. In the last few months, unauthorized bootleg recordings of Tupac Shakur's unreleased work have suddenly begun appearing. The sale of such bootleg tapes and CDs is illegal – a federal crime. No one knows yet – except perhaps those who are involved in or close to the situation – who is supplying the unreleased Tupac recordings for sale, or who is duplicating them for that purpose.

Obviously, there is no account reported with the sale of bootlegs. It's a total greed-fest. Among the many problems that surface from the sale of such illegal material is that the artist is not paid his proper percentage of royalties. In the case of Tupac's recordings, that would mean his estate is not being paid. Neither is the IRS.

When Afeni Shakur was interviewed on *Prime Time Live*, she made a statement that perhaps Tupac fans should consider before purchasing such illegal CDs and tapes. 'Please remember,' she said, 'that my great-grandmother was a slave, my grandmother was a sharecropper, my mother was a factory worker, and I was a legal worker, do you understand? And so this represents the first time in our life, in our memory, ever, that we have been able to enjoy the American dream, and that's what Tupac brought to his family.'

If Tupac Shakur, or his estate, particularly his mother, was not to be properly paid for the work he put in at the recording studio, nor to be compensated for royalties based on his sales figures, because of these bootlegs, it would be tantamount to slavery. However, that is precisely what is happening now with much of his work, due to the fact that someone is selling bootleg copies of rap music's biggest icon.

Afeni Shakur insisted to *Rap Pages*, 'Tupac could not and would not stand for his music to be bootlegged – past, present or in the future. Anyone involved in the bootlegging of his work on any level was and is taking money out of his pocket.'

Another question presented to Afeni involved the masters of Tupac's recordings. The answer was astonishing: 'The estate has not yet received any masters to which it is entitled. Death Row Records is still withholding the masters without any basis and not withstanding its agreement to turn them over some time ago.' In regards to this, negotiations are ongoing with Death Row.

> **'If Thug Life is real, then let somebody else represent it, because I'm tired of it. I represented it too much.'**
> **– Tupac**

Sadly, keeping Tupac's music safe from illegal recordings is now impossible for Afeni. The situation is clearly out of her control. With the masters remaining outside of her possession for safekeeping, there is seemingly little she can do to stop the plundering of her son's music. And if Tupac fans continue to consume the bootlegs in multitudes, her masters may ultimately be rendered void of value.

The unreleased material is being sold with such a vengeance, that the bootleg Tupac albums seem to have better distribution than most legitimately released products on independent labels. Throughout the country, bootleg copies of unreleased Tupac material have begun surfacing both on CD format and cassette tape formats. Album titles have appeared that include *Makaveli 2*

and *Makaveli 3*. One version of *Makaveli 3* is *Thugs Don't Die*. *Rap Pages* also obtained a CD titled *Makaveli 4*, a double CD comprised of primarily unreleased tracks.

There are different versions of these same album titles, containing various combinations of unreleased Tupac material. These bootleg CDs have appeared in Miami, Texas, California, Chicago, New York, Detroit, as well as other places throughout the country. One record store owner in Atlanta reported to a friend, 'Kids are asking for it [bootleg Tupac material] by the dozens.' In New Orleans, a double CD, sold discreetly in backrooms or kept quietly under the counter, can run as high as $50.

The availability varies with the location. A Tupac fan who had obtained one of the bootleg CDs, titled *Tupac Is Alive*, resides in the Deep South. He told *Rap Pages*, 'It was spooky. A friend of mine was told to call someone who would call someone else, and then meet yet another person at a Denny's parking lot three states away, in Texas. He did as he was told, and that's how we obtained this one.'

Some of the illegal recordings are crude-looking; others are neatly packaged in shrink-wrap; some of them actually have bar codes. At least one of the bootlegs bears artwork containing a threat against anyone who intends to make 'unauthorized' copies of it.

Perhaps the real definition of the term 'Gangsta Rap Recordings' should refer to illegally obtained recordings of rap music which are then put up for sale as, essentially, the true 'criminal' recordings.

Eric Nordquist is a recording engineer who mixes and produces albums. Among his studio credits, he has worked extensively with Bone Thugs-N-Harmony, and he mixed the song for the music video to 'Am I Dreaming?' featuring Old School and Xscape. *Rap Pages* joined Nordquist in the studio between sessions and let him perform an examination at the board with several Tupac bootlegs. Upon listening to the tapes and CDs, Nordquist observed, 'These don't sound like the bootlegs I listened to when I was growing up. These are much better quality.'

When asked if they sounded like a copy of a copy of a copy, he immediately responded, 'No. This one, for instance, sounds like all these songs had been mixed. They were put onto a cassette. And then someone took that cassette, or a copy of that cassette, and did this.' He added, 'These don't sound like rough mixes. They sound like they were good – the final mixes.' Ironically, one of the songs that appeared on one of the CDs was 'Thug Love,' a previously released track featured on Bone Thugs-N-Harmony's album *The Art of War*.

His reaction upon hearing it? 'The sound on this one is purposely not as good as the other CDs. I mean, I can tell it was taken off a tape. Why not just record the song off the Bone CD if this bootleg was made when the Bone LP had been out? Why do it off a tape? Someone may have doctored all of this one to make it sound like it was taken from a cassette.'

On other Tupac bootleg CDs, he noted, 'The quality is really pretty good. When I think of a bootleg, that's not what I think of. These are really clean for being bootlegs.' He added, 'Whoever did this knew what they were doing. They knew how to make a CD, and how to make this sound good.'

A few radio stations now have jumped on the Tupac bootleg bandwagon as well, playing some of the unreleased Tupac material. Is playing the illegally duplicated material really justified by a so-called demand from listeners, or is it, perhaps, merely a less-than-unethical ploy to hype up ratings in a competitive market?

Rap Pages contacted a radio station that is alleged to have started playing the bootleg Tupac material on the air. Vicky Preston, a music director at WJZZ FM in Detroit, told *Rap Pages*, 'Well, they [Amaru Records] haven't put out a single for a while. We are trying to play the music that our listeners are looking for. We're trying to stay fresh, current, ahead of the music game, because with that type of music [rap], it moves very quickly. It's always in need of something fresh. I'm looking for the next, the freshest, the newest, hottest thing.'

One might wonder, however, if Tupac's material is considered classic, why it would be so quickly disposable and in need of replacement and, thus, why, out of desperation, a bootleg should even be considered. Is this really love for hip hop? If this is the level of respect one holds for the music itself, why would there be any respect left for the artist?

When discussing the subject of radio stations playing bootleg Tupac material, a radio promotions employee at one successful rap label – who asked for anonymity – commented to *Rap Pages*, 'It doesn't surprise me. I've seen radio stations playing things, knowing full well that a cease and desist order will be coming in any minute.'

Also on the money trail, web pages on the Internet are now selling Tupac bootlegs. Others on the Net offer a free download of a sample of Tupac's unreleased material. Regarding the downloads surfacing on the Internet, Frank Creighton of the piracy division of the Recording Industry Association of America (RIAA) told *Rap Pages*, 'It's a violation of copyright law. People are under the misconception that it isn't, since they [the listeners] are not paying for the download, but that's not the case. In fact, there are probably one or two violations that are taking place before that download even takes place. Number one is copying that sound recording to a hard disk, which is a violation of the reproduction laws.'

Tupac at the first Annual Minority Motion Picture Awards, 1993. The aftermath of his death saw a deluge of posthumous bootlegs that diluted his legacy.

Creighton also stated of the Tupac cyber-boots, 'We have not brought any criminal actions, although we are currently seeking that out. The Net Act was enacted by the Clinton Administration that clarifies exactly these issues, pertaining to electronic delivery of sound recording.' Creighton says of the hobbyists who put up Tupac cyber-boot music on the Internet, 'Regardless of the demand for the fans, it's still the right of the artists and of the record companies as to how, when and where they distribute their materials. So if fans are receiving authorization from the artist and the record company to distribute this material, then so be it. If they're not, then it's absolutely illegal.

'We've sent cease and desist letters to over 500 Internet sites that offer these [bootleg] recordings to download.' He adds, 'I think the fans need to understand, a lot of them look at it like, This isn't going to hurt the big bad record companies or the artist, they have enough money. They need to understand that there are other people involved in the creative process of manufacturing a sound recording.'

Regarding Tupac's music, among those involved on that level is Afeni Shakur, who now heads Amaru Records, a label she formed to release her son's music, as well as that of new artists. Afeni's Amaru Records has been granted the right to re-release Tupac's four Interscope albums: *2Pacalypse Now*, *Strictly for My N.I.G.G.A.Z.*, *Thug Life* and *Me Against the World*. Amaru's first release was *R U Still Down? Remember Me?*

Clearly, the appearance of the Tupac bootlegs are a direct hit against the Amaru label. When Afeni was queried by *Rap Pages* about the financial implications of the bootlegs, the response was loud and clear. 'The estate is definitely being deprived of revenues that rightfully belong to it, and the wrongdoers are illegally profiting from the sales of Tupac's music.'

Publicist George Pryce, who once represented Death Row Records and now represents Amaru Records, told *Rap Pages*, 'I am amazed at the quality and the quantity of the bootlegged material.' It's expected that there will eventually be bootleg copies of bootlegs. Theories have arisen, and a few have surmised that perhaps the bootlegs are intentionally made to look as if they surfaced from different sources but, in actuality, they really came from basically the same place. One Tupac fan commented that it seemed strange that a Tupac bootleg CD contained unreleased material that was recorded shortly before Tupac's death, as well as older unreleased tracks: 'How would someone have access to all that?' One of the CDs, for instance, containing unreleased tracks that were recorded approximately three months before Tupac was murdered, also included an older track featuring Randy 'Stretch' Walker, who was fatally gunned down a year to the day after Tupac had been shot, when entering a recording studio in New York.

Among the collaborations found on certain bootlegs are Tupac and Notorious B.I.G. One of these is a freestyle 'Be the Realist,' while two others include 'Lost Soul' and 'Let's Get It On.'

Like vultures, a lot of people are trying to financially profit from this sad situation – ranging from Korean swap meet vendors in South Central Los Angeles who hawk the illicit tracks, to corrupt black record store vendors in New York City who hide the Tupac bootlegs under their counters. The greed has gotten out of control.

Afeni Shakur has made her attempts to put out the fires and stop some of this. Three Sacramento record producers were forced to scrap their plans to release an album containing two of the earliest recordings made by Tupac – 'I Thought U Knew' and 'Days of a Criminal' – when Afeni took them to court and blocked their release. Legal proceedings she filed called the producers' actions 'predatory' when discussing the unauthorized recordings. U.S. District Judge Lawrence Karlton issued a permanent injunction blocking their release.

Earlier this year, the Chicago police department confiscated 15,000 counterfeit CDs, tapes and videos worth more than $150,000, the *Chicago Tribune* reported. Among the findings were several Tupac bootlegs of unreleased material, most notably *Makaveli: The Lost Album*.

Will the appearance of Tupac's unreleased material on bootleg recordings devalue Afeni's later releases if she attains the recordings and wants to release them commercially through her Amaru label? Representatives for Tupac's estate notified *Rap Pages* that it expects to pursue its legal rights and remedies against bootleg operations selling Tupac's recordings. How many are involved in its tangled web is yet unknown.

Rap Pages contacted Death Row for a comment on the whereabouts of the master tapes, but no phone calls were returned.

WHO STOLE TUPAC'S SOUL?

by Allison Samuels

Terrance Combs scored one at a funky music shop on Melrose in Los Angeles. Kevin Jimmar got his at a fish market in Macon, Georgia. Jason Green copped one on a Miami street corner. And now they're among the thousands of lucky Tupac Shakur fans who own copies of the unedited, unauthorized Shakur albums that are variously titled *Makaveli II* and *III*, *Pac 4 Ever: Last Messages* and *The Last Words of Tupac Shakur*. 'It just feels real to me,' says the seventeen-year-old Combs. 'I just feel this is true 'Pac – plain, with no fancy videos and no flossing. Just 'Pac rapping from the heart.'

It's been two years since the charismatic 25-year-old rapper was murdered in Las Vegas, and still everyone – record execs, family members and fans – wants something from him. His mother, Afeni Shakur, who co-administers Tupac's estate, has been involved in a series of protracted and complex legal battles with Death Row Records, the rapper's former label, and its incarcerated CEO, Suge Knight. Two other authorized posthumous works – *Makaveli – The Don Killuminati: The 7 Day Theory*, which was a Death Row record, and *R U Still Down? (Remember Me)*, released by Afeni Shakur's Jive/Amaru – have gone triple and quadruple platinum, respectively.

Knight understands why Tupac's legacy persists. ''Pac was one of a kind,' he says from California's San Luis Obispo State Prison, where he's serving a nine-year sentence for a parole violation. 'He made music that was talkin' about something, and that's why people felt him so strongly. He'll never be forgotten, because he was a true black man that represented 100 percent.'

Now, the late rapper's unreleased work is beginning to pop up all over the country and is quietly becoming a hot black-market seller, though it's impossible to track the sales figures of such underground material. With tracks like 'Tear Drops,' 'Lost Soul' and 'Still I Rise,' the bootlegs offer up raw, gritty Tupac without the loopy, feel-good tracks like *R U Still Down*'s 'Do For Love.' Though *Makaveli II* and *III* are crudely recorded and come with amateurish or non-existent cover art, each full-length disc or tape fetches $10 at independent record stores, swap meets and flea markets. Someone is making a profit – enough of a profit, at least, to inspire the executors of Shakur's estate to investigate how music that they supposedly control made it to the streets in the first place.

And the material that has already surfaced is only the beginning. According to Knight, Shakur's voice will be heard for years to come. ''Pac was manic when it came to his music,' Knight says. 'He'd record all night, writing rhymes as he went. He never stopped – it was like he knew he was writing something to be remembered by.'

Indeed, no one's ready to forget. Determined to get their hands on any and all of Shakur's tracks, fans and retailers have bombarded Death Row's offices with calls demanding to know why they haven't been able to get copies. Retailers are angry that only a few stores have the tapes and CDs. 'People really believe this is some type of official release,' says one Death Row employee. 'When we explain that it's illegal, fans seem baffled and vendors proceed to give us the names of their competitors who are selling the albums.'

'I'm not sure how they decided who to come to,' one L.A. vendor says of his tight-lipped suppliers. 'We don't ask questions, and they don't offer any information. We just take them because every other person coming in is looking for it.' Even the major chains are pining for the popular LPs. 'I'd say every third person who comes in is asking for *Makaveli I* and *II*,' says Mykisha Thomas, a clerk at a Sam Goody in Fox Hills, California. 'We tell them Tupac has no new album, and they just think we're tripping. Sometimes I tell them it's at a swap meet.'

Not surprisingly, Death Row Records, which claims it is still owed one Tupac album, isn't taking the bootlegging in its stride; the company is planning an authorized Tupac record soon.

Since the rapper's unsolved murder in 1996, a number of disputes have erupted over the rights to anything and everything relating to Shakur – including more than 150 unreleased tracks recorded at Death Row's studios after he got out of prison. Both Death Row and the estate claimed the rights to the music; late last year, a settlement awarded all of the material to the estate. Death Row was in possession of the masters upon Shakur's death and was therefore responsible for transferring the music to the estate. In light of the recent developments, it appears clear that not all the music made it into Afeni Shakur's hands.

Richard Fischbein, the attorney for the Shakur estate, says bootleg sales of the unauthorized albums are causing the estate to lose revenue and promises that prosecution awaits all bootleggers. 'We're definitely going to get to the bottom of this, no matter how long it takes,' Fischbein says. 'We can only speculate on what could have happened to put it out there, and it only makes sense that it's a leak somewhere on the inside.'

But inside where? 'Anything could have happened in the transfer of those DATS,'

> **'He'll never be forgotten, because he is a true black man that represented 100 percent.'**
> **– Suge Knight**

says a source at Death Row.

'They were sent through the mail – who knows what fell out? People are saying it could have been an inside job, but we don't think so. What would Death Row have to gain from this? We're losing money, too.'

Knight thinks all the fuss over the bootleg releases is unfounded and that in the end all the finger-pointing might just lead right back to Shakur himself. ''Pac was always leaving tapes in cars, his friends' houses, anywhere,' says Knight. 'He probably just left one with somebody who decided to make some money off it. It's that simple. I mean, everybody knows the game, so if you're a friend with a tape, what you going to do? Give it back or make money?'

Knight should know. In 1996 Shakur's estate won a suit against Death Row and two other merchandizing companies for selling unauthorized hats and sweatshirts bearing Tupac's likeness. The estate was awarded more than $100,000, but that didn't end the bad vibes.

Despite the seemingly endless controversy, suits and countersuits, there are plenty of future profits in store for the Shakur estate, which is currently estimated to be worth at least $20 million. A major-feature biopic, an HBO documentary and a family-sanctioned biography are all in the works. And, if all the competing parties can find some common ground, there will be another LP, *Tupac's Greatest Hits*, ensuring that Tupac Shakur and his valuable legacy will continue to create a stir for years to come.

A ROSE BY ANY OTHER NAME
The Rose That Grew From Concrete

by Theresa Micalef

Published in 1999, with the help of Tupac's mother, Afeni Shakur, poet Nikki Giovanni and Tupac's manager, Leila Steinberg, *The Rose that Grew from Concrete* is a revealing collection of 72 poems written between 1989-1991, when 'Pac was eighteen-twenty years of age. Bursting with emotion, character and insight into the thoughts and fears of a young, yet compelling 'Pac, Steinberg thought it important that this work be presented to the public, because it bares a side of Tupac many never knew existed.

'Written when Tupac was nineteen, this poetry is free from the restraints of the music industry and all the monetary pressures. It is free of the anger that came from getting shot, betrayed, and thrown in jail for a crime I believe he never committed. It is Tupac before his fame,' says Steinberg in the book's introduction.

Following a preface by his mother, a foreword by poet and fan Nikki Giovanni and an introduction by his first manager and adult friend, the book is divided into four segments: 'The Rose that Grew from Concrete,' 'Nothing Can Come Between Us,' 'Just a Breath of Freedom,' and 'Liberty Needs Glasses.' His poetry focuses on poverty, struggle, love, politics, freedom and justice. Reproductions of Tupac's handwritten originals found on the facing pages of each printed poem add a personal touch.

Some of the most powerful poems are about 'Pac's mom, a Black Panther whose impact on her son's life is more than apparent in 'When Ure Hero Falls,' 'A River that Flows Forever' and 'Family Tree,' all dedicated to her.

Poems 'Just a Breath of Freedom,' 'Liberty Needs Glasses' and 'Government Assistance or My Soul' express the insight and passion 'Pac had for the issues he was all too familiar with. His numerous love poems, dedicated to Jada, April and Marilyn Monroe, among others, are uncharacteristic of the Tupac depicted by the media as a young man who personified roughness and vulgarity.

This book's major strong point is the hope conveyed within its pages, despite the obvious hardships 'Pac was experiencing. 'And 2morrow' epitomizes how and why this rose came up from the cracks, never mind the trampling from heavy feet above, becoming tangled in weeds and rooted in dirt.

Millions feel his absence in the game to this day and are left to wonder what could have been had he lived past quarter life. He spoke of 'death around the corner' many times in his rhymes, and now we learn that 'Pac's premonitions of an early death came even before he reached OG status and achieved industry recognition. Incredibly, he still managed to have hope for the future, even in the face of death. Maybe this is why he lived as he did; because there was so much he wanted to accomplish, in such a short time.

The rose that grew from concrete is the one that came up, that pressed on in the worst of predicaments and made it. This is the essence of Tupac. He will be forever missed. R.I.P. Tupac Amaru Shakur.

FOR HEAVEN'S SAKE

by Soren Baker

Behind every rap artist is a crew. In the case of 2Pac it was the Outlawz who had his back. After shining on Shakur's last posthumous LP, the battle-ready tribe has escaped from Death Row and is out for respect and a new record deal. Lord help them.

'Message to Eminem,' the Outlawz' E.D.I. explodes, 'Cut that shit out.'

E.D.I. (pronounced 'E.E. dee') and partners Napoleon, Kastro and Young Noble are situated in a lounge at Burbank, California's Enterprise Studios. The 2Pac protégés are explaining why they've got problems with Detroit's most famous rapper. The slightly pudgy E.D.I. sits between the bald-headed Kastro and the svelte Young Noble and a U-shaped couch, while the baby-faced Napoleon posts up across the room on a stiff-backed chair. But the crew might as well be in a boxing ring the way verbal jabs are being thrown around.

'You can talk about Christina Aguilera and all them,' E.D.I. continues angrily, 'but keep 'Pac's name out of your mouth, because that's dangerous to your health.'

See, the Outlawz didn't appreciate Eminem saying that he likes to 'Pop the same shit that got 2Pac killed,' on 'Busta Rhyme,' from Missy 'Misdemeanour' Elliott's 1999 album, *Da Real World*. And they certainly didn't appreciate 'Marshall Mathers,' the title cut from Eminem's new LP, where he says he's 'Leaning out a window with a cocked shotgun / Driving up the block in the car that they shot 'Pac in.'

'He says some shit that makes me think he's gay, because every time I hear him, he has 'Pac's name in his mouth,' Napoleon adds heatedly. 'We feel like he's on some disrespectful shit, because we don't hear him doing that shit about Biggie.'

'He's just annoying us right now,' E.D.I. adds, overstating the obvious. 'He's getting on our nerves.'

But the melanin-deprived rapper isn't the only one who has the Outlawz vexed. In fact, there's an entire list of ''Pac Biters' that the crew has issues with. 'Master P, he could've stole a 'Pac rap book from 1994,' Kastro fumes. 'He could have kicked 30 of them raps. His brother C-Murder, he took a song that was not even released, remade it on his last album and then dedicated it to 'Pac. He was like, "I'm going to steal your song, but I'm going to dedicate it to you." I don't know what they're thinking or what it was called. I don't listen to their music.

'Ja Rule, he don't know who he wants to be,' Kastro continues, sounding slightly calmer. 'Ja Rule will give it up and say, "'Pac influenced me," but Master P, C-Murder, they act like it's their own style. They'll say that C-Murder don't sound like 'Pac in every magazine, and now they've got Krazy, another fake 'Pac.' And the drama continues.

'We've got a hot list, people that if they don't holler at us, there's going to be problems,' Napoleon declares. 'Mobb Deep can't clear that up. Eminem, we want to hear what he's got to say. A lot of people don't know that we're listening. When they get on mix tapes and talk shit, our people call us.'

Like when Nas said, 'Thug Life is mine' on Mobb Deep's 'It's Mine,' from *Murda Muzik*. Those words, the Outlawz say, erased all the goodwill Nas established in 1999 with his shout-out to 'Pac on *I Am . . .*'s 'We Will Survive.'

'If you give it up and say that 'Pac is your favorite rapper, even Eminem, then it's cool,' E.D.I. says. 'We understand that. Everybody's got an idol. But they don't want to say it.'

In an age when any friend of a superstar seems to have a record deal the Outlawz are contractless, despite having been 2Pac's best friends. And despite the platinum success of *Still I Rise*, their 1999 album of tracks they laced with 'Pac. Today, the Outlawz are suing Death Row and still mourning the losses of 2Pac and group member Kadafi, both of them murdered.

For some, the Outlawz are the last link to 2Pac and his legacy. That's why their debut album is a do-or-die situation. They have to protect 'Pac's memory with a stellar album. They also need to prove that they're worthy of their affiliation with 'Pac. Like their mentor, the members of the Outlawz are associated with the West Coast, even though they hall from the East. Kastro, who is 'Pac's cousin, grew up in New York with E.D.I. in the late 1970s. Kadafi was 'Pac's godbrother. After 2Pac worked with Kastro, E.D.I. and Kadafi in 1992 as artists in their own right, Kadafi's mother kept telling 'Pac how a kid she knew could rap well and that when he was three, both of his parents were murdered in front of him.

''Pac heard the story of how he came up and it brought him to tears,' E.D.I. recalls. 'He was like, "I've got to meet this guy. He sounds like he's got to be with us."' 'Pac clicked with the rapper he later named Napoleon and invited him to join the group in 1994. Kadafi had also grown up with Fatal, whom he introduced to 'Pac and initiated into the crew in 1995. Young Noble, who had grown up around the other members in Montclair, New Jersey, joined in 1996. Other artists, including Mussolini and Kormaini, have also been associated with the Outlawz, although none of them are in the studio as the group works on its new album on this June evening.

Fatal, who released a 1998 album, *In the Line of Fire*, seems to be the only non-present member who is still affiliated with them. 'Nothing really happened to Fatal,' E.D.I. says. 'He's still family. He's doing a little time right now. He'd definitely be on our album. We're on his new album, on Rap-A-Lot. He chose to do his solo thing. He's a grown man and we're not going to stop him. The core of

the family is still together.'

It's a family that has been recording together for more than five years. Back then, E.D.I., Napoleon and Kastro almost signed with Interscope as Dramacydal, but the deal got nixed when 2Pac was about to get out of jail in 1995. 2Pac was super-loyal to Death Row's Marion 'Suge' Knight for balling him out, and he interacted with Death Row more than Interscope once he was freed. But his loyalty to the Outlawz never wavered. He featured them on both of his 1996 albums, *All Eyez on Me* and *The Don Killuminati: The 7 Day Theory*, his set as Makaveli.

The Outlawz say that 2Pac intended to sign them to his own future imprint, Makaveli Records, before he was shot and killed in September 1996 in Las Vegas. Kadafi witnessed that murder. A passenger in the car behind Suge's that night, Kadafi, nineteen at the time, was the only witness who told Las Vegas police he could identify the shooter.

Two months later, he himself was shot in the face at point blank range in Irvington, New Jersey. The Outlawz won't discuss the murders, except to say how difficult it has been for them to succeed under the circumstances. 'It's been hard without 'Pac and Kadafi,' E.D.I. says, 'but we're going to do it.'

After the tragic death of their leader, the Outlawz found their career in limbo. 'We were in the mix and we were in the process of signing and we thought we were going to be on Death Row,' Kastro asserts. 'But when he passed away, everything got fucked up. We moved away from California for a minute. As time passed, everybody was mourning, but there was just something that brought us to Death Row. We saw 'Pac's situation with them. In our eyes, he was on Death Row, so we've got to be on Death Row. It wasn't like Death Row was banging on our door, even though a lot of labels were. We banged down Death Row's door and they were like, "Come fuck with us."'

Adds Napoleon: 'We were confused. We were like, "'Pac rode for Death Row so we want to go back to Death Row and ride," because after 'Pac died and Suge got locked up, they were downing Death Row. We wanted to ride for them and bring them back, because basically that was what 'Pac was doing. But as time went by, we wanted to do our own thing. It isn't anything personal against Suge and Suge don't have nothing personal with us. We never disrespected him and he never disrespected us. But it got to a point where we wanted our own label. How could we work with someone who's locked up?'

At any rate, Rap-A-Lot Records' Lil' J was the only label owner who would record the Outlawz, placing them on the Geto Boys' 1998 album, *Do Good Do Bad & Do Ugly*. Although it was rumoured that Rap-A-Lot had signed the Outlawz, they now say they are not on the label, even though they say Death Row and Rap-A-Lot almost worked out a deal about a year ago that would have made that rumor reality.

Yukmouth, who put the Outlawz on at Rap-A-Lot, was a good friend of 'Pac and wanted to work with the Outlawz on his own music. He included them on 'Do Yo Thug Thang,' a street favorite from his 1998 solo album, *Thugged Out – The Albulation*. 'Those muthafuckas are 'Pac,' Yuk, who stopped by the Outlawz' recording session, says emphatically. 'The movement goes on. The Outlawz are the hardest shit moving. They're continuing with the the 'Pac legacy. Noble is one of the rawest ones. Napoleon has that street, hard shit. E.D.I., he got that straight-to-the-point hard shit with style. Kastro's got the lazy flow. It all comes togeth-

er like a pot of gumbo.'

It's a pot of gumbo that has proven to be worth millions of dollars. Interscope's *Still I Rise* from 2Pac + Outlawz has sold more than 1.3 million copies, even though it has been almost four years since 2Pac's death. Also, it marked the first time that the Outlawz shared top billing on an album.

The group members say that Interscope needed to offer fans a new version of 2Pac music, which is why they were featured prominently on the album. 'Interscope was putting out these 'Pac albums, and they were running out of formats,' Kastro opines. 'They were like, "Fuck it, let's put out this 'Pac/Outlawz album just to change it up and get us some sales."'

> **'I think being real is just being true. I'm the nigga that will wear a suit when everybody's got on khakis. I'll be baldheaded when everybody's wearing braids.' – *Tupac***

Plus, E.D.I. says, the group recorded too many songs with 2Pac for them not to be thrust into the spotlight. In fact, he says, the group has been an integral part of each of 2Pac's posthumous releases. 'We've been involved with every project that's come out since 'Pac passed, from the beginning to the mixing and everything,' E.D.I. says. '[*Still I Rise*] was another project coming up. Afeni, 'Pac's mother, made it so that nothing would come out without our hearing it and putting our approval on it because we know how 'Pac would want it to sound.'

And, largely on the strength of 'Pac's name, the album has gone platinum. 'On "The Good Die Young," you hear what he's talking about,' says E.D.I. 'All of the shit that he's talking about is still happening. "Babies catching murder cases / Scared to laugh in the sun." How many six-year-olds are shoot-

173

ing other six-year-olds?

'He saw that back in '96. Every time I hear that, it sends chills up my back because I'm like, "Where did that come from?"'

The same could be asked of the May lawsuit the Outlawz filed against Death Row, Suge Knight and Interscope Records, seeking damages in excess of $1 million for allegedly interfering with their career. According to published reports, the lawsuit alleges that the group signed with Death Row in March 1997 and delivered an album that the imprint refused to release unless the group turned over its publishing to Knight. It also alleges that the group's affiliation with Death Row ended in May 1999 and that Death Row instructed Interscope Records not to promote *Still I Rise*. 'All that lawsuit shit, that ain't personal,' Young Noble says. 'It's just business. That happens every day in the white offices. But they don't blow it up like that.'

On June 23rd, the Outlawz were granted an injunction that prohibits Death Row from interfering with the Outlawz' ability to contract for or market their services, according to Outlaw Recordz CEO, Big G. A Death Row spokesperson said that the Outlawz are still on the company's roster.

Adds E.D.I. of the lawsuit: 'It's just another thing that we've got to get over. It's been a long-ass road but ain't none of us ready to stop and ain't nothing going to make us stop. Whatever's in the way, it's just going to be there for a moment.'

For the moment, the Outlawz are focusing on their debut album, which they promise will be released on Outlaw Recordz by the end of October. Although the group would not say who its label will be affiliated with, they did say that 2Pac will not be featured on the collection.

'Right now, we can't really ride on his shoulders too tough,' Kastro says of 2Pac. 'I'm sure people are going to say, "We want to hear the Outlawz with 'Pac." But we can't

put out our album with him on there because we won't be able to establish our identity. That's what we really need.'

Later at the studio, Kastro excitedly emerges from the vocal booth. He's been working on an untitled song for the album, and his partners reward him with a series of pounds after he delivers a particularly punishing verse.

Completed songs such as 'Blessing' and 'Nobody Cares' ring with the type of emotion, promise and conviction that made 2Pac a hip hop favorite. The set's tracks, which were produced by mostly newcomers like 23 Productions, Femi, Mr. Lee, and Quimmy Quim, vary from placid and smooth to aggressive and driving.

While the Outlawz may have been schooled by 'Pac, their sound owes little to his more recent, most popular work. Where 2Pac's most famous beats and flows were smooth, radio-friendly and easily digestible, the Outlawz' album is filled with unbridled intensity, on both the lyrical and production sides. It appears to be a strong collection, one that will not be confused with anything 2Pac or his estate has put out in the last five years. By the group's count, this album will be the sixth that they have recorded, even though it will be their first release.

That's why, after recording and touring extensively with 2Pac and being in the limelight for several years, the crew remains driven, especially since many of today's chart-topping rappers bite their mentor's style. 'We haven't gotten ours yet,' Young Noble says forcefully. ''Pac has been gone and we've been on albums that have sold more than twenty million copies and we haven't put out our own record yet. We're hungry. We've got a definite spot in the game.

'The more people that are against us, the more we want to do it,' he continues. 'We haven't put out an album yet, but we're going to take the game over. Straight up.'

ETERNAL TRUTHS AND DEAD POP STARS

by Frank Ahrens

Jim Morrison is to Tupac Shakur as hallucinogens are to Glock 9s.

Both men were pop music icons of their generations. Both had fans that considered them prophets. Both wrote poetry. Both died because they trod the minefields of their times. Morrison's was the hedonist hellscape of drugs; Shakur's, the gunfire-strafed streets of gangsta rap.

Most similarly, both died under hazy circumstances – there was a three-day news blackout after Morrison's July 3, 1971, Paris death, followed by a closed-coffin funeral. Shakur was cremated only one day after his shooting death in Las Vegas – on Friday, September 13, 1996 – and no suspects have been apprehended. At the time of their deaths, Morrison was 27; Shakur, 25.

All of which has created a mythos around both Morrison and Shakur that lead a significant number of fans to believe that each is still alive. Theories that Shakur faked his own death outnumber even Elvis sightings.

Alexandria playwright and publisher Kwame Alexander has written a play about Shakur called *The Seventh Son*, which taps into the need to believe that the rapper is still alive. The title comes from African folklore, Alexander says: The seventh son of each family is meant to become its leader. Alexander posits Shakur as a seventh son of America, killed before he could reach his potential and uplift his followers.

The two-act play, set in Shakur's afterlife, opens tonight at the Rosslyn Spectrum Theatre in Arlington. One snowy day last week, Alexander took a couple of his actors and three of his play's monologues to Woodrow Wilson High School in Tenleytown and performed before 1,000 students, many of whom, by their show of enthusiasm, proved to be Tupac fans. That's where the similarities with Morrison end: Shakur still looms large over what he called the 'hip hop nation'; dozens of Web sites are devoted to proving he is still alive. Morrison's Dionysian epoch, by contrast, steadily recedes from relevance.

Alexander, 31, reminded the students that Shakur's stomach was tattooed with his mantra: 'THUG LIFE.' It was a purposefully contradictory acronym, Alexander said. Did anyone know what it meant?

One Wilson student offered: 'I don't have the "LIFE" part, but did "THUG" stand for "The Highest Under God?"'

'Hey, that's deep,' Alexander said, and handed him a free CD.

Another student got a burst of applause when she said, 'He got mixed up with the wrong crowd when he was young, and he felt that "Thug Life" was his family.' She also got a free ticket to the play.

'THUG LIFE,' explained Alexander, stood for: 'The Hate U Give Little Infants Fucks Everyone.' The tattoo was emblematic of Shakur's 'duality,' the complex character Alexander hopes to evoke in his play. He gave the students a further example:

Alexander, a former rap promoter, put on a Shakur concert in Charleston, SC, some years ago. After the show, Alexander drove his thirteen-year-old brother and Shakur to a party at a club. In the back seat with Shakur, the boy asked: 'How do I get in the rap game? I want to be just like you.'

'Don't do it,' Shakur said. 'It's shady. Stay in school. Go to college.'

Once at the club, however, Shakur abruptly switched gears, Alexander said.

'He went on the dance floor and got a girl and did some things that I don't want to tell you about,' he said. Then he asked the students: 'Why do you think that was?'

A boy in the crowd shouted out: ''Cause he was a hypocrite.'

Alexander smiled, seemingly pleased at the contentiousness stirred by his subject. Then he disagreed.

'It's because he was bold and truthful about who he was, whether you liked him or not,' Alexander said. 'The reason I wrote this play is because you don't know enough about the balance of Tupac's life.'

He mentioned various charitable works, such as day-care centers and Little League teams that the rapper supported. The ballet and poetry classes he took. But just then, the Tupac that these kids knew entered the auditorium.

The buzz built in the back of the room. Every head swiveled. There, or so it seemed, was Tupac Shakur, slowly, menacingly pimp-rolling down the auditorium aisles. Baggy jeans hung low. White muscle shirt underneath a long-sleeved denim shirt. Silver chain. Crablike hand gestures. Sad, sloe eyes under thick brows. And, atop a shaven head, the trademark blue kerchief, tied with the knot in the front.

Students called out to him – 'Yo! Tupac!' It was an uncanny bit of mimicry by New York actor Dennis White, 26.

He walked to the front of the auditorium and recited a rap-monologue from the play, dedicated to Shakur's mother: 'That's what your son misses most – I miss you, momma.' He read a poem that included none of Shakur's famously violent and misogynistic lyrics. It concluded with:
Sometimes I cry
no one wonders why.

Alexander's play is part of an image-rehabilitation effort underway to portray Shakur as more than your average gangsta, more than just a drive-by victim of an East Coast-West Coast rap war. A chapbook of Shakur's poems – written when he was nineteen – has just been published by Simon & Schuster. Titled *The Rose that Grew from Concrete*, it is a collection of juvenilia that shows a youthful sweetness absent from the ultra-violence of his last years, when his records sold tens of millions of copies. (Shakur's poems, it should be noted, are much more readable than Morrison's incoherent meter.)

Shakur was a tempestuous cauldron of better and worse natures, a convicted sex felon who had attended the Baltimore School for the Arts; a hustler on the streets of Oakland who earned critical reviews for his Hollywood roles. All of us, Alexander told the students, carry both natures. It may be less important to believe that Shakur is still alive (one web site posts what it claims are autopsy photos) than to examine his life, learn from it, and 'prevent what happened to him from happening to other potential Tupacs around.'

'Who knows,' Alexander speculated, 'he could have been president.'

From somewhere in the auditorium, the teenage voice of cynicism shot back:

'Not in your lifetime.'

The sentiment was clear: It's easier for at least some to believe that Shakur is still alive than to believe that a black man could be elected president.

ALL ODDZ ON ME
Think You Know Who Killed Tupac? Wanna Bet?
by Jordan Harper

I was lost late one night in Kansas City, totally lost on a road that seemed to get more decrepit and abandoned with each block I traveled. It was on this street that I saw a strange trinity painted on a wall: Martin Luther King, Malcolm X and Tupac Shakur. This was no piece of street graffiti; it was the well-manicured side of a church.

Tupac Shakur, who recorded under the name 2Pac, has reached the same quasi-religious status with inner-city blacks that Elvis had with poor Southern whites. I once owned a black-velvet painting of Elvis, a close-up of his face on which you could see the track of a single tear working its way down to his huge polyester collar. Hit any swap meet today and you'll find T-shirts with Tupac in the exact same pose. Why these men have been elevated to mythical figures is debatable, but one element is certain: a mysterious death.

As far as eerie deaths go, getting gunned down on the Vegas strip is a little more romantic than popping a gasket on the crapper. September 13 will mark the eighth anniversary of the death of 2Pac, who was shot six days earlier while cruising the Las Vegas strip with Death Row label-owner Suge Knight. The past eight years have seen 2Pac's rival, Biggie Smalls, shot down, followed by . . . nothing. No breaks in the case, no trial, no answers. On the long list of unsolved rapper murders (Jam Master Jay, anyone?), none invites more speculation or discussion than 2Pac's. Though none of the theories bouncing around have any hard evidence behind them, some have more weight than others. So while I can't tell you who really pulled the trigger, I'm willing to place some odds.

Theory No. 1: Suge Knight

Pros: In his book *LAbyrinth*, investigative reporter Randall Sullivan lays out in impressive detail the relationship between the feared Suge Knight and corrupt LAPD officers, going so far as to claim that Knight used Los Angeles cops to murder 2Pac, whom Suge owed a great deal of money. It's no stretch to envision murderous LAPD hitmen, and Knight is the closest thing hip hop has to a bogeyman. In the documentary *Welcome to Death Row*, a death-row security officer offers another piece of evidence: Knight told his bodyguard not to ride in his normal place in their car, sending him to another car before the shooting.

Cons: Knight was in the car when 2Pac was shot, catching a bullet fragment in his head. The gunman was firing directly at both of the men in the car (although 2Pac was the obvious target, and the fact that he tried to dive into the backseat may have been what saved Suge's life). No matter how much of a badass you think Knight is, can you really conceive of anyone planning a murder that puts them directly into the line of fire?

Odds: 6 to 1

Theory No. 2: The Crips

Pros: A few hours before he was shot, 2Pac and his posse badly stomped a Crip by the name of Orlando Anderson in the lobby of the MGM Grand. *Los Angles Times* writer Chuck Philips, in a 2002 two-part series, lays out the case against Anderson (who was murdered himself shortly after 2Pac's death) in great detail. Philips' argument is bolstered by the beating caught on security cameras, providing a crystal-clear motive that you can download on the Internet. If most people beat down a known gang member and were shot in a drive-by a few hours later, it would be an open-and-shut case.

Cons: Philips' piece is woefully lacking in verification, as it comes mostly from the unidentified mouths of gangbangers. You wouldn't buy a used car from an unnamed gang member, so why buy a murder rap?

Odds: 3 to 1

Theory No. 3: Biggie Smalls
Pros: After 2Pac was shot for the first time, outside a New York recording studio, the Notorious B.I.G. dropped a track called 'Who Shot Ya?' that was tacky to say the least. 2Pac had claimed in interviews and in songs that he had slept with Smalls' wife. The most public feud in rap history ended with both men dead when Smalls was shot to death during a visit to L.A.. This suggests that at least one person with a gun thought that Biggie had fingered 2Pac.

Cons: Absolutely no proof. Chuck Philips ends up compromising his article's credibility by including a ludicrous tale (once again, from an unnamed gangbanger) of Biggie and Orlando Anderson meeting up in Las

> **'By the next election, I'll be sitting across from all the candidates. I'ma be so far from where I am now in four years – God willin' I'm alive.' – *Tupac***

Vegas after 2Pac beat down Anderson. In this story straight out of a bad gangster movie, Smalls promises $1 million cash (!) to Anderson for committing a murder Anderson was going to commit anyway, then hands Anderson his pistol so that 2Pac will be killed with his own bullet. Silly beyond belief.

Odds: 10 to 1

Theory No. 4: 2Pac Lives!
Pros: Eleven, count 'em, eleven 2Pac discs have been released since his death. That's seven more albums than he released while alive. Proof beyond these increasingly poor releases is on the 'Paul is dead' level, involving dissecting and interpreting the smallest clues in 2Pac's lyrics.

Cons: Compare Jimi Hendrix's posthumous releases some time. Besides, all the other musicians who have 'faked their own death,' like Elvis and Jim Morrison, haven't popped up recently.

Need more proof? Got a strong stomach? Go to Google and type in '2Pac Autopsy color photos.' Any questions?

Odds: 1,000,000,000 to 1

179

HOOD SCRIPTURES

by Kris Ex

Tupac Shakur comes to us, searching for answers, searching for a worthy opponent, searching for the next word to his rhyme. His militant debut, *2Pacalypse Now* (1991), bursts at the seams with a pubescent grasp of black nationalism: broad-stroked diatribes against the police, heavy-handed denunciations of 'AmeriKKKA,' shout-outs to political prisoners and refugees, 'Words of Wisdom' is an incendiary blast of street corner punditry worthy of a young Farrakhan.

Despite the album's thick pedagogy, 'Pac is able to emerge as the nigga next door with 'If My Homie Calls' and 'Tha Lunatic.' But the best moments are 'Brenda's Got a Baby' and 'Part Time Mutha' where 'Pac assumes the position of observant storyteller. The result? Two songs that speak more about the black condition than all the fire-and-brimstone rhetoric spewed throughout the rest of the disc.

Where the overwhelming majority of music artists peak with their early work, *2Pacalypse Now* shows promise that 'Pac's best days are ahead of him. But things get worse before they get better.

Strictly 4 My N.I.G.G.A.Z. (1993) represents the nadir of 2Pac's musical career. The sounds are a hodge-podge of Cali crafts vying for New York novelty. 'Pac tries to be everything to everyone here: Then-Vice President Dan Quayle's boogeyman, the savior of the Black Nation, and friend to all MCs.

Possibly gassed from being called out by Quayle as Nigga Enemy No. 1, 'Pac thinks he found a style as the stuttering, sometimes constipated rhyme schemes of *2Pacalypse* give way to muddled badassness. He also stops wrapping his topics within musical concepts, save for 'Papa'z Song,' a first-hand rebuking of a deadbeat dad, and his two breakthrough hits: 'I Get Around' and 'Keep Ya Head Up.' The latter succeeds much in the same way as 'Brenda's Got a Baby.' When 'Pac notices that 'they got money for wars but can't feed the poor,' moments after reminiscing on Marvin Gaye, he's calm but not cold, detached but not distant, as if he just opened up his mouth and let God come out.

The group effort *Thug Life* (1994) is where the 2Pac legend begins in earnest. 'Pac, who started sporting a bald dome with *Strictly . . .*, takes to wearing the bandanas that would become his signature, perfects the rhyme technique that would appear in analog via countless imitators, and begins his fascination with glory-through-death on 'Pour Out a Little Liquor,' 'Bury Me a G' and 'How Long Will They Mourn Me?'

'Pac's transformation into a West Coast ridah is evident on *Thug Life*. Divided into an East Side and West Side, the LP uses all of the G-music staples: samples by the Isley Brothers, Curtis Mayfield and the O'Jays as well as Parliament and Bootsy Collins. On 'Stay True' 'Pac describes, 'Rolling down the 405 gettin' high / . . . Cruisin' in a 6-0 Impala, driving like I'm in a hooptie / . . . 'Cause I can make the ass drop / Make the front pop / And hit the three-wheel motion.' Still, he adds texture and a vulnerability to the gangsta archetype on 'Under Pressure,' when he rhymes, 'You wonder why I'm made this way / I wasn't turned-out / I was raised this way / . . . I'm stressed / Smoking weed and nicotine / But what a nigga really need is Thorazine.'

On *Me Against the World* (1995) ''Pac goes from ashy to classy. He discards his ultra baggy gear, gaudy, oversized rings and things, and covers up his numerous tattoos in favor of a button-down shirt, understated jewelry and spectacles; he flashes his winning smile. Likewise, his music – a smoothed blend of R&B bass and drums tweaked for hip hop consumption – begins to serve him. The tracks no longer overpower him, his flow becomes more relaxed and confident.

He sounds free on *Me Against the World*; as if he's making music to please himself for the first time. Gone are the pressures of living up to the expectations of his Black Panther family tree. Despite nihilistic numbers like 'Fuck the World' and 'Death Around the Corner,' 'Pac is ready to live on cuts like 'It Ain't Easy,' and 'So Many Tears.' With 'Dear Mama' and 'Can U Get Away' he zeroes in on a one-on-one dialogue absent from his earlier material, speaking directly to his mother and a fictional girl stuck in an abusive relationship. He's coming into his own.

'I won't deny it / I'm a straight ridah / You don't want to fuck wit' me.' These are the first words on 'Pac's mammoth Death Row debut *All Eyez on Me* (1996). The album is a paradox. Reveling in his own legend and acting under the aegis of the world's most notorious record label.

'Pac's never sounded better: but he rarely delves beneath the surface. 'What'z Ya Phone #' and 'How Do U Want It' are great in their documentation of conviviality, wantonness and carnality – you can hear the Alizé pouring, the panties dropping, the bed springs bouncing. Bolstered by the best beats Suge could secure, 'Pac rhymes like he could go on forever on 'California Love (Remix),' 'Ambitionz az a Ridah' and 'Got My Mind Made Up.' But on 'Heartz of Men,' 'Cant C Me' and 'Holla at Me' he sounds hollow and directionless as he rails against his 'enemies.' 'Shorty Wanna Be a Thug' comes off as a paint-by-numbers admonishment of the thug life.

Most of the elements on 2Pac's last conceived album, *The Don Killuminati: The 7 Day Theory* (1996) are his standard fare – gleeful helpings of debauchery ('Toss It Up'), overflows of dementia ('Krazy'), tirades against foes ('Bomb First [My Second

Reply]'), and the requisite ray of sunshine ('To Live & Die in LA'). But he comes full circle on 'White Man'z World,' asking his 'true sisters' to 'help me raise my black nation' and once again shouts-out political prisoners. When he screams 'Babylon beware / Comin' for the Pharaoh's kids' on 'Blasphemy,' you hear two voices: that of the thug and the revolutionary.

His concepts take a mature turn on 'Me and My Girlfriend,' a song long metaphor, on 'Just Like Daddy' he comes to realize that his true appeal to many women lies in his presentation as a surrogate father not as a sex symbol. He holds 'Against All Odds' to be 'the truest shit I ever spoke,' but nothing is as revealing as 'Hail Mary.' Here 'Pac is in love with the song of his own voice: he breaks into small flutters of breathy melody, secure enough in his artistry to simply end his chorus with a diatonic non-sequitur. Then he says: 'I ain't a killer, but don't push me.' It's a statement that pushes him beyond his rebel-without-a-pause caricature and into more tangible territory.

He's no longer martyr or messiah. He's just a nigga playing with the hand he was dealt.

It wasn't like we needed any more sticks in the nest of confusion surrounding Tupac's demise. The hard-headed and conspiracy-weary alike already had a stocked arsenal suggesting that 'Pac was somewhere sipping umbrella drinks with Elvis, Sammy the Bull and the third shooter from the grassy knoll: No memorial service, no body, that chilling 'I Ain't Mad at Cha' video, 'Pac's whole Niccolo Machiavelli fascination.

But then, just months after his death, the first of 2Pac's bootleg Makaveli series – full of unreleased material, from his Death Row tenure – began flooding the streets. Even the most level-headed persons became doubting Thomases, wanting to finger 'Pac's wounds for proof. As theories reached a convincing surreal fever pitch (recall Chuck D's 'Eighteen Compelling Reasons Why

Tupac is Not Dead'), 'Pac probably pinched himself and checked his own pulse to make sure he was, well, dead.

Now that the hubbub has subsided and (almost) everyone can agree that 'Pac is no longer with us in the physical, these works go a long way to fortifying his new millennium urban legend: '2Pac-was-the-Hardest-Working-Rapper.' One has to marvel at the tremendous amount of studio work he put in between October 1995 and September 1996, allowing him to drop more albums in death than the average rap artist drops in two lifetimes.

As bearers of the Tupac legacy, the Makaveli albums shine brighter than the cash-cow opportunism of releases like *1 in 21: The Tupac Shakur Story*, *The Lost Tapes*, *Legends*, the *Pac & Biggie You Never Heard*, and *Stop the Gunfight*. Those records are mostly deplorable jumbles of outtakes and remixes; the worst cases just retread rare vocals over bargain basement beats. Also, there's a raw, jagged-edged allure to the Makaveli series that's lost in the commercial sleekness of official posthumous collections like *R U Still Down? (Remember Me)* and *Until the End of Time*. Then there's questionable quality control endemic to all things black market: there are two versions of *Makaveli 5: Thug's Passion*; something sold as *Makaveli 7* contains no 'Pac at all – just a soundalike player paying tribute. *Makaveli 7* makes you cringe: Those ain't 2Pac vocals – what the fuck you done to that?

The best and most valuable album of the unofficial series, *Makaveli 2: Life Passion* features no song breaks – just segues from one song to another. Conceived by parties that had in mind to continue 'Pac's beef with certain East Coast parties, the LP contains interviews where 'Pac chastises the Notorious B.I.G. and reveals the genesis of his beef with Mobb Deep. ('Pac took a low-end ad-lib in the chorus for Mobb's 'Survival of the Fittest' ['Thug life, we still livin' it'] as a subliminal jab to his famous jailhouse renunciation of the thug life.) In song, 'Pac berates Jay-Z

(who gets a lion's share of harsh words throughout many of the series' earlier offerings with no explanation), L L Cool J, Da Brat, and Lauryn Hill. Radio gossip Wendy Williams gets threatened with a '$20,000 hit through Jenny Craig' on a foam-mouthed diatribe that ends 'Why U Turnin' on Me?' (Williams' name was omitted when the song was released on this year's *Until . . .*)

Makaveli 2's saving grace comes in its music: the jam session backing tracks for the social commentary of 'Never Be Peace' serves its topic well. Likewise, the lone horn that punctuates 'Words 2 My First Born' makes it more poignant than its *Until . . .* version; the included version of 'Black Jesus' flows smoother than its rendition on the Outlawz' *Still I Rise*. And, almost as if to prove 'Pac was not wholly anti-East Coast, there's 'Military Minds,' a collaboration with the Cocoa Brovas and Buckshot that bounces with menace.

All but five of *Makaveli 3*'s songs (or some semblance thereof) have since been made public, some on the *2Pacalypse Now*-era retrospective *R U Still Down*? 'World Wide Dime Piece' features Greg Nice, with Snoop closing the number out with silky pimp talk much like *All Eyez on Me*'s 'All About U;' 'Cause I Had To,' which interprets Bill Withers' 'Just the Two of Us,' is a pre-*Thug Life* justification for dealing drugs; ''Pac's Life' uses Prince's 'Pop Life' and interview snippets to tell his story.

Collaborations play a prominent role in one rendering of *Makaveli 5*, which also contains older vault material like 'Fuckin' wit da Wrong Nigga,' a rendition of 'Grab the Mic' (found on *The Pac & Biggie You Never Heard*) and 'Static' (mixes of which appear on *Legends*, *1 in 21* and *The Lost Tapes*). Many of the songs are from 'Pac's never-realised *One Nation* project: 'How Many Shots' featuring the Outlawz, the unfinished Big Daddy Kane duet 'Wherever You Are,' the reggae-hooked 'Let's Get It On' with the Cocoa B's and Buckshot. On 'Set It Off,' 'Pac, his Boot Campian comrades and Greg Nice

'I didn't create T.H.U.G. L.I.F.E., I diagnosed it.' – Tupac Shakur

borrow a chorus from Strafe's 'Set It Off' and Funkadelic's 'One Nation Under a Groove' ('getting down the for the smoke of it') in a round of microphone hot potato. 'World Wide Mob Figgaz,' bridged by snippets of *GoodFellas* and *Reservoir Dogs*, contains Outlaw lyrics different from its *Until . . .* version.

Makaveli 6 resorted to rejected tracks from his *Strictly 4 My N.I.G.G.A.Z.* and *Thug Life* days, some of which appear on *R U Still Down?* Then there's the female variant of 'Fake Ass Bitches' only featuring 'Pac on adlibs and dated stuff like 'Outta the Gutta' and 'Thug Bitch,' on which 'Pac doesn't do so much as fart. Still, there are some good moments: The haunting 'Hard on a Nigga;' 'Fuck All Y'all' which samples 'Breezin'' by George Benson; 'Throw Your Hands Up,' powered by Parliament's 'Funkentelechy.' Despite such aged music, *Mak 6* did its part to cement 2Pac's position as a thug immortal – dead or alive.

HIP HOP REQUIEM

by Neil Strauss   **Mining Tupac Shakur's Legacy**

On Monday afternoon Adam Gassman, a fourteen-year-old from Queens, stood amid a gaggle of teenybopper girls outside MTV's Times Square studios, as he does almost every day after school. While the schoolgirls begged producers to let them into the studio for the day's taping of *Total Request Live*, Adam looked on dour-faced. In his hand was a large white sign with two words sloppily scrawled in thin black marker: 'Tupac lives.'

At the same time on Fourth Street in the East Village, at the New York Theater Workshop, tickets were on sale for *Up Against the Wind*, a play about Tupac Shakur's life and 1996 death in a drive-by shooting. It opened last week, featuring an actor who looks remarkably like Shakur, along with others playing Puff Daddy, Suge Knight of Death Row Records, Jimmy Iovine of Interscope Records and other real-life characters.

Several blocks farther downtown, on Canal Street, street vendors were hawking eight separate volumes of posthumously released recordings (and two volumes of remixes) on Cochise Records from a late period in Shakur's career when he was recording under the pseudonym Makaveli (a vengeful character who raps that he is sicker than a Nazi) in addition to numerous Shakur bootlegs and recordings by an ever-increasing army of sound-alikes, among them Tha Realest and Krazy.

Shakur's latest legitimate posthumous album, the two-CD set *Until the End of Time* (Interscope), is Number One on the pop charts, having sold an impressive 427,000 copies in its first week. In Georgia the Tupac Amaru Shakur spring camp session for disadvantaged youths is under way. Land there has just been bought for a future Tupac Amaru Shakur Performing Arts and Cultural Center, a combination gallery, museum, performance space, community center and shrine planned by the Tupac Amaru Shakur Foundation.

Add to this a Quincy Jones-backed Hollywood feature on Shakur, an MTV special about his early days, a big-budget documentary film and volumes of additional official recordings to come, and you have a cultural revolution staged by a corpse. 'How long will they mourn me?' Shakur asked in the song of the same name. By the looks of it, a long, long time.

'He is going to be viewed as one of the most respected African-Americans of the last generation,' said Elliott Wilson, the editor of the hip hop magazine *XXL*. Michael Develle Winn, who wrote *Up Against the Wind*, said, 'Tupac is the closest thing in some ways to a revolutionary that we have had.'

That wasn't what many African-Americans were saying before he died at age 25. 'Case Brings Bad Image to Blacks,' proclaimed a headline in one African-American newspaper after Shakur was convicted of first-degree sexual abuse in 1995.

Like Shakur's music, which vacillated between glorifications of the thug life and beautifully moralistic elegies for the wages of that life, public opinion was sharply divided.

But in the four and a half years since his unsolved murder in Las Vegas, Shakur has progressively become a much greater symbol. The cover of his very first posthumous record depicted him nailed to a cross, a hip hop martyr.

'Now that Tupac is dead, people don't have to bother with the actual details of his life,' said Bill Adler, a former record executive and spokesman for rap groups like Public Enemy. 'He's going to be Jim Morrison, he's going to be Rambo, he's going to be whatever people make of him.'

The person who's been making the

most of Tupac has been his mother, Afeni Shakur, a former Black Panther who conceived her famous son while free on bail after she was charged with conspiracy to blow up several Manhattan buildings. (She was acquitted.) Because of her, her son is the first rapper with an estate and legacy that is being carefully, even obsessively, maintained and marketed.

Ms. Shakur is in charge of the Tupac Amaru Shakur Foundation, the Tupac Amaru Shakur Performing Arts and Cultural Center and Amaru Records, the only official home of her son's posthumous recordings. And her mark is all over his posthumous work. In the liner notes to *Until the End of Time*, his current Number One album, only one lyric has been blown up in large type, and it is a line in which he pays tribute to his mother.

Some have said that Ms. Shakur is trying to remake Tupac into the son she never had. Mr. Winn, the playwright, said, 'She's trying to show the world the son that she saw.'

In an interview this week Ms. Shakur said her responsibility as his mother was clear. 'People can like him or not like him individually,' she said. 'But I need for them to know that he was a person of substance, and he was worthy, and he was a good son and a good brother and a good participant in the community.'

She paused, and added: 'I just need to do 'Pac's work. I just need to. Maybe because I'm a recovering addict, I'm obsessed like that.'

Now, Shakur wasn't the best rapper of his time, nor are any of his albums masterpieces of the genre, though some of his singles are stellar. Many rap fans will admit that the Notorious B.I.G., who was gunned down in 1997, was a better rapper and lyricist. But Shakur was a better star, a more charismatic presence, a more gifted actor, a bigger lightning rod for trouble, a more complex visionary. And as the flurry of posthumous recordings has shown the world, he was incredibly driven.

'You don't think of Tupac as a traditional MC,' said Mr. Wilson of *XXL*. 'You think of

him as a workman. I don't know how he had time to make all these songs and do movies and run around with women and get in trouble. He had more hours in the day than most of us do.'

When her son died, Ms. Shakur fought in court, with Death Row Records, among others, to gain control of his music. With no experience she became the chief executive of her own record company. Running the label with the mind of a mother and idealist instead of as an executive and profiteer, she made sure that her son's artistic side was emphasized over the dark thug side that landed him in jail on several occasions. She released a book of his teenage poetry far more impressive and literary than, say, Jewel's and several months ago released a record of Danny Glover, Quincy Jones, Mos Def and others interpreting the poems, *The Rose that Grew from Concrete, Volume One*.

'Since the mother's involved, she's definitely trying to give it a more positive spin of what he represented,' said Mr. Wilson.

Perhaps there is some evidence of this in *Up Against the Wind*, because the script, for legal reasons, had to be condoned by Shakur's family. Both Ms. Shakur and Mr. Winn said that nothing in the play was censored but that changes were made at the suggestion of the family that they described as factual. Nonetheless, the play manages to walk a difficult line: it's knowledgeable enough to appeal to Shakur's fans without patronizing them, but at the same time it's clear and engaging enough to engage the straitlaced (outside of the constant stream of profanities).

Mr. Winn begins the story with the first main event leading to Shakur's downfall, his arrest on rape charges. Taking the story through his non-fatal shooting in Manhattan, his post-prison transformation into a swaggering, high-living, gang-affiliated member of Death Row (where, perhaps, he found a father he never had in Suge Knight), and his subsequent murder, the play portrays Shakur as a victim of celebrity,

For Tupac, it was highly possible that he viewed Suge Knight as the father figure that he had always lacked.

media vilification, the ruthless record business, his family, his own bad decisions and his destiny.

In the post-gangsta requiems that he specialized in, Shakur wallowed in a certain resignation to a tragic fate, even for those with the best of intentions. The circumstances leading to his death could easily have been just another one of his songs.

'The Tupac in my play is a guy who wanted to do something good,' Mr. Winn said. 'What he wanted to do was to change the public's opinion of who he was and where he came from. I think he wanted to change the way he felt about himself in the process. But he was dealing with a lot of pain. His mother prepared him for a different time. The commercialisation of our society doesn't allow for revolutionaries who can't back a product.'

This is Mr. Winn's Tupac. Many others, like Adam Gassman outside MTV's studios, have their own vision of a Tupac still living and breathing and inspiring them to pick up the microphone.

Tupac Shakur no longer belongs to Tupac Shakur. Soon he won't even belong to Afeni Shakur. He will belong to playwrights, filmmakers, novelists, television executives and other modern-day mythmakers. Soon a generation that has been weaned on his albums since 1992 will grow up. And Shakur will be their Motown or John Lennon or Malcolm X.

They will make pilgrimages to Georgia to see his cultural center, and petition Las Vegas to declare the stretch of road where he was shot a historical landmark. And thus he will become enshrined as a grand, idealized cultural idol, as selective memory erases the bad and vaunts the good, even if his art drew its power from exploring the ambivalent territory between the two.

So how long will they mourn him? 'We don't know how long they'll mourn him,' said Ms. Shakur. 'But we hope that one day they'll celebrate him.'

TUPAC RESURRECTION

by Rita Michel

Even though there has been a rash of Tupac related documentaries looking at everything from the last year of his life seen through the eyes of his bodyguard Frank Alexander (*Before I Wake*), to his record company (*Welcome To Death Row*), and including unlikely exclusive interviews (*Words Never Die*), *Tupac: Resurrection* stands out because it is, in fact, a resurrection. The film brings Tupac to life – his aura, his charisma, and his development, creating a real connection. Through graphics and the editing of the documentary footage which is primarily Tupac discussing his own life, the filmmaker Lauren Lazin, an Emmy-nominated editor, producer, and director, really allows the audience to eavesdrop on a very complex personality.

Rita Michel: *How would you describe Tupac?*

Lauren Lazin: Honest, charismatic, insightful, complicated, funny, and sweet; of course, my image of Tupac is frozen in time, he died at 25.

Rita Michel: *I got, not necessarily a chronologically exact portrait, but a sense of the growth of a person. Was that one of your first goals?*

Lauren Lazin: I'm happy that you picked up on that. When we were at a crossroads, 'how are we going to tell the story of the shooting?,' or 'how are we going to tell the story of going to prison?,' it was always: 'let's go back to his psychological state; let's go back to his psychological development. What clues do we have that tell us where his head was at, where his heart was at that time?'

Rita Michel: *Was that difficult to do?*

Lauren Lazin: He was someone who was deeply reflective, and it didn't matter where the interview came from. Anytime anybody asked him a question, he took it to heart and really thought about it and gave an interesting answer.

Rita Michel: *Your career basically began at MTV. Do they always have so much footage on a particular artist? Or was there some person that was carrying his footage specifically?*

Lauren Lazin: There are certain people whose careers we cover more extensively. Tupac loved talking to media channels. He loved to sit there and tell them what they were doing wrong and tell them what they should change. Dave Surelneck, who is my boss, is a big hip hop fan, he 'got it' very early on that Tupac was somebody that was going to be important. It was because of him we had so much footage.

Rita Michel: *What was the thought process behind scrolling his written words?*

Lauren Lazin: I wanted to do something more interesting graphically than any typical scene in a documentary. I wanted it to have a little design to it, a nice feel to it, that wouldn't be distracting but would still have some style to it. So we worked with these guys from Sony, Fred Salkind and Stephanie Mazarsky, and they came up with the whole graphic look of the piece. I really like it, I felt like his journals, his writing, they come alive. The chronotype, the titling type was all from Tupac's handwriting so that it would definitely have his feel.

Rita Michel: *The aerial shots throughout the movie, what was your intention?*

Lauren Lazin: To me it was just a beautiful way to shoot the film. I wanted it to look like a film, and not a TV show . . . I wanted this to feel bigger than TV. I think it's really up to the viewer to take away from that how it made them feel.

Rita Michel: *I'm a big one for past lives, present lives, I got that there's so much of Tupac's energy still in the world that it felt like the film is where he is right now. He's observing this with us as he's telling his story.*

Lauren Lazin: That was our hope, that people would feel that way. There are two Tupacs in the movie, there's the Tupac that's with us sort of telling the story, and there's the Tupac you are seeing living his life.

Rita Michel: *In the film he said that he liked women, you could have shown him going to a gala event with a woman on his arm, but you chose to show him about to close the door and do something personal with various women. Why?*

Lauren Lazin: He *loved* women; it was a big part of his identity. The photos that we used in the movie were like a fraction of what we found. When we were going through his vault, his personal materials, every phone number that someone gave him, he kept, as far as I could tell. Every letter a woman wrote him, every picture someone sent him, it was not something that he just tossed aside. He just loved his women fans.

I felt that footage was very provocative. He himself said, 'I'm a man, yeah I write this sensitive music, but I'm also just a guy.' How old was he, 23, or 24? Famous women were interested in him. I also thought that was an interesting bit of footage to include in the film before the charges of sexual assault. It just gives you a little bit of a window into what that world is like. There are women available, it's sort of ambiguous, do they want to be here, do they not? Are they here only because he's famous? To me it really set the stage for why things got very complex later. I just wanted to show the atmosphere that he was in so you weren't totally surprised when all of a sudden someone says I don't really want to be here, look what you made me do. He himself was very, very honest. He had deep loving relationships with many strong black women that he respected and loved. But he also says, 'I loved having sex without any emotional connections. I loved acting out all my fantasies.' He was a great sensualist, he had two sides and he didn't see them as conflicting.

> 'Tupac loved talking to media channels. He loved to sit there and tell them what they were doing wrong and tell them what they should change.'
> — Lauren Lazin

TUPAC'S BOOK SHELF

by Mark Anthony Neal

On April 17, 2003 a group of scholars, journalists and fans gathered at Harvard University to talk about hip hop. The occasion was the symposium 'Tupac Shakur and the Search for a Modern Folk Hero.' Sponsored by the Hip Hop Archive, the W. E. B. Du Bois Institute for Afro-American Research and the Program for Folklore and Mythology at Harvard, the event examined Tupac's legacy as an intellectual, a political figure and an urban folk hero. The Hip Hop Archive at the W. E. B. Du Bois Institute, currently under the leadership of Harvard anthropologist Marcyliena Morgan, was launched in January of 2002 and is one of the first scholarly archives devoted solely to hip hop music and culture. The symposium was yet more evidence of the current engagement between American academics and the burgeoning culture that had its birth in urban centers throughout the United States 30 years ago.

Scholars such as Michael Eric Dyson, who was the keynote speaker for the event, Tricia Rose and Todd Boyd have made careers out of being hip hop pundits. Dozens of courses focused on hip hop culture are taught at the nation's colleges and universities every semester. The Hip Hop Archive has documented the majority of these courses on their web-site. But 'Tupac Shakur and the Search for a Modern Folk Hero' struck a particularly strange chord because of its location at the pre-eminent American University and under the auspices of the leading African-American intellectual Henry Louis Gates, Jr., who directs the W. E. B. Du Bois Institute. Despite all of the books written about it, hip hop culture still bears the burden of having to defend itself as a legitimate site of scholarly inquiry. As one person commented to me shortly before the event, 'If Tupac is or could ever be an "urban folk hero" to anyone but a brain addled white kid from the suburbs, then much of our intellectual capital is already lost.' On the contrary, all of the scholars who congregated for the symposium proved that not only are the scholarly fields of African-American and Afro-Diasporic Studies thriving, but that Tupac Shakur and hip hop as a whole remain vital guideposts to black culture in the post-Civil Rights era.

The symposium was broken down into three distinct panels. The opening panel, titled 'Theoretical T.H.U.G. Battles: Mapping the Intellectual Legacies of Tupac Shakur,' featured Knut Aukrust and Northeastern Communications professor Murray Forman. In his talk titled 'Tired of Hearing These Voices in My Head: Baktin's MC Battle,' Aukrust, a professor of Culture Studies at the University of Oslo, described his introduction to Tupac while driving through an Italian city as his sons popped into the car stereo a copy of Tupac's *Makaveli – The Don Killuminati: The Seven Day Theory*. Aukrust conveyed his surprise that the dead rap artist had been well read in the works of the fifteenth century Italian writer Machiavelli (*The Prince* and *The Art of War*). Forman's paper, 'Tupac Shakur: O.G. (Ostensibly Gone),' discussed Tupac's after-life as an Internet icon. The author of the recently published *The 'Hood Comes First: Race, Space, and Place in Rap and Hip-Hop*, and co-editor (with myself) of the forthcoming *That's the Joint!: A Hip-Hop Studies Reader*, Forman argued that 'having transcended "the real" in death Tupac merges with the hyperreal – where he is arguably rendered more knowledgeable, more proximate.' A third presentation by myself (author of the forthcoming *Songs in the Key of Black Life*, June 2003) discussed Tupac's connection to the tradition of celebrity Gramscians (organic) intellectuals, such as the late Nigerian musician Fela Kuti and Bob Marley.

The following panel, 'Me Against the World: Tupac Shakur and the Hunger of Heroism,' placed Tupac's popularity within the context of the black urban folk hero. UCLA Ethnomusicologist Cheryl L. Keyes, author of the new book *Rap Music and Street Consciousness,* asserted in her paper 'Redefining the Meaning of Hero in Hip-Hop Culture,' that the mainstream 'often envisions a hero as someone who has saved another person.' In contrast, the hero in hip hop, she argued, 'is translated as someone who has stood against the odds and adversaries of life.' Like Keyes, Emmett G. Price III, placed Tupac in the tradition of black folk heroes like High John the Conqueror and Stagger Lee. In 'From Thug Life to Legend,' Price drew on his own training as a gospel musician and ethnomusicologist to examine Tupac's spiritual development, suggesting that the late artist had surpassed the legacies of John Coltrane and Mahalia Jackson as spiritual figures within the tradition of black music.

In the third presentation, Greg Dimitriadis, who wrote the groundbreaking ethnographic study of hip hop and youth culture (*Performing Identity/Performing Culture: Hip-Hop Text, Pedagogy, and Lived Practice,* Peter Lang), specifically drew from the comments of many of those youths he interviewed for his study about their own connections to Tupac as documented shortly after the artist's death. Dimitriadis revisits much of that study in his forthcoming *Friendship, Cliques, and Gangs: Young Black Men Coming of Age in Urban America* (September 2003).

The final panel, '"Keep Your Head Up": Power, Passion, and the Political Potential of Tupac Shakur,' brought together noted Harvard sociologist Lawrence Bobo, UCLA scholar Dionne Bennett, and journalist Bakari Kitwana, whose critically acclaimed book *The Hip-Hop Generation: Young Blacks and the Crisis in African-American Culture,* was published last year. Whereas Bobo locates Tupac as a voice of critique around the burgeoning Prison Industrial Complex or what Loic Waquant calls the 'carceral state,' Kitwana sees Tupac as the logical link to the Black Power politics of the late 1960s and 1970s.

But in the most provocative talk of the day, Dionne Bennett examined Tupac's role as a feminist agent. Bennett, who is the author of *Sepia Dreams: A Celebration of Black Achievement Through Words and Image,* was careful not to describe Tupac as a feminist, in the strict sense of the concept, but rather as someone who engaged in feminist labor. As she asserts, 'Just as [Tupac's] misogynistic lyrics informed a dehumanizing gender discourse, the lyrics in which he demonstrates a passionate identification with women present a model for a politics of empathy that both imbues and extends beyond culture.' Bennett cited the example of Tupac's 'Baby Don't Cry (Keep Ya Head Up II),' which features the Outlawz, as not only an example of the power of Tupac's empathy towards working class and disenfranchised black women, but also of his ability to reproduce that empathy among other male hip hop artists.

Dionne Bennett's paper powerfully tapped into the mythology that has been erected around the figure of Tupac. The Harvard symposium was very much about various contemporary thinkers imagining how a mature Tupac Shakur – as organic intellectual, urban hero, political organizer and feminist – would have impacted American life. Despite his brilliance as an actor and lyrical provocateur, it was clear that by the time of his death at 25, Tupac Shakur was still a work in progress. It was roughly the similarities between Tupac and a 25-year-old Martin Luther King, Jr., that led Michael Eric Dyson to suggest that the two had a more common spirit than most are willing to grasp. Of course King has been the most celebrated black icon of high moral fortitude, while Tupac was easily the most demonized black male of his generation. The mythologies that have exploded around Tupac's legacy may simply be the process of many folk attempting to recover his moral, spiritual, and intellectual value to the black community. As Dyson notes in his criti-biography *Holler If You Hear Me: Searching for Tupac Shakur*, 'Anonymous, ordinary individuals project their lives onto the legendary figure, merging with it where they can, fostering an even more intense identification with that figure. By contributing to the creation of a legend . . . ordinary people are in fact creating themselves.'

And what exactly are black intellectuals and others creating when we fashion our own mythologies of Tupac? Clearly many of us see Tupac as a politically engaged intellectual. As Marcyliena Morgan noted during the symposium, many of us take comfort in the idea that Tupac Shakur read some of the same books that we do. Tupac's book collection became one of the recurring themes at the Harvard symposium. Tupac's relationship with Leila Steinberg, who befriended Tupac in the late 1980s and became his mentor, was crucial to his development as a reader.

According to Dyson, 'the most important role Steinberg played in Tupac's life was that of a literary soul mate . . . it was as reading partners that Steinberg and Tupac most profoundly shaped each other's lives.' The pair spent hours in the Bohdi Tree Bookstore in L.A. On a bookshelf in Steinberg's apartment, she keeps copies of the books that Tupac read (Tupac lived with her for awhile). Included in that collection are books such as J. D. Salinger's *Catcher in the Rye*, Jamaica Kincaid's *At the Bottom of*

> **'It was clear that by the time of his death at 25, Tupac Shakur was still a work in progress.' – Mark Anthony Neal**

the River, Herman Melville's classic *Moby Dick*, Eileen Southern's *Music of Black Americans*, and the feminist writings of Alice Walker (*In Search of Our Mother's Gardens*) and Robin Morgan (the now classic *Sisterhood is Powerful: Anthology of Writings from the Women's Liberation Movement*).

Many of the texts cited above were read before Tupac reached the age of twenty. Tupac's bookshelf was indeed the bookshelf of a young man who, at his age, was extraordinarily well-read and well-rounded intellectually – likely more so than the average student entering in the first year class of most Ivy League institutions. Dyson argues that 'Tupac's profound literacy rebutted the belief that hip hop is an intellectual wasteland . . . Tupac helped to combat the anti-intellectualism in rap, a force, to be sure, that pervades the entire culture.' This is the version of Tupac that made him such a compelling choice for Dyson to examine in a full-length text – a book that is the best-selling of Dyson's eight books in print. The success of Dyson's *Holler If You Hear Me* is not only evidence of Tupac's significance as a cultural figure, but suggests that the late rapper's core audience are themselves readers.

Tupac Shakur was a legitimate public intellectual – the organic intellectual that Antonio Gramsci describes in his *Prison Notebooks*. I can't help but think that those of us who are scholars, and do the work of deconstructing the myth and symbols of Tupac Amaru Shakur, are somehow hoping that we can be as relevant to the folks on the street corner as he was – and still remains to be.

THE TUPAC UPRISING
by George Wehrfritz — Outlaws With A Cause

The West Side Outlaws rule the western suburbs of Honiara, and always leave a calling card. 'War zone,' they scrawl on thatch huts newly 'cleansed' of migrants from Malaita. '2 PAC OUTLAWZ, KILL 'EM ALL,' they scribble on a nearby roadblock built of oil drums and old timber. Hip hop music fans will recognise the graffiti as lyrics by Tupac Shakur, America's most flamboyant gangsta rapper. A swaggering talent who topped US charts until his murder in 1996, Tupac lives again as the patron saint of this teen gang on the beautiful South Pacific island of Guadalcanal. 'Tupac was a man of action,' says a bare-chested gang member in cut-off blue jeans. 'He wasn't afraid of dying.'

Strange but true, Tupac is the troubadour for teen gangs that have joined Guadalcanal's Aboriginal uprising against Malaitan settlers. Youths copy Tupac's strut, hand gestures and tattoos. They study Tupac lyrics and identify with his troubled life. Born to a member of the radical Black Panther Party, Tupac went to art school, dealt crack, made films, dominated America's hip hop scene and died in a Las Vegas drive-by shooting – all by the age of 25. 'We, too, are outlaws,' says a teen rebel, in the shade near a postcard-perfect tropical beach. 'So when outsiders come in and try to boss us around, like Malaitans and the police, we cop a Tupac attitude.'

Most of these teens had never heard of Tupac until after he was dead. Honiara, the isolated capital of the remote Solomon Islands, didn't even get television until 1992. As locals tell it, Tupac's music first came to Guadalcanal three years ago, in the luggage of islanders returning from Australia. 'Someone would bring back a CD and we'd copy it 50 times,' says the son of a former prime minister. Chinese merchants began importing Tupac T shirts and $1 bootleg cassette tapes. Soon, the country's only private radio station, ZFM, was getting requests. 'Kids would call up and say, "Play Tupac for me and the homies,"' recalls DJ Gareth Porowai.

Tupac's popularity got an inadvertent boost from a 1997 police crackdown on reggae lovers and their marijuana farms. When the Outlaws responded by planting rows of marijuana to spell out WEST SIDE on a hill overlooking Honiara, the drug raids intensified. 'We used to be into Bob Marley, who sings, "Get up, stand up, fight for your rights,"' says one of the gang members. 'But when we stood up, the police shot at us. Then we became outlaws, like Tupac.'

The Guadalcanal Revolutionary Army started its uprising late last year, and the teen gang joined in. They chased off Malaitans at gunpoint and torched villages. A few Outlaws have been arrested, but most are free to roam. On a recent afternoon, four militants strutted along the beach wielding machetes. They wore high-top basketball shoes, baggy knee-length shorts and T shirts with the sleeves torn off – a South Pacific take on American hip hop fashion. 'These boys see Tupac as a symbol of militancy,' says Francis Orodani, a local chief. 'They're very revolutionary.' And these gangstas don't just sing it.

[reporting by Dorothy Wickham in Honiara]

SYMPOSIUM ANALYZES, CELEBRATES 'THUG'

by Ken Gewertz

Few spaces at Harvard are more burdened by symbols of the University's glorious past than the Barker Center's Thompson Room.

While the room itself is not particularly large, everything in it is on a grand scale, from the towering grandfather clock to the walk-in stone fireplace topped by a bust of John Harvard, both prominently inscribed with Veritas shields. Standing portraits of Theodore Roosevelt, Percival Lowell, and other Harvard notables hang from the floor-to-ceiling oak paneling, in which names such as Emerson, Longfellow, Bulfinch, and Agassiz have been carved in bas-relief.

But for one day last week (April 17 2003), these dignified totems of authority and rectitude were all but effaced by portraits of a young black man, his head shaved, his muscular arms and torso heavily tattooed, and his heavy-lidded eyes conveying an expression both menacing and soulful. In several photos he brandished a handgun, and in one he wore a large automatic tucked into the waistband of his boxer shorts.

The occasion was an academic symposium titled 'All Eyez on Me: Tupac Shakur and the Search for the Modern Folk Hero.' It was co-sponsored by the Hiphop Archive, the W .E. B. Du Bois Institute for Afro-American Research, the Program of Folklore and Mythology, and IKS University of Oslo, Norway.

Shakur, a rapper and film actor, died in 1996 at the age of 25, the victim of a drive-by shooting outside a hotel in Las Vegas. Like James Dean and Elvis Presley before him, he is believed by many of his fans to have faked his death and to be living secretly somewhere, perhaps Cuba.

If anything, his devotees have grown more numerous and adoring since his demise. Tupac Web sites abound, offering discussion groups, downloadable recordings, photos, and forums for conspiracy theorists. Dozens of books have been published about the rapper, ranging from popular biographies to speculations about his death to scholarly interpretations of his music and his significance as an icon of popular culture.

Mark Anthony Neal, an English professor from the State University of New York, Albany, gave a talk titled 'Thug Nigga Intellectual: Tupac as Celebrity Gramscian,' in which he argued that Shakur could be seen as an example of the 'organic intellectual' who expresses the concerns of his group, a concept articulated by Antonio Gramsci, the Marxist political theorist.

Murray Forman, a professor of communications studies at Northeastern University, discussed the 'Tupac lives' theory in its myriad manifestations, a task that must have required hundreds of hours surfing through Tupac sites on the Internet.

'Tupac's murder provided a catalyst for his re-emergence in digital form,' Forman said. 'His fans have succeeded in resurrecting Tupac as an ethereal life force.'

Knut Aukrust, a professor of culture studies at the University of Oslo and a visiting scholar in the Program on Folklore and Mythology at Harvard, described his first exposure to Shakur's music while driving to Florence, Italy, to conduct research on the Renaissance writer Niccolo Machiavelli – an odd coincidence, he proposed, since Shakur renamed himself 'Makaveli' on one of his albums.

In a similarly open-ended way, Aukrust pointed out that Shakur's birthday, June 16, coincides with Bloomsday, the fictional 24-

'Pac's enduring status was emphasized by the Harvard symposium 'All Eyez on Me: Tupac Shakur and the Search for the Modern Folk Hero.'

hour period that forms the time frame for James Joyce's *Ulysses*.

Reaching for suggestive parallels between Shakur and literary figures of the past or applying the ideas of theorists like Gramsci and Mikhael Bakhtin to the rapper's output were symptomatic of the difficulty all the presenters seemed to have with finding a suitable approach to this undeniably fascinating artist. While it seemed impossible to fit Shakur into a neat framework, all agreed that his music as well as his tumultuous life justified the effort of scholarly inquiry.

Tupac's mother, Afeni Shakur, was a prominent member of the Black Panther party, but later became addicted to crack cocaine. A high school dropout, Shakur read

widely, familiarizing himself with the work of many contemporary social theorists, a fact that has surprised many who know him only as a rapper. Others are offended by that surprise.

'How do we end up thinking that Tupac didn't read books?' asked Marcyliena Morgan, director of the Hiphop Archive. 'What is that assumption? And then why do we think, "Oh, he read that. So did I. Isn't he special?"'

'I think reading those books is impressive for anyone of that age,' replied Forman.

One member of the audience asked the panelists what they had to say about the glorification of violence and abuse of women in Shakur's lyrics.

'Well, he's a walking contradiction,' Neal said. 'But because of that, he makes the process of being an intellectual accessible to ordinary people.'

Emmett Price, an ethnomusicologist from Northeastern, traced the evolution of trickster figures in African-American folk tales to the urban badman of the post-slavery period, an archetype to which Shakur's public persona conforms.

And yet he was more than that, Price asserted, characterizing Shakur as a prolific artist driven by a terrible sense of urgency who struggled to unify mind, body, and spirit. 'He was also very similar to the rest of us – a work in progress.'

Greg Dimitriadis from the University of Buffalo's Graduate School of Education spoke about his interviews with young fans of Shakur and their beliefs about the rapper and his death. These ranged from blind faith ('Tupac's not dead, 'cause I just know.') to anger and a feeling of abandonment because of Shakur's failure to reveal himself and confirm the fact of his survival.

Cheryl Keyes, an ethnomusicologist from the University of California, Los Angeles, said that Shakur's life 'reflects living on the edge. His life wasn't very different from those of other black men. It was just that he lived his in the public spotlight.'

But the guy who blew everyone away was the keynote speaker Michael Eric Dyson, Avalon Professor in the Humanities and African American Studies at the University of Pennsylvania and author of *Holler If You Hear Me: Searching for Tupac Shakur*. Speaking in an intense, cadenced, crescendoing style that clearly derived from black preaching, Dyson combined the vocabulary of post-structuralist theory with the language of the streets while quoting liberally from Tupac, Notorious B.I.G., Snoop Dog, Nas, and Mos Def.

Dyson, who has written books on Martin Luther King, Jr. and Malcolm X, as well as issues in contemporary culture and race relations, said that when colleagues heard he was writing a book on Tupac Shakur, they asked 'Why would you waste time and energy writing about this thug?'

Dyson's answer was that 'Tupac spoke to me with brilliance and insight as someone who bears witness to the pain of those who would never have his platform. He told the truth, even as he struggled with the fragments of his identity.'

Although Shakur was 'deeply and profoundly self-destructive' and that in looking at his life, 'you can see his rush toward the grave,' it is important to note that 'the heroic character of Tupac was not predicated upon his moral perfection.'

A reader of theologians like Teilhard de Chardin, Shakur was obsessed by the problem of evil, Dyson said, and through his music, 'got at the heart of the hurt and suffering that was going on in human society and gave it a voice.'

Hearing Dyson's words, one wondered whether the heroes of Harvard's past whose images adorned the Thompson Room's walls were convinced of the heroism of this thug poet. But on further reflection, one found resolution in the thought that in the world of shades, perhaps superficial differences held less importance than we in the living world suppose.

G.O.A.T.

by Kris Ex

When most of us took notice of Tupac Shakur for the first time, he was sitting in royal fashion, rocking African garb and flowing like a b-boy ('Now I clown around when I hang around with the Underground.') in the video for Digital Underground's 'Same Song.' He was at once who we were – badasses of movement, rhythm and words; and who we believed we were – kings and queens of history, science and knowledge. With the black-rage-against-the-machine and power-to-the-people leanings of his debut, *2Pacalypse Now*, 'Pac fit the spirit of the times without falling to overbearing pedagogy, condescending militancy, or outright corn. He railed against the evils of AmeriKKKa with a proud black fist and sagging jeans, talking unity with the same mouth that downed 40's and puffed blunts.

He was the embodiment of a picture that would later appear on the inside jacket of Ice Cube's *Death Certificate*. With G's in oversized black gear chilling on one side and sharp-dressed FOI standing sentinel on the other, Cube stood in the middle reading *The Final Call*; the paper's headline read 'Unite Or Perish.' In the days when 2Pac emerged, Cube was still in his *AmeriKKKa's Most Wanted* phase. The nigga we loved to hate had just parted ways with NWA, was still rocking a greasy jheri curl, and made a record where he pondered on kicking a girl who may have been pregnant with his child in the belly. Understandably, 'Pac became hip hop's shining black prince.

Truth be told, for most of his career, 'Pac was a marginal lyricist. He largely eschewed the use of simile as a creative device. When he did go that route, the results were elementary – he 'hustled like a crack fiend,' 'hit switches like I was fixed with hydraulics.' He could never hang with the Holy Trinity of rhyme: Biggie, Jay-Z and Nas. He didn't have

Big's ability to construct interlocking rhyme schemes laden with hidden corridors; was no rival for Jigga's deceptively simple wit or wordplay; couldn't conjure Esco's sage observations and unique rhyme couplets. For the craft of the matter, the Hot Boys are better line-for-line MCs. Fabolous, who's yet to drop an album, has more inventive *bon mots* in his résumé than 'Pac.

Take 'Hit 'Em Up,' 'Pac's scathing Biggie/Bad Boy diss, for instance. It's one of the most searing, titillating, memorable diss records of all time. But it's indelibility lies in the shock value of its name-calling and hits below the belt. Stylistically, it lags leagues behind the studied precision of Common's 'Bitch in Yoo,' anything in Eminem's war on white rappers, Jay shots to Ma$e and Harlem World's Meeno, or Mobb Deep's retaliatory 'Drop a Gem on 'Em.'

None of this means that 'Pac may not be the greatest MC of all time. As LL Cool J proved, that crown doesn't necessarily go to the 'best' MC; it goes to the one who can make the best argument for wearing it. Think: Would the words of DMX, Ghostface Killah or Noreaga be so damned inviting if those guys weren't X, Ghost and Nore? And, if you ask anyone without a backpack, Canibus is weed, Black Thought is what Malcolm X was on, and Ras Kass is . . . that Ethiopian King that started dreadlocks? The only MCs with technical skills out the anal and the record sales to match are Biggie, Jay-Z and . . . Eminem.

In terms of bulletproof love, 'Pac had (and still does have) big bank – enough to escape scrutiny for his avoidance of time-honored hip hop staples. Not to say he wasn't talented. He was prodigious. Gifted. He didn't just flow, he roared like white-water rapids; rained like Exodus 9:23-25. But he was strictly about flow, almost to the exclusion of

'Pac spits more than rhymes, New York, July 1994.

all other tools in the MC arsenal; more about mood and emotion than analogy and imagination. He made rhymes without similes like the Israelites made bricks without straw.

He tapped into a small garden of evergreen topics and rarely strayed outside of its confines. His early work revolved around loyalty, honor and duty (and women – wayward or otherwise); his later stuff dealt with loyalty, honor and betrayal (and women – wayward or otherwise). But he mined those sentiments for all they were worth and served them up with verve and spirit. He talked like he believed every word that came out of his mouth. Moreover, he made you believe it and made you believe he believed it. He radiated a sense of concentrated self and indomitable will that infected you. Listening to him was beyond catharsis like ejaculating is beyond urinating.

As opposed to slick turns of phrase, 'Pac relied on adages, aphorisms, and arrogance. He used vagueness to tap into universal human needs like an accomplished motivational speaker or a great ad campaign. Plan your goals. Just Do It. Ride on your enemies.

There are parallels for 'Pac's success in other genres of music. In rock 'n' roll, the Ramones became heroes through attitude not skill – but are still revered as fathers of punk rock. In R&B, no matter how many ingénues-of-the-moment come and go, Mary J. Blige remains the Queen of Hip-Hop Soul, not by being the most accomplished singer, but because she's, well, just Mary.

Yet 'Pac was turning an artistic corner before his death. He began spitting 'spiritual lyrics like the Holy Qu'Ran' and moving towards surreal imagery that cooked the Bible in a cauldron under a street lamp. 'Have you ever seen a crackhead?' he asked. 'That's eternal fire.' He drank so much he 'swore I saw the Devil in my empty glass of Hennessey.' And, while the gun-as-girlfriend exercise 'Me and My Girlfriend' lags behind earlier gun metaphors like Nas' 'I Gave You Power' and Organized Konfusion's 'Stray Bullet,' it was a move towards higher creativity.

Given his vigorous work ethic during the last months of his life, 2Pac was experiencing growth in leaps and bounds. With as little as another half year at the rate he was going, he may have well had that greatest of all time title locked down.

TUPAC SHAKUR'S LEGACY

by Lucy Morrison

On its surface, the music of Tupac Shakur (1971-96) appears to maintain the sexism, violence, and drugs associated with 'thug life' – in keeping with gangsta rap's ideology. Tupac's works explore the culture of his African-American environment and address problems stereotypically assigned to it, while simultaneously drawing upon street myths to create his own legend. Silenced by a gun in September 1996, Tupac's murder may seem to many to be a fitting end to the violent lifestyle depicted in his work, but his voice sings on in defiance of the life he saw, lived, and recorded. Even though gangsta rap is frequently viewed as a transient genre of the late 1980s and early 1990s, significant principally in its elucidation of white stereotyped African-American culture, Tupac's music transgresses such a restrictive border. Indeed, I suggest Tupac's music is unique in its positive address of African-American women and their struggles in society and, as such, should be considered to be what *Newsweek*'s Alison Samuels identifies as Tupac's true 'poetic legacy.' What I wish to address is neither the larger issue of why rap music has caused such controversy, nor how gangsta rap swept the nation and intrigued so much of America's youth, especially the white audience which, according to the *New Yorker*'s Connie Bruck, makes up 70 percent of rap's consumers. Rather, I would like to counter the attacks which have been consistently made upon Tupac's work for its unsuitability in our society. In this article, I explore the complex contradictions inherent in Tupac's music, particularly the dialogue between his misogyny and his enlightened views of women.

Before I look closely at several songs, though, it is necessary to acknowledge that Tupac's lyrics are deeply ingrained with the misogyny and 'thug life' so typical of gangsta rap and that this article is not an attempt to deny that position. Most criticism of Tupac focuses on the negative and violent aspects of his works, such as 'Hit 'Em Up' and its infamous insult to the Notorious B.I.G. While it is surely too simplistic to situate such a complex artist within the reductive categorization of 'gangsta,' I do not hesitate to agree that his work can easily be bracketed as offensive and misogynistic. But simultaneously, as *Rolling Stone* journalist Kevin Powell points out in his retrospective of Tupac's life and career, 'Shakur's lyrics were all over the map. Sometimes you didn't know if he loved black people or if he absolutely despised them.' Tupac's music also exposes the white stereotypes that African-American women have to fight to escape, revealing his own struggle and, perhaps, failure to defeat the African-American stereotype imposed upon him.

Bruck noted that, 'unfairly or not, Tupac Shakur's name has become synonymous with violent rap lyrics and "thug life."' Such an association has become even more entrenched since his death, for he can no longer respond to his critics directly, as he did so powerfully during his brief life, although his music still makes his arguments. Why is it that 'blame' for gangsta rap, for the violence and misogyny it depicts, has been pinned so consistently upon Tupac? Part of it perhaps rests upon his tragic and yet representative life story – a young man raised without a father who found his own identity peddling drugs on the streets of Los Angeles before successfully breaking into the music industry and catapulting to stardom. Part of it equally likely rests upon his handsome appearance and his sultry voice, as well as upon his success as an actor and as an artist, his records selling in numbers unprecedented for a black rapper. Part of it, too, lies in his own personal mythology, from his birth to a former Black Panther to the mystique he built around his own life by taking street events and making them his. And part of it must rest upon his 1995 conviction for sexual abuse.

But, surely, most of the condemnation heaped upon Tupac is for his depictions of women, his leading critic being C. DeLores Tucker of the National Political Congress of Black Women. Tucker, who denounced Tupac specifically in her campaign against rap music as degrading black women, probably (and ironically) assisted his sales. But her accusations do not consider the whole picture. I am not going to attempt to deny that Tupac was clearly misogynist in much of his lyrics, although we should understand his apparent sexism as an authentic evil in what author and cultural commentator Venise Berry defines as 'very real images and messages in the everyday world of the rapper and his original fan: the black urban youth.' Rap is, above all, an account of the inner city with which most of its dominantly white listeners are unfamiliar, and, as such, it is necessarily and simultaneously an act of documentation, exaggeration, and of mythologizing. Both Tupac's life and art were involved in aspects of the form of expression he chose. But, although sexism is easily apparent in his lyrics, what I want to highlight are the specifically positive aspects of much of his work and its inspirational address of African-American women, since, as *Newsweek*'s John Leland observes, 'for all his wanton machismo, Tupac rapped passionately about the strength of black women.'

In considering Tupac's lyrics as poetry, I am also not attempting to divorce them from their original context. But without the rap music, many of Tupac's lyrics can stand alone as purposeful narrative poems. His lyrical proficiency is widely acknowledged, and, immediately before his death, he was working on his first book of poems; he wooed his fiancée, Kidada Jones, by sending poems to her house every day. Admittedly, much of the power of Tupac's lyrics lies in

the music which surrounds them. In considering Tupac's lyrics as poetry and in asserting their positive address of African-American women, contrary to most criticism of Tupac's works, I ask that Tupac's work be given another, alternative look, one which furthers our understanding of a rap culture so removed from many of its listeners. It quickly becomes evident that, alongside the frequent uses of the terms 'bitches' and 'hos' to which Tucker so strenuously objects, and which should be considered in context, Tupac addresses women positively.

Tupac's first commercially successful single, 'Brenda's Got a Baby,' was from his 1991 debut album, *2Pacalypse Now*. Apparently based upon a newspaper article Tupac read, it relates the story of a twelve-year old girl who gave birth to a child fathered by her cousin and, not knowing what to do, but having hidden the pregnancy from her family, she threw the baby down into an incinerator. Immediately, the multiple horrors of this situation are apparent even in a brief summary, but Tupac's sympathies lie squarely with Brenda and he accuses both her family and the larger society for its lack of assistance for the young girl. Noting that Brenda 'never really knew her moms and her dad was a junky,' Tupac relates that when she became pregnant by her cousin, her family cared little, 'as long as when tha check came they got first dibs.'

Clearly, Tupac indicts the family for being remiss in their duty to care for their own. As he relates how Brenda had the baby alone and 'didn't know what ta throw away and what ta keep,' he also indicts the larger society for its lack of education of young African-Americans. He notes: 'The girl can hardly spell her name, that's not her problem; that's up to Brenda's family / Well, let me show you how it affects tha whole community.' Tupac concludes his tale by relating that Brenda's family rejected her and that she was unable to get a job. She tried to make a profit by selling crack, but her attempts ended when she was robbed.

Ultimately, she is forced on the streets to find her existence: 'there ain't nothin' left ta sell, so she sees sex as a way of leavin' hell.' Tupac does not use the word 'bitch' in this song, and even the unjust summary of the bare details of the narrative which I have given reveal that Tupac sympathizes with the twelve year old girl.

Tupac's attitude toward African-American women as confined and entrapped by their societal environment is a consistent theme on each of his albums. In 'Keep Ya Head Up,' which *Esquire*'s Ivan Solotaroff has called an 'inspirational ode to black women,' Tupac addresses 'my sisters on welfare' and advises them to ignore African-American men's behavior toward them: 'Forgive but don't forget, girl keep ya' head up / And when he tells ya' you ain't nothin', don't believe him.' He encourages women to affirm and value their own independent individuality before confirming; 'And since we all came from a woman, Got our name from a woman, and our game from a woman.'

Time magazine's Christopher Farley observes that this song is 'chivalrously supportive of black women,' and indeed, Tupac's message to African-American women is that they must believe in themselves and not allow African-American men to position them constrictively as necessarily secondary within society. In this song, then, Tupac criticizes himself and male African-American society for maintaining its sexist attitudes toward women. At the same time, he encourages African-American women to take control of their own lives and to defy society's stereotyping of their roles.

On *Thug Life Volume 1* (1994), Tupac notes that 'Mama told me, "son, there'll be days like this,"' as he relates the deaths of so many of his friends. In his autobiographical 'From the Cradle to the Grave' on the same album, he recalls his 'Mama always workin' tryin' to make ends meet,' and notes that his existence is an homage to and a voice for 'the mothers that cried' whose sufferings find no release. Indeed, mothers in Tupac's music, while real, are also idealized and earn his utmost respect – the mother figure in Tupac's songs is usually a positive one. His music records his understanding of his own mother's endeavors and ultimately elevates her in his respect as a woman who struggled consistently and successfully raised him, a task he recognizes as a challenge for any single mother. He records that 'for a woman, / It ain't easy tryin' ta raise a man' in his most eloquent tribute to his mother and one of his most acclaimed songs – 'Dear Mama,' from his 1995 album *Me Against the World* – a song which Farley terms 'a surprisingly tender tribute.' Tupac recalls how he ran wild as a child and recognizes the pain he must have caused his mother, while retrospectively acknowledging the vital discipline which shaped his behavior: 'Runnin' from tha Police, that's right, Momma catch me, put a whoopin' to my backside.' Later in the song, he continues, 'Ya always was committed, a poor single woman on welfare.'

Throughout the song, Tupac expresses his recognition of his mother's sacrifices and applauds her strength: 'But tha plan is to show ya that I understand – You are appreciated.' He notes that his father's absence meant that his mother was both parents for him. Even when he moved out when her drug habit became too much for him to bear, he still ensured that she had money for rent while recalling that 'when I wuz low, you was there for me, / Ya never left me alone, coz ya cared for me.' He recalls how she always managed to find enough for the children to eat, making 'miracles every Thanksgiving,' and that 'all my childhood memories are full of all the sweet things ya did for me.' What most critics of Tupac's music conveniently overlook is this consistent portrayal of his own mother as a strong African-American woman for whom he has the ultimate respect. Certainly, in 'Brenda's Got a Baby,' Tupac criticizes a society which permits young African-American women to

Tupac with Quincy Jones' daughter, Kidada Jones, at the Versace party during Milan Fashion Week, 1996.

become single parents without being old enough to realize the consequences of their actions; he sympathizes with the victimized African-American title character. In many of his songs, and especially in 'Dear Mama,' Tupac demonstrates his respect for and admiration of African-American women who overcome their secondary position in society and who raise their children with strength and commitment, despite the odds against them. Tupac demonstrates his appreciation of his own mother's efforts and applauds her consistent devotion to him and to his half-sister. As in other songs, Tupac recognizes and depicts the day to day hardships of many women's lives in the inner city, noting their strength and the respect which should be accorded to them.

It is evident that Tucker and others' condemnations of Tupac's music, based upon the misogyny exhibited therein, is only one side of the issue. Turning to 'Wonda Why They Call U,' from *All Eyez on Me* (1996), I suggest that Tupac's use of the word 'bitch' does not necessarily have to be pejorative – a possibility that Tucker (among others) apparently overlooks – but can be viewed as a term that African-American culture has re-addressed and reclaimed. Of course, 'bitch' has traditionally been seen as a slang term degrading to women, but 'Wonda Why They Call U' surely suggests alternate connotations. Tupac's use of the word 'bitch,' then, is as problematic as his conflicted address of women. In some songs, he uses the term in a pejorative sense, but in others, the word is negative only insofar as the song's protagonist succumbs to the stereotype attached to the word, rather than rising above it.

'Wonder Why They Call U' is a narrative

addressed to a young woman whom Tupac has seen grow up and change. At the outset, he remarks that, 'In the locker room, all the homies do is laugh. / High fives coz anotha nigga played your ass.' He asserts that, of course, she can do as she wants to with her body, even though she is called 'sleazy' and 'easy,' but he suggests that, rather than 'play[in'] tha game,' she 'get mad and change.' Tupac notes that she is looking for a way out from the position in which society has placed her and suggests that there is a way: 'Keep your mind on your money, enrol in school, / And as the years pass by, you can show them fools.' But the girl doesn't seem to hear his advice as she gets ready to go out, 'still lookin' for a rich man . . . got your legs up tryin' to get rich.' He points out that she needs to 'switch' from the conventional negative expectation of what an African-American woman can do to succeed, noting that her adherence to the stereotype is what has led to her being called a 'bitch.'

> **'Keep your mind on your money, enrol in school, / And as the years pass by, you can show them fools.' – *Tupac***

As Tupac continues to follow her actions, he notes that she leaves her children at home as she goes to a club to look for a rich man, and pleads with her to look beyond the limits of her environment: 'It's like your mind don't understand: You don't have to kill your dreams, plottin' schemes on a man / Keep your head up, legs closed, eyes open; either a nigga wear a rubber or he die smokin'.' Clearly Tupac is speaking out against not only selling your body, but also telling this woman that her life does not have to revolve around being with a man. And, if she cannot break away from this traditional belief, then he advises her to remember that

sex can kill her: if she cannot see beyond sleeping with men as a way to rise up in the world, then at least she should ensure that there will be a life left to live.

As her life continues and she becomes pregnant again, Tupac watches her receiving more welfare money, which she spends on getting her hair done before she goes out to meet another 'trick,' intimating that, whereas she might formerly have been sleeping with men solely for self-advancement, now she has become a prostitute relying upon their payment for financial support supplementary to that forthcoming from the county. Tupac momentarily recalls her in high school, when she was innocent of the world and of the opportunities before her, before concluding his narrative of her decline: 'Let the ghetto get the best of you and baby, that's a shame / Called HIV and now you're 'bout to be deceased and finally be at peace.'

Having recounted her rise and fall, Tupac concludes the narrative noting that she succumbed to the ways of the inner city, giving up on herself and on her abilities to break out of stereotypes – she succumbs not only to prostitution, but, furthermore, dies alone of AIDS. For Tupac, this tale of a young African-American woman with her whole life ahead of her, who succumbs to her culture's low view of her gender and uses her sex to try and move forward, is a tragic one. Simultaneously, in exploring aspects of this stereotype, noting that her fall into prostitution is a hard cycle to break, Tupac provides a powerful indictment of a culture which offers little alternative to inner city African-American women. With no encouragement and without positive reinforcement of her own identity, this young African-American woman saw herself as society positioned her, as a body, and tried to use this body as a way to break free. Not hearing Tupac's emphasis upon the possibilities, on the need to stay in school, to keep her 'head up, legs closed, eyes open,' this young girl became yet another victim. And, as Tupac reiterates throughout the song, her behavior earned her the epithet of 'bitch.'

But, given that this song endorses education and demands alternatives for African-American women in the inner city, protesting against a culture and men who maintain women's secondary position based upon their gendered biological makeup, the epithet of 'bitch' seems reinvented. For Tupac demonstrates that 'bitch' is applied as a matter of course to women who adhere to societal expectations and stereotypes. At the conclusion of his rap, Tupac addresses Tucker directly, asserting that this song explains why he refers to women as 'bitches.' And his conclusion is not angry at women such as the one whose tale he narrates in the rap; rather, the 'bitch' figure is a protest against the limits placed around African-American women's potential within society. Tupac concludes that 'it ain't personal' but rather that he is trying to explain: using 'bitch' does not have to be a negative term but instead reconstitutes the epithet designed to injure. It then acts as a protest against a dominant white society and its African-American subculture in which

African-American women are constrained as doubly penalized, both for their race and for their gender.

Kevin Powell, writing after Tupac's death, asserts that 'to me, Shakur was the most important solo artist in the history of rap . . . because he, more than any other rapper, personified and articulated what it was to be a young black man in America.' Indubitably, Tupac's is a voice which calls to his own culture and to that of the larger dominant culture for urgent reform. His 'Thug poetry,' such as 'Brenda's Got a Baby' and 'Wonda Why They Call U,' narrates the stereotypical existence of many young African-American women who, trapped in their culture's constrictive societal positioning, turn to drugs and prostitution. But, as Tupac carefully informs his audience, including Tucker, there are alternatives to such a lifestyle, and Tupac's rapping highlights such alternatives in the form of carefully crafted rhythms and rhymes which reflexively reinforce their content. The strength of Tupac's music and poetry have led to the first university course in his life and works, offered at the University of California at Berkeley, where students study his writings in context and where, perhaps, Tupac's hitherto negative media depictions will finally be re-evaluated. An angry voice within a minority culture, Tupac emerges as an artist deploring African-American inter-destruction, instead offering alternatives and hopes for reformation. As such, his music merits serious attention as lyrical poetry which spans and embraces both mass and high culture.

TUPAC'S CONTINUING CAREER

by John Jurgensen   **A Matter of Grave Importance**

Despite lingering rumors to the contrary, it's safe to say that Tupac Shakur is dead. So why does he keep putting out records?

The rapper's latest posthumous release, *Loyal to the Game*, shows up in stores this week in time for the holidays. It's the seventh 2Pac record (not including greatest-hits and remix collections) to emerge since he was shot down in Las Vegas eight years ago.

Shakur's output in death can be explained by how prolific he was in life. The man who helped canonize the West Coast gangsta sound committed loads of unreleased material to tape before his unsolved murder. The demand for those songs is understandable. When Shakur was gunned down – at the age of 25 – he was one of America's most famous musicians.

But by dying young and famous, he joined a much more exclusive club. Like Elvis, Marilyn, Jimi and John, Shakur became one of those celebrities whose career continues to flourish and even diversify in death.

In 2002, Shakur entered Forbes' list of top-earning deceased celebrities at Number Ten. His rank dwindled slightly on the latest list, published in October, but he still came in with a respectable $5 million in 2004, edging out Frank Sinatra at Number Twenty.

People have bought more than 30 million of his records since he died in 1996 – several times more than he sold as a living artist. And that tally will grow with this latest

> 'Like Elvis, Marilyn, Jimi and John, Shakur became one of those celebrities whose career continues to flourish and even diversify in death.'
> – John Jurgensen

release, thanks in part to the participation of Eminem, who produced the album and also raps on it, along with 50 Cent and other word-slingers who weren't even a twinkle in Tupac's eye.

Could the dead rapper owe part of this posthumous glory to Elvis Presley?

When the King died in 1977, death was still a career killer. Within a few years, however, the Elvis estate (directed by his ex-wife, Priscilla) began to strategically cash in on his legacy. By promoting and licensing Elvis' image and work – while fiercely defending it from infringement – Elvis Presley Enterprises can still haul in $40 million a year. Needless to say, Elvis consistently tops the Forbes chart.

Mark Roesler helped gild the King's retirement from life. In 1981, he became the licensing agent for the Elvis Presley estate and went on to shape the industry with his own company. As head of CMG Worldwide, he manages the market presence of some of the biggest late stars in the business, including Princess Diana, Malcolm X, Babe Ruth and Buddy Holly. He helped the heirs of such celebrities to lay claim in court to their famous legacies.

A violent death stemming from the thug life he endorsed took Tupac Shakur out at the top of his game, but his icon status is sealed by his music, which hardcore fans interpret as scripture. What's also important

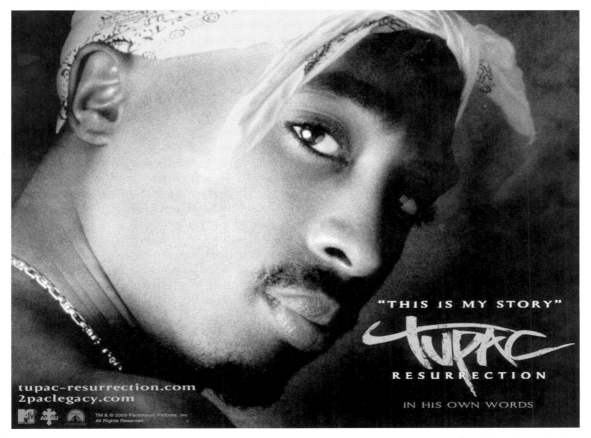

Laurin Lazin's bio-pic Tupac Resurrection *(2003) featured previously unseen home movie footage of the slain star.*

– and puts the rapper in league with his contemporary, Kurt Cobain – is the timing of his rise and fall.

'Tupac was American royalty at a time when hip hop was making that transition from underground culture to mainstream pop culture. Even though before him and possibly after him there were better artists, he continues to benefit from that in a way that other artists don't,' says Bakari Kitwana, a former editor of *The Source* magazine and author of the forthcoming book *Why White Kids Love Hip Hop*.

Successful lawsuits and a deal with the record label that puts out Shakur's music gave his mother, Afeni Shakur, a former Black Panther, control over his unreleased work and the lucrative merchandising of his image. She is a co-producer of the new album, and her savvy business moves have led the estate into other ventures, including fashion.

But not everybody is happy with the way the Tupac 'movement' is unfolding.

'I think they're just taking the legacy in the wrong direction,' says R.B., who writes for rap news sites on the Web under the name Robert. He also runs a site dedicated to Shakur called *ThugLifeArmy.com*.

Robert is especially upset about the way Eminem has manipulated the words Shakur recorded in a different decade.

'They're twisting it to sound like Tupac is saying things that he wasn't saying, and that's wrong,' Robert says.

CONTRIBUTORS

Frank Ahrens is the *Washington Post*'s business reporter for the media and entertainment industry.

Frank Alexander is Tupac Shakur's former bodyguard, whose recollections can be found in his book *Got Your Back*, which was published by St Martin's Press in 1998.

Ruby Bailey is the Washington correspondent for the *Detroit Free Press*.

Soren Baker is a writer, producer and author based in Los Angeles.

James Bernardinelli is a prolific reviewer of films and webmaster of the ReelViews site, which is the largest non-commercial movie site on the net (http://movie-reviews.colossus. net/master.html).

Veronica Chambers is a journalist, novelist, editor and playwright, whose writing has appeared in such publications as *Esquire*, *The Village Voice*, the *New York Times*, *Vogue* and the *Los Angeles Book Review*, as well as many others.

Davey D is a hip hop historian, journalist, DJ and community activist. Much of his work is collected on his website: www.daveyd.com

Roger Ebert is America's best known film and television commentator. In 1975 he became the first film critic to receive a Pulitzer Prize for criticism. He is a film critic for the *Chicago Sun-Times* and has also written many books on cinema and several screenplays, most notably *Beyond the Valley of the Dolls* (1970).

Kris Ex has written for *Rolling Stone*, *XXL*, *Vibe*, the *New York Times* and many others. He has co-authored *From Pieces to Weight* (with 50 Cent), *Ghetto Superstar* (with the Fugees' Pras Michel) and *How To Draw Hip-Hop* (with artist Damion Scott). His first collection of short fiction, *Stay Low and Keep Firing,* is set for release in fall 2005.

Bronwyn Garrity is a writer and journalist whose work has appeared in *The Nation*, contributed to Nely Galán's self-help workbook, *The Swan Curriculum: Create a Spectacular New You with 12 Life-Changing Steps in 12 Amazing Weeks* and is a producer of websites and DVD-ROM content at Canned Interactive, an interactive design agency based in Los Angeles.

Ken Gewertz is a staff writer for the *Harvard Gazette*.

Mikal Gilmore is a long-time music writer and contributor to *Rolling Stone*. In 1999 his anthology, *Night Beat: A Shadow History of Rock 'n' Roll* was published. He has also written *Shot in the Heart,* a memoir recounting his relationship with his brother Gary, who was executed for murder in 1977.

Ernest Hardy writes about film and music from his home base of Los Angeles. His criticism has appeared in the *New York Times*, *Rolling Stone*, *Vibe*, the *L.A. Weekly*, the *Los Angeles Times*, the reference book *1,001 Movies You Must See Before You Die* and the hip hop anthology, *Classic Material: The Hip-Hop Album Guide*, among others. He's currently working on a book of criticism that will be published by Redbone Press in Fall 2005.

Jordan Harper is music editor of *Riverfront Times*, the news and arts weekly of St. Louis, Missouri.

Chris Hicks is the movie critic for Salt Lake City's *Deseret Morning News*.

Johnny Ray Huston is the arts editor for the *San Francisco Bay Guardian*.

Benjamin Meadows Ingram is the lifestyle editor at *Vibe* magazine.

June Joseph is a New York-based music journalist who has contributed to publications such as *i-D*, *MixMag UK*, *MTV*, *Hip-Hop Connection*, *Billboard* and *Vibe*. Since 1998, she has also established herself as a popular club DJ.

John Jurgensen is a staff writer for the *Hartford Courant*.

Dana Kennedy has been MSNBC's entertainment editor since April 2000. She also appears regularly on CNBC's *The News with Brian Williams*. Previously, she was an anchor and correspondent on the Fox News Channel and entertainment reporter for ABC's *Good Morning America Sunday*.

Amy Linden is a music journalist whose writing has appeared in such publications as *XXL*, *The Source*, *Vibe*, and *People*.

Veronica Lodge is the author of *Our Gang: The Criminal Element in Professional Sports and Entertainment*.

Theresa Micalef is a Canadian writer with a passion for hip hop and an understanding of the relevant social issues surrounding its dominance in youth culture today. She works as a publicist for community arts organizations such as the Roaring Truth Theater Company and the Toronto Urban Music Festival, and endeavors to use her ability to communicate through the written word to inspire, encourage and empower others, especially young people.

Rita Michel is a journalist and filmmaker, whose writing has been featured in such publications as *NY Arts* and *Film Festival Today*.

Lucy Morrison is an Assistant Professor of English at Salisbury University, Maryland, where she specializes in British Romantic literature. She is co-author of *A Mary Shelley Encyclopedia* (2003) and has published articles in her field.

Mark Anthony Neal is Associate Professor of American Studies at the University of Texas, Austin. A prolific cultural and arts commentator, he has also written a number of books including *Songs in the Key of Black Life: A Rhythm and Blues Nation, Soul Babies: Contemporary Black Popular Culture and the Post-Soul Aesthetic* and *What the Music Said: Black Popular Music and Black Public Culture*.

Chuck Philips is a Pulitzer Prize winning journalist who writes primarily for the *Los Angeles Times*.

Kevin Powell is a public speaker, activist, poet, journalist, hip hop historian, and author. He has had a number of books published, most notably *Who's Gonna Take the Weight: Manhood, Race, and Power in America* (2003). His journalism has been published in such publications as *Essence, Ms.*, the *Washington Post, Newsweek, Rolling Stone*, and *Vibe*.

Ronin Ro is a journalist and the author of several books including, *Raising Hell : The Reign, Ruin, and Redemption of Run DMC and Jam Master Jay, Have Gun Will Travel, Bad Boy: The Influence of Sean 'Puffy' Combs on the Music Industry* and *Tales To Astonish : Jack Kirby, Stan Lee, and the American Comic Book Revolution*.

Bryan Robinson is an associate editor at *Court TV Online*.

Micah Robinson is a journalist and film reviewer whose work can be found on CHUD.com and the Rotten Tomatoes website.

Joshua Rubin is a California-based writer and journalist who has contributed to such publications as *XXL* and the *New York Times*.

Alison Samuels is a Los Angeles-based journalist and author who has written for *Newsweek* and *Rolling Stone*. She has also written a children's book, *Christmas Soul: African American Holiday Stories*.

Danzy Senza is a prolific writer on issues of race, identity, and gender. She currently holds the Jenks' Chair of Contemporary American Letters at the College of the Holy Cross in Worcester, Massachusetts, and has had several novels published.

Cathy Scott is a full-time police reporter for the *Las Vegas Sun* and has received more than a dozen journalism awards. Her work has appeared in the *Los Angeles Times* and the *New York Times*. She is the author of *The Killing of Tupac Shakur* and *The Murder of Biggie Smalls*. She also has her own website at www.cathyscott.com

Michael Small is the executive editor of *Entertainment Weekly Online*.

R.J. Smith is a senior editor and media critic for *Los Angeles Magazine*. He was a visiting scholar at the Getty Research Institute and has been a visiting community scholar at the University of Southern California's Center for Multiethnic and Transnational Studies. He has written for *The Village Voice, SPIN, New York Times Magazine* and *Grand Royal*.

Daniel Smyth is an occasional contributor to *Spin* magazine.

Neil Strauss is the Los Angeles-based co-author of *The Long Hard Road Out of Hell* (with Marilyn Manson), *How to Make Love Like a Porn Star* (with Jemma Jameson) and *The Dirt* (with Motley Crue). His journalism regularly appears in the *New York Times* and *Rolling Stone*.

Sway is a New York-based DJ and broadcaster.

J. H. Tomkins is a contributing editor for the *San Francisco Bay Guardian*. His blog can be viewed at www.artsjournal.com/tommyt/

George Wehrfritz is *Newsweek* magazine's Tokyo bureau chief.

Armond White is film critic for the *New York Press* and author of *The Resistance: Ten Years of Pop Culture that Shook the World* and *Rebel for the Hell of It: The Life of Tupac Shakur*.

P. Frank Williams has written for such magazines as *King, America* and *Complex*. A former executive editor of *The Source* and *Los Angeles Times* reporter, he was a writer/producer for the 2004 Olympics on NBC, the NAACP Image Awards on FOX and *Hip Hop Honors* on VH1. He currently works as a producer in TV development at VH1 in Los Angeles. An Oakland native, he is also the story editor/writer for the new video game *25 to Life*.

British Library Cataloguing in Publication Data

Tupac : a thug life
    1.Shakur, Tupac, 1971- 2.Rap Musicians - United States -
    Biography
    782.4'21649'092

    ISBN-10: 0859653757

Printed in Great Britain by Scotprint, Haddington
Cover and book design by Rebecca Martin
Cover photograph by Jeffery Newbury/Corbis Outline

Acknowledgements

The following articles appear by courtesy of their respective
copyright holders: 'Bury Me Like a "G"' by Kevin Powell, © Kevin
Powell 1996. Reprinted with the permission of the author c/o
The Wylie Agency, UK. 'An Interview with Tupac's Mom' by Davey
D, KMEL Radio, 19 April 1996. 'My Brother' by Benjamin
Meadows-Ingram, XXL, October 2000. All rights reserved. 'The
Music is the Message' by Bromwyn Garrity, Los Angeles Times, 22
April, 2002. 'On the Line with Tupac Shakur' by Davey D, KPFA
Radio, June 1991. 'Asking for It' by Michael Small, © Michael
Small. 'Violence is Golden' by Danzy Senza, Spin, April 1994.
Reprinted by permission of Spin and the author. All rights
reserved. 'Dreaming America' by Daniel Smyth, Spin, April 1994.
Reprinted by permission of Spin and the author. All rights
reserved. 'Thug Life' by June Jospeh, first published in Hip-Hop
Connection #71, January 1995. www.hiphop.co.uk. 'Q&A with
Tupac Shakur' by Chuck Philips, Los Angeles Times, 25 October
1995. 'Interview on the Westside Radioshow' by Sway, KMEL
radio, 19 April 1996. 'Have Gun Will Travel' by Ronin Ro ©
Quartet Books 1998. 'King of Stage' by Joshua Rubin, XXL,
October 2001. All rights reserved. 'Conversations with Tupac' by
Veronica Chambers, Esquire, December 1996 © Veronica
Chambers. Juice review by Roger Ebert, Chicago Sun-Times, 17
January 1992 © Roger Ebert. Poetic Justice review by Roger
Ebert, Chicago Sun-Times, 23 July 1993 © Roger Ebert. Above the
Rim review by Chris Hicks, Deseret News, 14 April 1994. 'Got
Your Back' by Frank Alexander, © Frank Alexander, 1998. Bullet
review by Micah Robinson, CHUD.com, 4 October 2003. 'Rebel
for the Hell of It' by Armond White, © Quartet Books 1997.
Gridlock'd review by Roger Ebert, Chicago Sun-Times, 31
January 1997 © Roger Ebert. Gang Related review by James
Bernardinelli, Reelviews, October 1997. 'The Living End' by Frank
Williams, The Source, November 1996 © P. Frank Williams. 'All
Eyes On Him' by R. J. Smith, Spin, December 1996. Reprinted
with the permission of Spin and the author. All rights reserved.
'The Day After Tupac Shakur Died' by Amy Linden, © Amy
Linden, 1996. 'Easy Target' by Mikal Gilmore, from Rolling Stone,
31 October, 1996 © 1996 Rolling Stone. All rights reserved.
Reprinted by permission. 'Rap Wars' by Dana Kennedy, © 1996
Entertainment Weekly Inc. Reprinted by permission. 'Who Killed
Tupac Shakur?' by Chuck Philips, the Los Angeles Times,
September 6, 2002. 'Who Killed Tupac Shakur? Epilogue' by
Chuck Philips, the Los Angeles Times, 7 September, 2002. 'Dead
Men Tell No Tales' by Tommy Tompkins and Johnny Ray Huston,
San Francisco Bay Guardian, 18 September 2002. 'The Tupac
Shakur Murder Investigation' by Bryan Robinson © 1997, cour-
tesy Court TV. 'The New Tupac Fans' by Ruby Bailey, Detroit
News, 26 October 1996. Reprinted by permission. 'Deadly
Business' by Dana Kennedy, © 1996 Entertainment Weekly Inc.
Reprinted by permission. 'Dead Poets Society' by Cathy Scott,
George Magazine, October 1998 © Cathy Scott. 'Interview with
Suge Knight' by P. Frank Williams, The Source, June 2000 © P.
Frank Williams. 'Biggie & Tupac Remix' by Ernest Hardy, LA
Weekly, 4-10 October, 2002. 'Jackin Beats' by Veronica Lodge,
RapPages, September 1998. 'Who Stole Tupac's Soul' by Allison
Samuel, Rolling Stone, 25 June, 1998 © 1998 Rolling Stone. All
rights reserved. Reprinted by permission. 'A Rose by Any Other
Name' by Theresa Micalef, Word, June/July 2003. 'For Heaven's
Sake' by Soren Baker, XXL, October 2000 © Soren Baker. 'Eternal
Truths and Dead Pop Stars' by Frank Ahrens © 2000 The
Washington Post, reprinted with permission. 'All Oddz on Me' by
Jordan Harper, originally published in Riverfront Times, 8
September 2004, the news and arts weekly of St. Louis, Missouri.
'Hood Scriptures' by Kris Ex, XXL, October 2001 © Kris Ex. 'Hip
Hop Requiem' by Neil Strauss, copyright © 2001 by The New
York Times Co. Reprinted by permission. 'Tupac Resurrection' by
Rita Michel, Film Festival Today, Spring 2003. 'Tupac's Book
Shelf' by Mark Anthony Neal, PopMatters.com, 1 May 2003. 'The
Tupac Uprising' by George Wehrfritz from Newsweek, 16 August
1999 © 1999 Newsweek, Inc. All rights reserved. Reprinted by
permission. 'Symposium Analyzes, Celebrates 'Thug'' by Ken
Gewertz, Harvard University Gazette, 24 August 2003. 'G.O.A.T'
by Kris Ex, XXL, October 2001 © Kris Ex. 'Tupac Shakur's Legacy'
by Lucy Morrison, article originally published in To The Quick,
Fall 1999 © Lucy Morrison. 'Tupac's Continuing Career' by John
Jurgensen, Baltimore Sun, December 2004 © 2004 The
Baltimore Sun. Used by permission.

    It has not been possible in all cases to trace the copyright
sources, and the publishers would be glad to hear from any such
unacknowledged copyright holders.

    We would like to thank the following film companies, picture
agencies and individuals for providing photographs: Michael
O'Neill/Corbis Outline; Mitchell Gerber/Corbis; Bettmann/Corbis;
Tim Mosenfelder/Getty Images; Danny Clinch/Corbis Outline;
Ernie Paniccioli/Retna; Steve Eichner/Retna; Ron Galella/
WireImage; Michael Benabib/Retna; David Corio/Retna; John
Spellman/Retna; James Leynse/Corbis; Jeffery Newbery/Corbis
Outline; Lawrence Schwartzwald/Corbis; Polydor; Dana Lixenberg/
Corbis Outline; Jim Smeal/WireImage; Steve Granitz Archive/
WireImage; Malcolm Payne/Time Life Pictures /Getty Images; Stan
Honda/AFP/Getty Images; Kimberly Butler/Time Life Pictures/
Getty Images; Barry King/WireImage; Bellis Agencie De
Bellis/Empics; Frank Wiese/Empics; Bebeto Matthews/Empics.